ETHICS IN PUBLIC SERVICE FOR THE NEW MILLENNIUM

Ethics in Public Service for the New Millennium

Edited by
RICHARD A. CHAPMAN
Durham University Business School

Ashgate

Aldershot • Burlington USA • Singapore • Sydney

© Richard A. Chapman 2000

All rights reserved. No part of this publication may be reproduced, stored in a retrieval system, or transmitted in any form or by any means, electronic, mechanical, photocopying, recording or otherwise without the prior permission of the publisher.

Published by
Ashgate Publishing Ltd
Gower House
Croft Road
Aldershot
Hants GU11 3HR
England

Ashgate Publishing Company
131 Main Street
Burlington
Vermont 05401
USA

Ashgate website: http://www.ashgate.com

British Library Cataloguing in Publication Data
Ethics in public service for the new millennium
  1.Civil service ethics
  I.Chapman, Richard A. (Richard Arnold), 1937-
  172.2

Library of Congress Control Number: 00-133534

ISBN 0 7546 1063 2

Typeset by Owain Hammonds Associates, Ebeneser, Bontgoch, Talybont, Ceredigion, Wales SY24 5DP. Telephone (01970) 832014.

Printed and bound by Athenaeum Press, Ltd., Gateshead, Tyne & Wear.

Contents

Notes on Contributors   *vii*
Workshop Participants   *x*
Acknowledgements   *xii*
Abbreviations   *xv*

1. Introduction   1
   Richard A. Chapman

2. Corruption in Local Government – some ethical issues of the last twenty-five years   9
   Rodney Brooke

3. Parliament and Ethical Behaviour   23
   Michael Hunt

4. The Ethics of Equal Opportunities   35
   Susan Corby

5. Courts, Parliament, and Public Authorities under the British Human Rights Act 1998   51
   George J. Szablowski

6. The Public Interest: A Political and Administrative Convenience?   71
   Barry J. O'Toole

7. Setting Standards in a New Organization: The Case of the British Civil Service Commission   93
   Richard A. Chapman

8. The Inherently Unethical Nature of Public Service Ethics   111
   Lawrence Pratchett

9. Is Democracy a Substitute for Ethics? Administrative Reform and Accountability   127
   B. Guy Peters

10 Democratic Accountability and Models of Governance:
   Purchaser/Provider, Owner/Trustee   141
   Colin Campbell

11 Contracting, the Enterprise Culture and Public Sector Ethics   165
   Martin Painter

12 Between Autonomy and Accountability:
   Hong Kong's Senior Civil Servants in Search of an Identity   185
   Anthony B.L. Cheung

13 Ethics, Governance, and Constitutions:
   The Case of Baron Haussmann   203
   John A. Rohr

14 Ethics in Public Service for the New Millennium   217
   Richard A. Chapman

Index   *233*

Notes on Contributors

Rodney Brooke is Senior Visiting Fellow at the School of Public Policy, University of Birmingham; Deputy Lieutenant of Greater London; and a Freeman of the City of London. He was formerly Chief Executive of West Yorkshire County Council and of Westminster City Council; Secretary of the Association of Metropolitan Authorities, Chairman of Bradford District Health Authority and a consultant with Ernst and Young. He was appointed CBE in 1996 and holds the Order of Merit of France and Germany.

Colin Campbell is University Professor of Public Policy at Georgetown University in Washington D.C. From 1990 to 1998 he served as Director of the Georgetown Public Policy Institute. Campbell has authored or co-authored eight books which between them have won four national awards in the United States. The most recent is *The U.S. Presidency in Crisis* which won the 1999 Levine Prize for the best book in the areas of comparative public policy and administration. Campbell was founding co-editor of the journal *Governance* and founding co-chairman of the Structure and Organization of Government Research Committee of the International Political Science Association. In 1999 he was elected a Fellow of the National Academy of Public Administration. His current research has focused on Corporate Strategic Planning in the U.S. Air Force.

Richard A. Chapman is Emeritus Professor of Politics, University of Durham. He previously taught at Carleton University in Canada and the Universities of Leicester, Liverpool and Birmingham; before that he was a civil servant. He was Chairman of the Public Administration Committee (PAC) of the Joint University Council 1977-81. His most recent book is *The Treasury in Public Policy Making* (Routledge, 1997). In 1999 he was elected a founding Academician of the Academy of Learned Societies for the Social Sciences (Ac.S.S.).

Anthony B.L. Cheung is Head and Associate Professor of the Department of Public and Social Administration at the City University of Hong Kong. An ex-civil servant, a former Hong Kong legislator and a specialist in public administration, he has published extensively in books and articles on privatization, civil service and public sector reforms, and government and politics in Hong Kong and China. His recent books are *Public Sector Reform in Hong Kong* (co-edited with Jane Lee) (The Chinese University Press, 1995) and *The Civil Service in Hong Kong: Continuity and Change* (co-authored with Ahmed Shafiqul Huque and Grace Lee) (Hong Kong University Press, 1998).

Susan Corby is a Senior Lecturer in Human Resource Management at the University of Greenwich. She has published widely on various aspects of industrial relations in the civil service and the National Health Service, in both of which fields she was previously a full-time union offficial, and on equal opportunities in the public services. Her book, co-edited with Geoff White, *Employee Relations in the Public Services* was published by Routledge in 1999.

Michael Hunt is a Principal Lecturer in Public Administration at Sheffield Hallam University. He has particular research interests in open government and in ethics, and these form the principal focus of his publications. He was joint editor with Richard A. Chapman of *Open Government: A study of the prospects of open government within the limitations of the British political system* (Croom Helm, 1987) and, with Barry J. O'Toole, of *Reform, Ethics and Leadership in Public Service: A Festschrift in Honour of Richard A. Chapman* (Ashgate, 1998). He has edited *Teaching Public Administration* since 1993.

Barry J. O'Toole is Reader in Politics at the University of Glasgow. From 1991 until 2000 he was Editor of the PAC journal *Public Policy and Administration*. He has written widely on ethics in public service and his publications include: *Private Gain and Public Service* (Routledge, 1989); *The Next Steps: Improving Management in Government?* (edited with Grant Jordan) (Dartmouth, 1995); and *Reform, Ethics and Leadership in Public Service* (edited with Michael Hunt) (Ashgate, 1998). His 1990 *Public Administration* article on 'T.H. Green and the Ethics of Senior Officials in British central government' has been reprinted twice in edited collections.

Martin Painter is Associate Professor and Head of the Department of Government and Public Administration, University of Sydney, where he teaches courses on public policy analysis and public sector management. His current research interests include intergovernmental relations in federal systems and public sector reform. His books include *Politics Between Departments* (1979), *Steering the Modern State* (1987), *Managerialism: the Great Debate* (1997) and *Collaborative Federalism* (1998).

B. Guy Peters is Maurice Falk Professor of Government at the University of Pittsburgh and Distinguished Visiting Professor at the University of Strathclyde. His recent publications include *The Future of Governing* and *The New Institutionalism in Political Science*.

Lawrence Pratchett is Senior Research Fellow in the Department of Public Policy, De Montfort University, Leicester, where he specialises in local government research. He has written widely on local government and democracy, and is co-author (with David Wilson) of *Local Democracy and Local Government* (Macmillan, 1996) and editor of *Reviewing Local Democracy? The Modernisation agenda in British Local Government* (Frank Cass, 1999). He is also convenor of the Urban Politics Specialist Group for the Political Studies Association.

John A. Rohr is Professor of Public Administration at the Center for Public Administration and Policy at Virginia Polytechnic Institute. He has written and lectured extensively on questions of ethics and constitutionalism in public service.

George J. Szablowski is Member of the Bar of Quebec and Professor Emeritus in the Department of Political Science, York University, Toronto, Canada. His research and professional interests are in the fields of international human rights, judicial review, and European integration. He is the author of numerous publications and, most recently, co-author of *Final Appeal: Decision-Making in Canadian Courts of Appeal* (James Lorimer, Toronto, 1998).

Workshop Participants

Dr Peter Barberis
Manchester Metropolitan University

Mr Rodney Brooke
formerly, Secretary, Association of Metropolitan Authorities

Mrs Jeanne Caesar
Secretary, Joint University Council

Professor Colin Campbell
Georgetown University

Professor Richard A. Chapman
University of Durham

Dr Anthony Cheung
City University of Hong Kong

Miss Susan Corby
University of Greenwich

Mr John Dickens
University of Luton

Mr Peter Gabbitas
Chief Executive, West Lothian Healthcare NHS Trust

Dr Barry Gower
University of Durham

Professor Andrew Gray
University of Durham

Mr Paul Gray
Department of Social Security

Mr Jeffrey Greenwell
formerly Chief Executive, Northamptonshire County Council
Hon Secretary, Society of Local Authority Chief Executives

Miss Kirstin Howgate
Commissioning Editor, Ashgate Publishing Limited

Mr Michael Hunt
Sheffield Hallam University

Dr Peter Laverty
University of Luton

Professor Ian Leigh
University of Durham

Mrs Joyce Liddle
University of Sunderland

Dr Barry J. O'Toole
University of Glasgow

Professor Martin Painter
University of Sydney

Professor B. Guy Peters
University of Pittsburgh

Dr Lawrence Pratchett
De Montfort University

Professor Charles Raab
University of Edinburgh

Professor John A. Rohr
Virginia Polytechnic Institute

Mr Tony Stott
De Montfort University

Professor George J. Szablowski
York University, Toronto

Mr Bryan Watson
Management consultant (formerly Personnel Director, Greater London Council)

Professor Robert J. Williams
University of Durham

Acknowledgements

This book is a successor to *Ethics in Public Service* (Edinburgh University Press, 1993) – itself the result of a conference in Durham, in 1990, of the International Political Science Association Research Committee on the Structure and Organization of Government (SOG). The book, which was also published as a paperback in North America by Carleton University Press, 1993, was well received by reviewers, and in 1997 most of the contributions to it were translated into Hungarian and republished in *Kozszolgalat Es Etika* (Helikon Kiado, 1997). By 1997 the print run had almost sold out and I was encouraged to consider preparing a successor to it, with entirely new contents.

The arrangements were similar to those in 1990. First, there had to be sponsorship. On this occasion the leading sponsor was the Public Administration Committee of the Joint University Council (PAC/JUC). This was appropriate because the 1993 book appeared in the 'Public Administration in the 1990s' series of volumes edited by Michael Hunt on behalf of the Joint University Council. The PAC was keen to support the project and the JUC approved a Workshop grant towards the costs. SOG again agreed to be associated with the arrangements and recognized the Workshop as a SOG Affiliate Conference. A small contribution towards expenses was also received from the University of Pittsburgh. With these indications of financial and academic support, an application was made to the Garfield Weston Foundation, which generously gave a grant to the JUC for this purpose. The contributors wish to record their thanks for all this support: without it the project would not have been possible.

A number of participants in the 1990 conference expressed the hope that we would again be able to meet in Durham Castle – which houses University College, the oldest college in the University of Durham. We are grateful to the Master and Staff of the College for ensuring that the accommodation and domestic arrangements were to such a high standard. The Director of Durham University Business School offered administrative assistance, through the Centre for Public Sector Management Research, and members of the University of Durham Centre for Applied Ethics and Relational Studies were also encouraging. Ashgate Publishers were positively supportive from an early stage in the planning, and we were particularly grateful for participation in the Workshop from Kirstin Howgate, the Ashgate Commissioning Editor for the Social Sciences. Sir Kenneth Calman, the Vice-Chancellor, hosted a reception on behalf of the University of Durham, and we were grateful for his encouragement as well as for the University's hospitality.

From the outset it was decided that the Workshop would be on a small scale, with the participants all playing active roles. Most of the papers discussed in Durham were offered as a result of announcements through the networks of the academic sponsoring organizations; others were the result of personal invitations from the editor to ensure that what appeared to be obvious gaps would be covered. In a number of cases adjustments to proposed topics were made following discussion between the editor/convenor and the participants. The main criterion for inclusion was what participants felt were important topics for consideration at the present time in the field of ethics in public service. The themes that emerged were therefore the result of considerable thought and discussion among the participants. In addition to the academic participants, we invited a small number of distinguished public servants to join us, thus ensuring that our discussions did not overlook practical perspectives.

All the participants had roles to play: there were no free-riders. Participants preparing papers consulted widely before and during the Workshop. All the papers were revised, not only after the Workshop sessions, but also again after further comments had been sought from the Workshop discussants, who acted as peer referees, and the editor. During the Workshop, at a special session devoted to publication plans, it was agreed, after discussion, that certain themes would be given more attention and that attempts would be made to interrelate the contents of the individual contributions. A co-operative team spirit emerged, and the project has benefited accordingly. Consequently, all the contributions have been specially written for this book, none has been published elsewhere, and all have been revised after extensive discussion and consultation.

The authors of the individual chapters accept full responsibility for what they have written. All, however, wish to express their thanks to the other Workshop participants, especially the discussants who subsequently acted as referees for each individual chapter. We have all benefited from this collegial process of discussion and consultation. The passages on the First Division Association in Barry O'Toole's chapter derive from access he was afforded to the Association's files during the early 1980s. He wishes to gratefully re-acknowledge the permission he was then granted to use those files. In addition, George Szablowski wishes to thank Aisling Reidy, of University College, London, for comments on an earlier draft of his chapter; and Richard Chapman wishes to thank the Leverhulme Trust and the Economic and Social Research Council for their financial support for his research on the Civil Service Commission. Crown Copyright is reproduced with the permission of the Controller of Her Majesty's Stationery Office. This applies to the note at the end of Chapter 14.

RAC
Durham, September 1999

Abbreviations

AC	Appeal Cases
APS	Australian Public Service
CDO	City District Office
DETR	Department of the Environment, Transport, and the Regions
DOC	Department of Conservation
EC	European Community
ECHR	European Convention on Human Rights
ECJ	European Court of Justice
ECR	European Community Reports
EHRLR	European Human Rights Law Review
EU	European Union
FDA	Association of First Division Civil Servants (or First Division Association)
FEA	Fair Employment Act
GLC	Greater London Council
GPRA	Government Performance and Reports Act
HM	Her Majesty
HRA	Human Rights Act
ICAC	Independent Commission Against Corruption
ICS	Indian Civil Service
JUC	Joint University Council
LCC	London County Council
MBC	Metropolitan Borough Council
MDC	Metropolitan District Council
NPM	New Public Management
OECD	Organization for Economic Co-operation and Development
PAC	Public Administration Committee
QC	Queen's Counsel
SAR	Special Administrative Region

SCR	Supreme Court of Rights (Canada)
SOG	Structure and Organization of Government (Review Committee of the International Political Science Association
SRA	Strategic Results Areas
UK	United Kingdom
US and USA	United States of America
WCC	Westminster City Council
WLR	Weekly Law Reports

1 Introduction

Richard A. Chapman

The previous volume, *Ethics in Public Service,* began with the clear but general statement that ethics in government refers to moral standards in the public service. This conveys the impression that the scope of the topic is broad – as, indeed, it is; and the impression was intended. At the outset of that project the participants agreed that the focus would be narrowed to concentrate on the behaviour of officials, though it was recognized that there was also plenty of scope for a book that might concentrate on the behaviour of politicians; it was also agreed to focus on public service in western style democracies, in the belief that it would not be viable to cover all types of political system. What emerged in practice, in preparing the previous volume, was an emphasis on how the behaviour of public officials was affected by ethical constraints, and especially the way in which their behaviour was seen by others when considering ethical perspectives. What seemed to be of primary importance, in any discussion of ethics in public service, was what officials felt they ought to do when they were exercising the discretion they have. All officials are faced with this question: discretionary decisions have to be made all the time, they cannot be avoided, even if the detailed rules and codes of guidance intended to minimize the difficulties are well drafted. There is no way for individual officials to avoid making discretionary decisions. The focuses that emerged in the volume, therefore, were how officials behaved in such circumstances, what constraints there were on their behaviour, and how their behaviour was affected by various facets of the environment in which they worked.

The focus for this present volume is again that of moral standards in public service, with special attention to the role(s) of officials. It presents discussion and analysis of some of the issues that seem to the contributors to be of pressing importance at the present time and that seem to have relevance for public service in the new millennium. Although the issues discussed are somewhat different from ten years ago, the focus is again primarily on public officials, and the constraints imposed on them by the political environment in liberal democracies. It is these constraints that are of so much interest at the present time, and this is not surprising since the chief differences between management decisions in the public service and management decisions in other contexts result from the political environment within which public service exists and must operate.

This is clearly evident in the chapter that follows this, in which Rodney Brooke presents reflections, based on his keynote talk at the Workshop, on how he sees the subject of ethics from his long and distinguished career in local government. Brooke considers how officials in British local government have developed new roles because the constitutional position of local authorities and of their officials has changed, and because it is often now the case that officials do not have jobs for life. In the opinion of some politicians and management enthusiasts, public sector employees should, indeed, be more like employees in other contexts and should not have jobs for life: they must welcome change and be agents for change. This approach is increasingly found throughout the public service in Britain and elsewhere, and it has important consequences for ethics in public service. In Britain, these consequences include the implications for local government administration of the increasing politicization of officials and of the changing relationships between officials and elected representatives. These changes have far reaching consequences for elected representatives as well as for officials. They can be observed in practice throughout the public sector at the present time; and because they affect the political environment and because, as Brooke puts it, they raise 'issues of ethics and probity beyond those for which the current rules are devised' (p.20) they serve to emphasize matters of increasing concern to public service in the new millennium.

Within the scope of this topic, however, not everything should be seen on the scale of individual or personal behaviour. Standards approved by institutions and groups within society are important, as are the wider standards to be observed in society at large. This is emphasised by Michael Hunt, who draws attention not only to the ethical standards expected of individual Members of the British Parliament, but also to the standards expected by the House of Commons as an institution – as expressed in its rules and procedures. In a democracy the will of the majority should prevail whilst the rights of minorities should be protected, but all too often attention is focused on the ethical dilemmas of individuals and minority groups whilst the behaviour and standards of majorities and thereby of institutions largely escape examination. A plea is made for more attention to the standards of majorities and to the effectiveness of Parliamentary structures, procedures and processes, which are often and easily given general support, though with little critical attention to their actual working arrangements. To adapt a phrase of Ellen Wilkinson in another context: 'Nothing is so dangerous in a democracy as a safeguard which appears to be adequate but is really a facade' (Wilkinson, 1932). Perhaps there should be requirements to subject Parliamentary institutions, procedures and processes to regular health checks to ensure that they keep pace with wider public expectations and are assessed against perfection as conceived in the world of ideas.

Some of these issues are considered by Susan Corby in her study of equal opportunities – presented here as an illustration of key issues in public service ethics. It is clear from her chapter that the questions on which she has written are far more complex than may at first appear. Partly, this is because nearly all ethical problems are difficult to resolve in terms of agreed approaches, but partly it is also because even good intentions that have wide support, and that lead to laws and procedures, are not easy to implement in practice. Institutions and procedures need much more than good intentions if they are to achieve their objectives; they also need continuous vigilance and revision so that they are not, in effect, counterproductive. Furthermore, institutional structures and legal requirements have roles to play in ethical issues – and their roles have to be continuously evaluated and reviewed from ethical perspectives.

An example of how difficult this can be in the context of structures and intentions is provided by George Szablowski in Chapter 5, on the British Human Rights Act 1998. This act was intended to make it unlawful for a public authority to act in a way which is incompatible with rights laid down by the European Convention on Human Rights. In effect, it is, as Szablowski says, a major step towards the convergence between, on the one hand, UK law and the UK judiciary, and on the other hand, the European regime for human rights enforcement. Some of the peculiarities of the United Kingdom constitution are highlighted in his chapter, which also draws attention to some of the difficulties in implementing the provisions of the Human Rights Act. Szablowski's critical and provocative analysis recognizes the growing importance of human rights and the value of expressing them in charters and conventions. The Human Rights Act is an important part of the UK 'modernization' programme of changes in democracy, and its provisions are intended to be fully operational early in the new millennium. However, this measure to protect human rights is likely to have significant effects within public sector institutions, and in relationships between them, as well as in the work of public sector officials.

Moreover, there is likely to be an increase in work for courts and lawyers. The Act will probably result in changes in the British system of government of considerable constitutional and political importance, with effects on the daily work not only of lawyers but also of all public sector officials.

Whilst some aspects of public service are being sensitized to human rights and are being affected by constitutional and political change, there is still the expectation that public servants will be motivated to serve the public interest. It is therefore valuable to have, in Chapter 6, Barry O'Toole's exposition and analysis of this concept, with reference to both modern practice and its use by philosophers going back to the time of the ancient Greeks. O'Toole argues that, in public service, a belief in the public interest is necessary for ensuring the practical application of democratic principles; and also that it is part of the public interest in liberal democracies that there are responsible public servants who will seek to put the public interest before their personal interests and before the interests of groups. Only in this way, he suggests, can liberal democracies flourish to the benefit of all citizens.

Chapter 7 is a case study of the creation of the British Civil Service Commission. The ethos of the unified British civil service was to serve the public interest as O'Toole suggests it ought to have been: indeed, when mottoes were in vogue, the motto of the original Society of Civil Servants was 'We serve the state'. In developing the ethos of public service in the United Kingdom, an important part was played by the Civil Service Commission, created in 1855. The Commission became, through its practice of recruiting civil servants on the basis of openness, fairness and impartiality, and usually through competitive examinations, an important institution for developing a unified civil service which expected its officials to devote themselves to the public interest. The chapter considers how the Commission became established, how standards were set and achieved, and what insights and lessons might emerge from its experience.

In Chapter 8 Lawrence Pratchett considers the significance of institutionalized values and procedures that may have the effect of diminishing the scope for ethical behaviour. If rules are developed to such an extent that they greatly minimise the scope for officials not only to make mistakes but also to exercise discretion, then it must follow that the scope for individual ethical judgments is limited. Rules and procedures have their part to play in, for example, sensitizing decision-makers, making sure that relevant factors are not overlooked, and ensuring that irrelevant factors are excluded from the decision-making process. Indeed, as the 1990 project appreciated, ethical codes have important roles to play in the education and training of officials (see Jackson, 1993). Nevertheless they cannot eliminate the important responsibilities that must be peculiarly associated with public service. Judgments still have to be made about which objectives, procedures and values should be given priority in given circumstances, and also about what to do when objectives, principles and values are in conflict. Institutional codes and procedures are important, and their significance should not be underestimated. Similarly, institutional values and procedures have a special role to play when questions are asked about where they come from, how they achieve importance, and how they are applied in practice to ensure that their intentions are achieved. In relation to all these considerations, care must also be taken to apply them with common sense, otherwise officials may behave like unthinking machines, applying rigid rules to individual cases, with the consequence that responsibility is, in effect, denied. It is because of the procedures for democratic accountability and the constraints of the political environment that public service is sometimes more bureaucratic than business practice, and that is why Pratchett believes the scope for ethical decision-making is in danger of being undermined.

Nevertheless it should be emphasized that discretion is the essence of administrative ethics, and this is emphasized by Guy Peters in Chapter 9. The exercise of discretionary decision making is so important in modern democracies that much effort is devoted to ensuring that the frameworks within which such decisions are made is appropriate. Discretionary decision makers normally operate within the constraints of official hierarchies that ensure accountability; but towards the end of the twentieth century features of the new public management have resulted in public services being offered outside the traditional structures of government departments. Not only have agencies been created to give greater flexibility and autonomy to parts of government, some functions are now contracted out to business organizations that spend only part of their time on public service work. This leads to a large number of questions which have not attracted agreed answers but which will have to be given more attention in the new millennium. Peters draws attention to these questions and also considers some of the tentative answers that have been offered.

An aspect of discretion that is increasingly important is considered in Chapter 10 by Colin Campbell. He draws attention to the relationship between the political and administrative culture and the exercise of discretion, and he argues for the wider recognition and, indeed, the protection of administrative discretion as a valuable facet of democracy. A healthy democracy *needs* responsible administrators who, within the context of democratic accountability, make discretionary decisions. Some

6 *Richard A. Chapman*

of these sentiments echo those of O'Toole in Chapter 6, Pratchett in Chapter 8 and also Peters in Chapter 9, but Campbell's comparative approach pays special attention to the dangers of procedures influenced by the rise of public choice theory and lessons that may be learned from New Zealand. He notes the increasing emphasis on 'ownership' as a concept in public choice, intended to aid the achievement of desirable outcomes; but he proposes the adoption of 'trusteeship' rather than 'ownership' as a way forward that recognizes the importance of ethical behaviour in modern democracies. As Campbell, in effect, puts it, it is citizens, not politicians or bureaucrats, who, in the end, own the productive apparatus of the state in a democracy. Wider recognition of the sort of responsibilities generally expected of trustees may be a valuable feature of an administrative culture that seeks to protect democratic values and protect opportunities for responsible administrative behaviour. Moreover, consideration of these issues in a trustee context may provide a constructive framework for reviewing ethics in public service and also for influencing the way public sector work may be expected to develop in the new millennium.

Some of Campbell's concern for democratic values and accountability arises because of the emphasis on ownership in modern approaches to management theory. These approaches encompass public choice theory and the practice of contracting out some of the functions of government. The implications of these approaches are considered further by Martin Painter, who uses some of the experience of the Australian Public Service to illustrate his argument and, in doing so, refers to some of the comments and evidence presented in Australia on recent developments in this direction. He concludes that the prognosis for ethical conduct is not good: indeed, the Australian experience, mirrored in other modern democracies, indicates a threat to the basis of ethical conduct in the management and delivery of public services.

Whilst the implications of ownership, contracting, and other recent approaches to public sector management have led to a number of issues in terms of the ethical behaviour of officials in western style democracies, a different set of issues arises in Hong Kong. There, as Anthony Cheung demonstrates in Chapter 12, it is by no means straightforward for civil servants to be politically impartial and accountable – yet political impartiality and accountability are two of the features which emerge in this book as characteristics requiring attention in the new millennium. Difficulties arise because Hong Kong, as a former British colony, and with some features of the British system of government, has little experience of democratic politics, and is now a Special Administrative Region of China.

The administrative traditions of Hong Kong are expected to adjust to the new political environment, but tensions are sure to arise as adjustment occurs. The study by Cheung of a political and administrative system with British colonial traditions and very limited experience of the practice of democracy, presents contrasts with the other chapters and also stimulates questions about ethical behaviour that may with advantage be considered in other contexts.

Another example of ethical behaviour in a context other than that of a liberal democracy is provided by John Rohr. In his chapter on Baron Haussmann, Rohr considers the nature of the ethical behaviour of an individual in an authoritarian regime, and he provides valuable insights as a result of his comparative study. It would be arrogant and wrong to assert that ethical behaviour is only to be observed within what are constitutionally regarded as liberal democracies. A clear view of the public interest and the practice of ethical behaviour may be found in authoritarian regimes. Rohr is a well known advocate for the importance of constitutions for ensuring that a system of government is good and acceptable, but, as he demonstrates, there *are* lessons to be learned from experience in other contexts.

The essays in this volume are on topics that the authors, both individually and as a group, believe to be some of the most important issues concerning ethical behaviour in public service at the present time. Each chapter stands as a study in its own right, but each is part of an inter-related whole so that common themes emerge. As with the previous volume, *Ethics in Public Service*, it is relevant to emphasize that ethics in government refers to moral standards in public service. This places an important emphasis on discretion and duty. Ethics in public service is about making decisions where judgment has to be applied. Such decisions are not easy; they cannot be made according to formulas. Ethical codes and statements of standards have a part to play, but they can never absolve individuals of responsibility. In this volume, as in the previous one, the focus is primarily on administrators rather than on politicians or other facets of political and administrative processes; the focus is also restricted to concentrate primarily on practice in modern liberal democracies. This is not to say that there is no place for ethical behaviour in other types of political system, but it is to recognize that limitations of space preclude developing a wider view. Globalization may have been a popular or fashionable concept towards the end of the second millennium and the approach has left its mark. In the new millennium, however, if some of the underlying themes in this volume are a reliable guide, the emphasis may be somewhat different. Of almost overwhelming significance, as these chapters indicate, there is now a focus on the political environment which is so important for appreciating the ethical behaviour of officials in public service. Crucially, however, the emphasis is increasingly on the ways in which democratic standards are expected, and on ways in which a new emphasis on accountability is also expected.

References

Jackson, M.W. (1993), 'How can ethics be taught?', pp.31-42 in Richard A. Chapman (ed), *Ethics in Public Service*, Edinburgh: Edinburgh University Press.

Wilkinson, Ellen (1932), Annex VI in *Committee on Ministers' Powers, Report*, Cmd. 4060, London: HMSO.

2 Corruption in Local Government – some ethical issues of the last twenty-five years

Rodney Brooke

Introduction

This month (March 1999) the Society of Local Authority Chief Executives held a seminar. It was one of a series to get to grips with the government's new local government agenda. It was on ethics and propriety.

Billed to appear was the new leader of Doncaster, Councillor Malcolm Glover – the Mr Clean who had taken over to hose out the Augean stables of municipal corruption in that town. Within seven days of advertisement of the seminar Councillor Glover had himself become the twelfth Doncaster councillor to be arrested, himself implicated in the abuses he had pledged to stop.

Simultaneously the police were investigating an entirely unconnected matter: the leaflet which the council had issued just before the May 1998 election. In it Councillor Glover boasted of how the council had put itself to rights, expunging the old corrupt practices. The council's monitoring officer, buttressed by a QC's opinion, had advised that this was an illegal practice. Nevertheless the leaflet was issued.

At the same time the leader of adjacent Wakefield MDC left his position and was de-selected by the Labour party over corruption allegations. The former Wakefield chief executive was suspended from his post-retirement job as Clerk of the West Yorkshire Police Authority as a result of matters arising out of his service as chief executive. The deputy leader of nearby Rotherham MDC and others were suspended pending police investigations involving the payment of prostitutes out of public funds.

Poulson and aftermath

This seems like a time-warp. Twenty-five years ago I joined the new West Yorkshire County Council, arising out of the ashes of the old West Riding. A suite in my department was reserved for a team of Scotland Yard detectives led by Commander Crane (later to reappear in County Hall as Chief Inspector of Constabulary Sir James Crane with the task of investigating failings in the search for the Yorkshire Ripper).

Commander Crane was investigating the scandal surrounding architect John Poulson. The country had been rocked by the evidence of corruption disclosed at Poulson's bankruptcy proceedings. The Yorkshire architect had been active in precisely the same territory as the protagonists in the present scandals. From the unlikely base of Pontefract, he had been responsible for developments ranging from the Aviemore Highland Centre to a hospital in Malta. He had built up his nationally prominent practice by showering gifts and hospitality on those who might put contracts his way.

Among those implicated were Home Secretary Reginald Maudling and the charismatic Newcastle leader T. Dan Smith. Other national and local politicians had been caught up in Poulson's web. A Scottish Office undersecretary, George Pottinger, was jailed. Sir Bernard Kenyon, a director of a Poulson company while still West Riding county clerk, was still under investigation at the time of his death.

The consequences of the Poulson investigation spread widely and unexpectedly. Eddie Newby, leader of Bradford City Council was a mill overlooker, living modestly in a terrace house. He would work nights so as to lead the council during the day. He received a suspended prison sentence for accepting a free trip to Paris. He was advised by the Labour Party's northern organiser, T. Dan Smith, to go there to see new social housing. The bill was paid by Poulson. It was never alleged that he had taken any steps to award a contract to Poulson. Indeed Poulson never worked for Bradford City Council. The sentence was seen as harsh in the extreme, especially in the context of practice elsewhere in the public service. After all, ministers seem able to accept holidays and the loan of Tuscan palazzi without comment. When Councillor Newby resigned as leader (by this time of West Yorkshire County Council), he received a standing ovation from all parties.

The Poulson affair caused such a furore that it led to two national enquiries. The Prime Minister set up a committee on local government rules of conduct under the chairmanship of Lord Redcliffe-Maud (Redcliffe-Maud, 1974). When it became clear that Poulson's tentacles had reached into central government a Royal Commission under Lord Salmon examined standards of conduct in public life (Salmon, 1976). These led to the introduction of a national code of local government conduct, misnamed since it applied only to members. Overlaid with amendments over the years, it became 'complicated, even impenetrable, inconsistent' (Nolan, 1997, p.17).

For a quarter of a century and until the new series of Yorkshire cases, the spectre of financial corruption seemed to have disappeared from local government. Occasional councillors would claim benefits or expenses to which they were not entitled, but that was all. The creation in 1994 of the Committee on Standards in Public Life, the Nolan Committee, was triggered by parliamentary and central government scandals. In local government the Nolan Report found that in no sense was corruption widespread (Nolan, 1997). In the resulting consultation paper on ethics, the Government echoed that conclusion (DETR, 1998).

Ethical implications of central and local government clashes

In the place of financial corruption new ethical issues arose. Some of them stemmed from the hostility between the government of the day and local government. The 1973 refusal of the Clay Cross councillors to implement Conservative government policy on housing rents was followed by the refusal of South Yorkshire County Council to obey the Labour government's instruction to cut public transport fares. The advent of Mrs Thatcher's government in 1979 intensified the enmity. Councils declined to implement the government's policy on sales of council housing. Government decisions were challenged in a series of judicial reviews.

The great war took place over local government finance, as the government tried to rein back spending. Militant-controlled Liverpool refused to set a rate unless the City received more government aid. In a government climb-down, Environment Secretary of State Patrick Jenkin sent more cash (Widdicombe, 1986, vol.4, ch.2). In 1984 a humiliated government took powers under the Rates Act to cap the rates. Outraged constitutionally and encouraged by past successes, the Labour-controlled rate-capped authorities began to meet. Under the leadership of Margaret Hodge and Ted Knight, leaders respectively of Islington and Lambeth, the co-ordinating committee agreed a commitment to non-compliance. During the winter of 1984-5 this crystallized into a strategy of not setting a rate, so that the government would be forced to intervene. Solidarity broke down as the threats increased. By June only Liverpool and Lambeth had yet to make a rate. Without backing from national party leadership, they eventually succumbed in July. In due course the District Auditor decided that loss had resulted from the delay and councillors were surcharged (*Lloyd v McMahon*, 1987, 2 WLR 821).

Electoral corruption

The climate of hostility and partisanship prompted a scandal rivalling Poulson in news value. It surrounded council housing, that perennial bone of contention between the parties. Conventional thinking used to be that council tenants voted Labour and owner-occupiers Conservative. The more council dwellings, the more likely an authority to be Labour controlled. Deep inside Conservative thinking is the belief that Herbert Morrison, leader of the London County Council, conspired to 'build the Tories out of London' through the LCC's social housing programme. There is no evidence that Morrison ever said such a thing but certainly voters in LCC dwellings played their part in making the council a safe Labour fiefdom. The LCC was abolished in 1965 and replaced by the Greater London Council. Its wider boundaries embraced leafy suburbs and were designed to make the authority safe for the Conservatives. In practice it was from time to time controlled by Labour, most famously under the leadership of Ken Livingstone. His group ran the council from 1981 until 1986, when Mrs Thatcher's infuriated government abolished the authority in its turn.

In the meanwhile the old London County Council housing was progressively transferred to the boroughs. Unsurprisingly distribution of dwellings did not correspond to borough needs. Wandsworth, for example, had 42,000 units. When the council, previously Labour, came under precarious Tory control in 1978, the new controlling group transformed the electoral map of the borough by an aggressive policy of selling off council dwellings. The middle classes moved into the vacated council flats and Tory control became permanent. The borough's housing chairman, Christopher Chope, was accused of social engineering by Labour but became a Conservative hero. Later Council Leader, he entered the House of Commons in 1983 and soon become a Department of Environment minister in Mrs Thatcher's government.

Across the Thames from Wandsworth lies the august city of Westminster, covering almost all of tourist London. Its area stretches from Lords cricket ground in the north to the Palace of Westminster in the south; from Kensington Gardens in the west to Covent Garden in the east. It had always been Conservative-controlled. In 1983 its traditional Conservative leadership was replaced by the very different regime of Lady (Shirley)

Porter, later Dame Shirley. Consciously modelling herself on Mrs Thatcher, Lady Porter expected a 'can do' philosophy from council officers.

In the 1986 London borough elections there was a strong swing against the Conservatives. Dislike of abolition of the Greater London Council accentuated the normal mid-term swing away from the party of government. In Westminster the normally rock-solid Tory council tottered on the brink of Labour control. Ward after ward fell. Up on the Camden border in Fitzrovia the crucial contest was in the Cavendish ward. The Conservatives hung on by the skin of their teeth. Fewer than a hundred and twenty additional Labour votes would have handed over the country's wealthiest authority to Labour control.

The consequences would have been unthinkable. The Labour opposition were pledged to rename Trafalgar Square: Nelson's column would have found itself in Nelson Mandela Square. The GLC might have been a thorn in the government's flesh: a Labour-controlled Westminster Council would have been a dagger in the heart.

To Lady Porter the brush with defeat looked like a personal indictment. The next London borough elections were in 1990. Votes had to be won by then. She determined to learn from Wandsworth, but Westminster had only half as many council dwellings – 24,000 compared to Wandsworth's 42,000. It also had a major problem of homelessness and a demand for tenancies which exceeded supply. A generalized sales programme on the Wandsworth scale was out of the question.

Sales would have to be targeted in the key marginal wards. Estimates were made of the dwellings required in each ward in order to deliver sufficient votes for electoral victory in 1990. Targets were set and tenants offered grants of £15,000 to leave.

In order to deliver the programme – code-named 'Building Stable Communities' – Lady Porter recruited as head of her policy unit a senior civil servant, Bill Phillips, from the Department of the Environment. He guided a secret meeting at her Oxfordshire house. Instructions were given to 'stop rehousing in marginal wards' and to introduce 'political control' over housing allocations. The planning system should be 'used for social engineering'.

The motive for the policy was clearly improper. Officers took advice from leading counsel. He advised that it would be wrong to target wards for electoral advantage. To camouflage the motive, therefore, an authority-wide strategy was put together. This kept the target figures for gentrification in the marginal wards but added extra sales in non-key wards as a disguise.

To reinforce his influence Phillips recruited a colleague from the

Department of the Environment, Nick Reiter. Working through the Deputy City Solicitor and the Housing Director the policies were laboriously put in place. Tenants were moved and their flats boarded up pending 'gentrification'. Well before any possible electoral benefit might have accrued the policy was detected and investigated by the District Auditor.

In his provisional findings (Magill, 1994) ten councillors and officers were found guilty of misconduct and due for surcharge: Leader Lady Porter; Deputy Leader, David Weeks; Chief Whip Barry Legg; Housing chairs Peter Hartley, Judith Warner and Michael Dutt plus four officers: Phillips; Housing Director Graham England; the Deputy City Solicitor Robert Lewis; and an assistant housing director, Paul Hayler.

In the auditor's final findings (Magill, 1996) Legg, Warner and Lewis were exempted, Legg (by then an MP) and Warner for the rather peculiar reason that they did not realize that they were 'under a duty to disclose the unlawful and improper conduct' (Magill, 1996, pp.675 and 695).

By this time Dutt had committed suicide. The remaining six were surcharged £31m, being the District Auditor's final estimate of the loss suffered by the council. A series of reasons to justify the finding of illegality were given, but crucial to the decision for surcharge was that those surcharged were motivated by – or knew that the policy was motivated by – electoral advantage for the majority party, an unlawful motive.

The High Court considered appeals from five of the six. Hayler, the sixth, had a breakdown and was subsequently exempted following the High Court's findings. The High Court in its judgment referred to 'an atmosphere of fear' at Westminster. It referred to 'the attitude of the majority party to the WCC officers, for whom it could not have been pleasant working at this time. We take into account that such pressures may well have had an insidious effect on the officers, making them, consciously or unconsciously, reluctant to speak out robustly'. *Inter alia* officers provided the minority party with 'wholly misleading answers to what appear to us understandable and wholly proper questions.' Members had 'an inappropriate approach to the role of officers' and 'a contemptuous state of mind ... towards officers and their views'.

The Court's decisions on individuals are illuminating: The Director of Housing was exempted from criticism for the reason that he honestly believed that the council's policy was lawful. Chairman of Housing Peter Hartley was found to have been guilty of misconduct in that he was promoting a policy which was infected by an improper purpose (electoral advantage). 'His action was still unlawful and amounted to misconduct, despite his own proper motive, because of the improper motive of others of which he was aware. But we are prepared to believe that he did not appreciate the unlawfulness of his own conduct and genuinely believed that his own proper purpose rendered his actions lawful'.

Phillips, originally Head of Policy, was later appointed as 'Managing Director', a title intended to give him support in securing the illegal policy adopted by Lady Porter. The court took the view that 'he knew that what was proposed would give effect to an improper purpose, and he was therefore guilty of misconduct. But he was not advised that it was unlawful and accordingly we are not prepared to conclude that he must have known that what he proposed was unlawful'.

In the case of the Leader and Deputy Leader, 'their purpose throughout was to achieve unlawful electoral advantage. Knowledge of the unlawfulness and such deliberate dressing-up both point to ... wilful misconduct'. Both are currently fighting the ruling in the Court of Appeal.

Naturally the Westminster case was a godsend to a Labour party shrugging off Labour sleaze. At every debate when Labour sleaze was mentioned Labour hurled back accusations about Tory Westminster. Parliamentary debates on local government descended into arguments about which party's councils were more corrupt than the other.

The auditor's report threw a long shadow over Westminster. There were many ramifications. The policy had extended from 'Building Stable Communities' – the targeting of housing sales in marginal wards – to 'Quality of Life', where improvements were to be concentrated in marginal wards and a relaxed planning regime would encourage luxury flats. 'Quality of Life' prompted another investigation by the District Auditor.

Another scandal arose from the presence in flats of asbestos. By the early 1980s the danger had been recognized. Two council blocks – Hermes and Chantry Points on the Elgin/Walterton estate – were especially dangerous. The Council pursued a policy of removing tenants from the flats over a period of five years in order that they could be completely emptied and the asbestos safely removed. As the homes for votes policy took root and shortage of housing for the homeless became acute this policy was reversed in February 1989. The homeless were moved into the asbestos-ridden flats. The campaign by locals became a national issue (Rosenberg, 1998).

After political pressure for an enquiry, the council commissioned an independent inspector, John Barratt, to investigate the charges. He reported in March 1996. He found that Westminster Conservative councillors were 'influenced by considerations of party advantage' in rehousing homeless families in the asbestos-ridden blocks. 'Despite the availability of the clearest advice to the contrary, those acting on behalf of a public body took risks...with the health of people.' The majority party chairman's group took the decision though nominally it was taken by senior housing officials. The issue was never put to the council's housing committee. According to Mr Barratt, the 'detailed informal political control of executive action was becoming excessive and stifling' (Barratt, 1996).

Careers were damaged, and not only of those directly involved. In May 1996, just as the Auditor's final report was published, Graham Farrant, former assistant housing director at Westminster and by now chief executive of Birmingham's Aston district was appointed as Chief Executive of Norfolk County Council. Though he had not been mentioned in the 'Homes for Votes' report, Norfolk County Council revoked its offer of a job.

In January 1999 the newly appointed chief executive of the Shetland Islands, Nick Reiter, stood down after six months suspension. The reason: he had been head of policy in Westminster during the homes for votes saga. Though never surcharged, he had produced a paper on targeting which showed officers working for a Tory victory.

The neutrality of officials

According to Professor Martin Loughlin 'the most shocking aspect of the Westminster affair, however, concerns the role of officers. In other examples of politicisation in local government, officers have strived to maintain their professional position. Here, however, the impression formed is of officers acquiescing in, or even helping to promote partisan policies' (Loughlin, 1994).

Ironically it was a Conservative Secretary of State, Patrick Jenkin, who first publicly challenged the impartiality of officers. At the time the abolition of the metropolitan counties was going badly. The publicity war had been lost by the government. Officers – particularly myself – had stood up in defence of the doomed authorities. Although the government had said that the motive for abolition of the metropolitan counties was not political, the Secretary of State said that officers who defended the authorities were politically motivated.

The Government's annoyance prompted it to set up the Widdicombe Committee on the conduct of local authority business. Announcing its creation, Mr Jenkin told the 1984 Conservative Party conference:

> There is a cancer in some local councils which runs much deeper than extravagant spending. In some of our cities local democracy itself is under attack. The conventional checks and balances are scorned. Councils squander millions on virulent political campaigns.

Officers are selected for their political views; the rights of minorities are suppressed; standing orders are manipulated to stifle debates... (*The Guardian*, 11 October 1984).

In British local government decision-taking is vested in the council as a whole. The officers have a responsibility to the entire council: unlike civil servants they do not serve the party of government only. They have a duty to carry out council instructions unless they are clearly unlawful. If they carry out unlawful instructions, they are liable to be surcharged. If the authority fails to take decisions required to stay within the law, then officers have a duty to so inform the council. However, if the council still refrains from taking the decision, then officers cannot invent it. Councillors then take sole responsibility for the consequences.

This constitutional relationship was established in the days before tight political control of local government. It prompted officers to keep councillors at a discreet distance. In order to avoid a personal meeting, my first town clerk (1955-62) would leave the town hall if he saw the leader of the council entering. He was not untypical. Many town clerks would not meet the leader of one political party on the council unless the leader of the other were also present 'to avoid even the possibility of the appearance of favouritism' (Headrick, 1962, p.128).

In the period of post-war recovery town halls frequently enjoyed a comfortable atmosphere. Conservative governments were as eager as Labour to push council house building. Local government spending grew year on year. Since the parties largely shared a common agenda, private meetings between a majority party and the officers were not essential. The formal system in local government functioned adequately. The professionalism of officers was 'the greatest single force which enables local authorities to carry out, with much efficiency, the considerable tasks entrusted to them' (Griffith, 1966, p.534).

Neither the formal system nor officers' professionalism were proof against the policy tensions of the 1970s, especially since these were coupled with a change in the nature of councillors. The moral dominance of the old aldermen disappeared with their abolition in 1974. Many other old guard politicians left when they found uncongenial both the new confrontational politics and the rumbustious style of the big new post-reorganization authorities. More aggressive councillors arrived, with a clear political agenda. The majority parties took a firmer grip on more and more councils. Opposition parties ceased to share power and began to see their role as opposing the controlling group, following Westminster practice.

However, unlike central government, the institutions of local government are corporate not adversarial. The result was to put officers in a distinctly ambiguous position as they developed relationships with the party in power while retaining the duty of serving the council as a whole. Controlling groups naturally wished to have a private dialogue with officers on the development and implementation of policy. In order to permit that dialogue one-party groups and committees became common.

By the time of the Widdicombe Committee, chief officers were agreed that, 'given the realities of modern politics, their prime responsibility must be to the ruling party group' (Laffin and Young, 1985). Even the Conservative Party's National Local Government Advisory Committee said:

> Too many officers being neither wise nor weak, have tried to obstruct the new practices of determined political leaders and have created tensions within their authorities which could have been avoided. They have failed to recognise that the demand for exercising power by the elected leaders has to be accommodated if it exists, and that in those circumstances the practices and conventions of local government need to be adapted to ensure that the power is exercised wisely and that the political management is efficient (quoted in Brooke, 1986).

In politicized authorities this was nothing new. Herbert Morrison, when leader of the LCC, said that officers should rarely, if at all, speak in committee, placing responsibility where it should lie – with the elected member. But opposition parties frequently failed to accept the new conventions, even when these were codified. Arguments started over what advice officers should give an opposition party. Should it be confined to factual information on request? Could officers work up options on behalf of an opposition? Should they warn the majority party of areas of opposition interest of which they became aware?

Members started to influence the drafting of reports and to control the agenda of committees, suppressing items they found unpalatable. Treasurers became involved in creative accounting: 'I have to be prepared to bend my pure accountancy skills to the need of the particular authority', said one (quoted in Laffin and Young, 1985). The behaviour which Professor Loughlin found shocking in the Westminster case was by no means unique. Mrs Thatcher welcomed 'can do' civil servants. Not surprisingly local politicians liked the same. One party meetings encouraged members to describe political objectives which officers would translate into practical programmes. About the rate-capping protest, Margaret Hodge, then Islington Leader, said that 'you could tell those officers who were for us and those who were against'.

In its advice to councillors, a leading firm of local government consultants said 'No council can be successful if it does not have co-operative and resourceful officers to put policies into practice and develop policies which make the best of the manifesto objectives...Leading councillors are likely to be looking for a new type of loyalty in their senior staff...Senior officer appointments may be made on criteria linked to known political activity or views of the candidates' (Young, 1986, pp.127-8). No more overt invitation to appoint fellow-travellers could have been made. What price the 'impartiality' of officers?

Top jobs, hitherto safe for life, were truncated if the controlling group found their occupants not to their taste. Short-term contracts became common if only as a way of finding an easy way of disposing of an unwanted chief officer. Not surprisingly compliance with the majority party's requests became more frequent. The truculent independence of the old county clerks – holding office for life – became a thing of the past.

Generally new-style officers reinterpreted their duty as being to ensure that all councillors knew the relevant facts (though that could be open to interpretation). But they saw no need to make the council at large aware of their own views unless these were strictly professional. Most crucially they believed that, whatever members' political reasons for taking a decision, officers would be entitled to implement it if there was a proper local government reason for doing so. As the Westminster case made clear, the District Auditor did not agree. With the Ombudsman, he declined to accept that officers had anything other than a duty to speak out, however unpopular their advice might be and however it might imperil their jobs. The drift towards a quasi-civil service relationship seemed temporarily imperilled until the High Court decision on the Westminster case.

In a handful of predominantly small rural authorities, the relationship between officers and members has not changed much over the last quarter century. Elsewhere most chief executives do not now see their predominant duty as being to the council as a whole (Norton, 1991). Instead it is to promote and implement the policies of the majority party. It is on that criterion that they will be judged. The understanding of the obligations of officers has changed out of all recognition in the last quarter-century.

Conclusion

As Guy Peters (Chapter 9) points out, the traditional way of dealing with new ethical issues is to introduce new rules. The consequence of the problems of the last twenty-five years has been a succession of tightening rules on local government conduct, starting with legislation following the Widdicombe Committee's reports in 1985 and 1986. They culminated with the publication last week of the Government's draft Bill on ethics in local government. Despite the Government's denial of any major problem, the Bill proposes the creation of a Standards Committee, to include non-Council members, for each Council; a national Standards Board; a corps of Ethical Standards Officers; and Adjudication Panels with powers to remove errant members from their council.

When implemented, the Bill will also bring new ethical challenges, as it moves towards removing the committee system by which local authorities are governed. In its place authorities will choose between a directly elected mayor, a cabinet – which can be one party – or a council manager with executive powers. The proposals would remove the compulsory participation of minority parties in formal decision-taking. There are obvious implications for corruption. The Government propose to counter these by requiring the creation of Scrutiny Committees with powers to question the decisions of the executive. There will be new issues of openness when decisions are taken by one person or behind closed doors. When power is formally vested in a political executive, what is the duty of officers towards the rest of the council? What part should they take in aiding the Scrutiny Committee to challenge the executive's decision? As John Rohr (Chapter 13) makes clear, a code of ethical standards depends on the administrative setting in which it is based.

Also raising fresh problems are the tensions caused by a mixed economy of service delivery: outsourcing, management buy-outs, the private finance initiative, decentralized budgeting, local management of schools, joint ventures with the private sector, local authority companies. Martin Painter (Chapter 11) exemplifies the contradictions. They raise issues of ethics and probity beyond those for which the current rules are devised. The same problems arise in other parts of the public sector.

A striking feature of the topic is the way in which local government rules differ from those in other parts of the public sector. Civil servants, for example, have a clear allegiance to their minister: they do not have to weigh the ambiguity of a simultaneous responsibility to Parliament. Nor do they seem inhibited in implementing 'political' decisions: there seems to be no requirement for them to question motives as the Westminster case implies is necessary in local government. As Sir Brian Cubbon said: civil servants will help ministers make the system work in pursuance of their political aims (Chapman, 1993, p.9). Above all, public servants outside local government are not under threat of surcharge, a penalty removed from the civil service in 1981. If ministers contemplate an illegal action, civil servants do not have to argue the issue in public: a note on the file suffices. In due course it will be picked up by the Public Accounts Committee.

Parliamentarians and councillors work under very different regimes for accepting gifts. It seems possible for MPs to accept favours which would be illegal if taken by councillors. The elaborate machinery proposed by the Government to watch councillors is in stark contrast to the regime of self-discipline enjoyed by Parliamentarians – though this may change as a result of the Human Rights legislation, as George Szablowski foreshadows in Chapter 4.

The Nolan Committee is, however, prompting some convergence of rules for different parts of the public sector. The machinery of government unit in the Cabinet Office is currently requiring non-departmental public bodies to adopt a code of conduct similar to that imposed on local government. The Nolan Committee, in recommending the abolition of surcharge, proposed its replacement by an offence of misuse of public office, to apply to all parts of the public sector (Nolan, 1997). The Government has accepted the recommendation in principle but has yet to bring forward plans for its implementation.

Following the 1990 Ethics in Public Service conference, Richard Chapman wrote: 'What is acceptable in one place or at one time may differ from what is acceptable in another place or a different time' (Chapman, 1993, p.1). It is clear that ethical rules in the public sector are still evolving. Despite the substantial amendments over the last twenty-five years, they will continue to change as new problems manifest themselves. The next twenty-five years will be as eventful as the past.

References

Barratt, John (1996), *Report of a documentary review into the use by Westminster City Council of Hermes and Chantry Points, Elgin Estate, for housing purposes*, London: Westminster City Council.

Brooke, Rodney (1986), 'Management Aspects of Widdicombe', *Local Government Studies*, Vol. 12 No. 6, November/December 1986.

Chapman, Richard A. (ed.) (1993), *Ethics in Public Service*, Edinburgh: Edinburgh University Press.

DETR (1998) Consultation Paper: *Modernising local government: A new ethical framework*, London: Department of the Environment, Transport and the Regions.

Griffith, J.A.G. (1966), *Central Departments and Local Authorities*, London, George Allen and Unwin.

The Guardian (11 October 1984), quoted in Loughlin (1994).

Headrick, T.E. (1962), *The Town Clerk in English Local Government*, London: Allen and Unwin.

Laffin, Martin and Young, Ken, (1985), 'The Changing Roles and Responsibilities of Local Authority Chief Officers', *Public Administration* Vol. 63, Spring 1985.

Lloyd v McMahon (1987), 2 WLR 821.

Loughlin, Martin (1994), 'Abuse of Power in Local Government: The Auditor's Action against Westminster City Council', *Public Law* Summer 1994.

Magill, J.W. (1994), *Westminster City Council Audit of Accounts 1987/88 and Subsequent Years. Designated Sales. Note of the Appointed Auditor's Provisional Findings and Views*, London: Touche Ross.

Magill, J.W. (1996), *Westminster City Council Audit of Accounts 1987/88 to 1994/95. Designated Sales. Report of the Appointed Auditor under Section 15(3) of the Local Government Finance Act 1982*, London: Deloitte & Touche.

Nolan, Lord (1997), *Third Report of the Committee on Standards in Public Life: Standards of Conduct in Local Government in England, Scotland and Wales*, Cm. 3702, London: HMSO.

Norton, Alan (1991), *The Role of the Chief Executive in British Local Government*, Birmingham: Inlogov.

Redcliffe-Maud, Lord (1974), *Report of the Prime Minister's Committee on Local Government Rules of Conduct*, Cmnd. 5636, London: HMSO.

Rosenberg, Jonathan (1998), *Against the Odds*, London: WECH, 416 Harrow Road, London W9 2HX.

Salmon, Lord (1976), *Report of the Royal Commission on Standards in Public Life*, Cmnd. 6524, London: HMSO.

Widdicombe, David (1985), *Interim Report of the Committee of Enquiry into the Conduct of Local Authority Business*, London: Department of the Environment.

Widdicombe, David (1986), *Report of the Committee of Enquiry into the Conduct of Local Authority Business*, Cmnd. 9797, London: HMSO.

Young, Arthur (1986), *The Arthur Young Councillors' Handbook*, London: Harrap.

3 Parliament and Ethical Behaviour

Michael Hunt

In his essay 'The Pursuit of the Ideal' Sir Isaiah Berlin suggests that the attempt to impose ideals is wrong in itself. Ideals cannot be imposed but exist in 'an uneasy equilibrium, which is constantly threatened and in constant need of repair' (Berlin, 1998, p.16). Ethics, to the extent that they reflect the (ideal) moral standards by which men relate to one another, are thus also in a constant process of development – a development which changes in response to stimuli from external environments.

Such a perception is valuable when considering the development of ethics in relation to the House of Commons. The current procedures for considering ethical behaviour arise out of the culture of the House which has always assumed that a mixture of traditional rights and privileges should determine the way in which ethical behaviour is moderated (even if some of these rights and privileges have become increasingly archaic). However, a number of well publicized events in the 1990s have indicated that the long established rules and practices which have governed the behaviour of Members, particularly in relation to financial matters, are no longer sufficiently rigorous or sufficiently comprehensive. It is only recently, therefore, that the House has accepted the need for a code of conduct in relation to its members and one, moreover, which recognizes that ethical behaviour concerns rather more than simply the declaration of information about financial interests.

The importance of ethics to Parliament can hardly be overstated. The democratic process offers one of the principal safeguards against corruption – those who are elected by that process must therefore be above personal suspicion. Corruption may relate to financial probity but it is also more than that, it relates to proper standards of behaviour in relation to the way in which particular roles are performed. There are, therefore, a range of concerns that might come under the label 'moral issues'. How well, for example, are individual constituents represented? What sanction do they have against an MP who appears to represent their interests badly? What recourse might individuals have against a possible bias in the way they are represented which might allow some (powerful) interests to be better represented than those that are less powerful? How well are constituency interests represented when an MP becomes a minister and is thus unable to publicly pursue problems in the way that might be expected of a backbencher? The response that MPs are accountable to their electors through the quinquennial sanction of the ballot box is unsatisfactory. Quite apart from the delay involved, such a sanction offers no constructive assistance to a constituent concerned about the way in which an MP performs the tasks for which he or she was elected. Further, of course, most MPs are elected under a party banner at elections and it is rare for an individual's behaviour to be a significant factor in his or her re-election prospects. The unusual exceptions of John Browne, who lost his seat following adverse publicity surrounding his failure to disclose business interests to the House, and Neil Hamilton, after similar publicity about his involvement in the 'cash for questions' affair, merely serve to prove this rule. Finally, the Burkian argument about MPs being representatives rather than delegates implies that the behaviour of an MP is, in most material respects, beyond criticism by individual constituents.

It is, of course, dangerous to assume that MPs share a common perception about the ethical standards appropriate to their work. Their role is not precisely defined and remains largely a matter for individual discretion and preference; many, of course, feel that the nature of that work should not exclude the possibility that it might be combined with other work outside Parliament. In addition there are structural differences imposed by the adversarial nature of proceedings in the House which affect the ethical behaviour of MPs. The normal British practice of electing governments with a majority on the floor of the House means that the behaviour of the government, in terms of the way in which it treats the House and controls its business, must affect the behaviour of the House and the way that individual MPs determine their roles and the appropriate ethics that accompany those roles. For members of the government and, to a lesser extent, their backbenchers, Parliament is a necessary part of the process of ensuring the implementation of their policies. Their task is to ensure that this process is completed as easily as possible and they are able to do this by ensuring that the procedures of the House are oriented to that objective. Such objectives are not shared, of course, by other MPs whose primary task is to be the 'constant critic of those who do govern' (Ryle, 1994, p.647).

In addition to structural differences there are also differences of attitudes amongst MPs. Maureen Mancuso (1993) has demonstrated that, even on the narrow issue of conflicts of interest, there is a wide disparity of views about what constitutes acceptable behaviour. Her differentiation of four different sets of attitudes on this issue, ranging from the 'puritans' to the 'entrepreneurs' (and including the 'muddlers') offers a useful reminder of both the inadequacy of the rules in the mid 1980s, but also of the different interests of those elected to Parliament. A similar variety of views might be determined by examining some of the recent cases drawn to the attention of the Select Committee on Standards and Privileges.

The multiplicity of objectives, roles and perceptions in the House means that it is extremely difficult to produce a set of ethical guidelines that meets the needs of Members as well as the wider voting public. General guidelines seeking some ideal of 'public service' are unhelpful since they ignore the infinite variety of kinds of public service imposed by different structures and different roles. More dangerously, they may seek to impose ideals that are related to one role that has proved able to dominate both processes and structures. The 'Seven Principles of Public Life' advocated by the Nolan Committee (Nolan, 1994a, p.14) might therefore be deemed unhelpful to those concerned about the wider issue of MPs' ethical behaviour partly because they seem to deal primarily with financial issues and partly because some of the principles seem to apply more to members of the executive than to their (parliamentary) critics. This lack of specific relevance increases the danger, noted in Chapter 8 by Lawrence Pratchett, that codes (or principles) may act as surrogates for true ethical behaviour.

Whilst the ethics adopted by individual MPs are important, there is a danger in treating the ethics of Parliament as solely concerned with the individual ethics of its members, thus ignoring the wider issue of the ethics of the House itself. The rights and privileges that the House claims, which include the right to deal as it deems fit with transgressions by its members, clearly reflect a particular (and corporate) code of ethics. However, these rights and privileges, which originate from distant and totally different environments, have often not been adapted to the changed environment of the twentieth century. They ignore, for example, the extension of the franchise in the later part of the nineteenth century and the beginning of the twentieth century and the rise of mass parties. They also ignore the wider educational opportunities that are now available and the huge increase in methods of communication. They may also ignore changes in membership of the House, including the advent of different values, beliefs and backgrounds in the Members who attend. Nonetheless, these rights and privileges, inculcated in generations of MPs by a process of socialization, may encourage a belief that, providing particular behaviour is not apparently offensive to one's colleagues, then it must be publicly acceptable. There is no reason to believe this belief is correct, as the evidence presented to the first report of the Nolan Committee amply demonstrates (Nolan, 1994b, p.1). The past decade has witnessed a real public concern about the ethical behaviour that the House appears willing to sanction. Such fundamental concern is not solved simply by the House finding new ways to regulate the activities of its members – it is the attitudes that the House itself inculcates that need to be examined and discussed, and clearly by a wider audience than MPs themselves.

Rules governing ethical conduct

The House has consistently argued that it is capable of regulating its own affairs, using the privileges committee procedure to deal with any problems concerning the conduct of its members. However, until comparatively recently, the rules covering the ethical conduct of Members (including conduct relating to conflicts between their financial interests and their duties as an MP) were limited and lacked precision. Although there is a long standing rule that MPs cannot vote in a debate which might affect their financial interests, guidance about the information MPs should give about those interests when speaking in debates has, until recently, been extremely sparse. A resolution of the House in 1965 had prohibited 'the offer of money or other advantage to an MP' (Select Committee on Members' Interests (Declaration), 1970, Evidence by Sir Barnett Cocks, p.2). Rather more recently, in a case involving the decision by a trade union to cease offering support to an MP with whose policies it was becoming increasingly disaffected, the House noted that 'It is inconsistent with the dignity of the House ... for any Member ... to enter into any contractual agreement with an outside body controlling or limiting the Member's complete independence and freedom of action in Parliament'. Further, 'the duty of a Member is to his constituents and to the country as a whole rather than any section thereof' (H.C. Deb, 1947). A few years later, Speaker Morrison noted that a custom had developed whereby MPs informed the House of any interest they might have in a matter under discussion. He went on to explain that this was more a courtesy than anything else (H.C. Deb, 1953). Thus, as Alan Doig notes, until 1974 the House 'took its guidance from an uncoordinated set of resolutions and precedents which gave little detail or explanation of what was required of Members to keep their private interests separate from their Parliamentary duties' (Doig, 1983, p.329).

The reasons for the lack of rules governing conflicts of interests are not hard to find. The House has always taken the behaviour of its members very seriously but has not sought to probe into matters which were not its concern, and has preferred to believe that its members could be trusted to behave honourably – at least until there was evidence to the contrary. The Select Committee on Members' Interests (Declaration), 1969-1970, considered the need for a register of Members' interests but came to the conclusion that a formal register could not be made to work, partly because of the problem of deciding what precisely should form part of the register and what should not. In any case, it thought a register unnecessary because it would unnecessarily reveal information which would only be of consequence in the context of a debate – when most Members could be relied upon to abide by existing conventions. Many members of the House no doubt shared the views articulated subsequently by Enoch Powell when speaking against the motion to establish a register of interests in 1975; that it was unnecessary partly because members of the closed circle of the House tended to know what interests other members represented, partly because a formal register reflected on the individual honour of MPs and partly because it would, in any case, be ineffective (H.C. Deb, 1975, cols 742-743).

The Register of Interests

The origins of the Register may be seen directly to lie in the Poulson case of the early 1970s which involved three MPs: John Cordle, Albert Roberts and Reginald Maudling. Whilst the House appeared disinclined to be over censorious in relation to Roberts and Maudling it took a firm position in relation to Cordle who, it felt, had engaged in conduct amounting to contempt of the House in pressing claims in relation to The Gambia without making clear his own financial interests (Select Committee on the Conduct of a Member of the House, 1976-77). However the scale of the problem went rather further than the misdemeanours of three MPs; the House had already acknowledged the wider concern about standards of conduct in the public sector by making a formal ruling that Members should declare their interests in 'any debate or proceedings of the House or its committees' (H.C. Deb, 1974). In addition, it had established a Select Committee on Members' Interests (Declaration), whose recommendations, debated in the House in 1975, included the establishment of a Register where MPs might voluntarily record their interests. As Edward Short, Leader of the House, made clear, this was intended to supplement rather than replace the obligations on a Member to declare his interests as and when the occasion arose. He added that he did not see the need for a cumbersome machinery to cover this issue and that it would remain the responsibility of individual Members to decide what should or should not be added to the Register (H.C. Deb, 1975, cols 737-739).

The value of the Register should not be dismissed, even if some Members consistently chose to ignore it. The Select Committee faithfully reported various (relatively minor) breaches of the Register's provisions drawn to its attention by Members (although it is perhaps significant that the two most serious cases that it dealt with – those of Mr Browne and of the participants in the 'cash for questions' affair – were brought to its attention by journalists). However, as Doig notes, its reports were rarely debated in any meaningful way, still more infrequently were MPs subject to any sanction, and 'the 1989 Browne case was the first time since the Committee's establishment in 1975 that a report had gone to the House for a decision' (Doig, 1998, p.13). He further notes that it was a weak and ineffectual committee and comments, in a telling phrase, that 'it was ultimately shown to be a part of the world of nuance and influence that characterizes much of the manipulation of government business'. If any evidence were needed to confirm the latter assertion it was amply provided by the attempt by a junior Whip, David Willetts, to influence the outcome of the Committee's inquiry into Neil Hamilton's role in the 'cash for questions' affair (Select Committee on Standards and Privileges, 1996-97). In any case, the committee lacked the capacity to deal with major issues. It did its best to unravel the intricacies of the Browne affair whilst acknowledging that it was unable to get to the heart of the matter (Select Committee on Members' Interests, 1990). Whatever the outcome of its investigation, such comments hardly inspire confidence in the procedures available to regulate the activities of Members

It is unsurprising, therefore, that such a committee should be found lacking in public or parliamentary confidence when faced with the challenges of the 1990s. Indeed, it may be argued that its failure to establish a credible reputation was in part responsible for some of these problems; many MPs obviously felt it unnecessary to comply with the spirit and, sometimes, the letter of the Register. On the other hand, its low profile undoubtedly reflected the wishes of a House not yet prepared to grapple with some of the potential problems that might emerge and which preferred to turn the blind eye that it always had to problems involving the individual behaviour of its members.

The Commissioner for Standards

The recommendation that the House appoint a Commissioner for Standards arose from a range of allegations about the behaviour of members of the House including the 'cash for questions' affair, the failure by some MPs to properly register their interests and suggestions that some Members were accepting 'favours' from business organizations for ill defined purposes. More important, perhaps, was wider public disquiet about the behaviour of those in positions of power and authority in public life, which included concerns about financial impropriety in government, the processes of appointing members of the boards of Non Departmental Public Bodies and continuing revelations of sexual misbehaviour. This combination of concerns ultimately led the Prime Minister, John Major, to establish a committee to inquire into standards of conduct in public life, under the chairmanship of Lord Nolan. Although this report devoted a chapter to discussing the standards of conduct to be expected of MPs it focused almost entirely on issues relating to the failure by some MPs to disclose personal interests in matters coming before the House (including interests arising from payment for asking Questions). Much of the discussion in this chapter went over old ground; there is now little debate about whether MPs should have paid outside interests – it is generally accepted that the House benefits from the diversity of backgrounds, as well as the contemporary understanding, that such interests bring. In any case, it would be extremely difficult to decide which outside interests were acceptable and which were not. In addition, MPs have always represented particular interests and it is right that they should. However, the figure quoted by the Committee, that nearly 70% of MPs (excluding members of the government and the Speaker) 'have financial relationships with outside bodies which directly relate to their membership of the House', provides evidence of the scale of a different problem (Nolan, 1994a, p.22). The size of this figure almost certainly has less to do with the venality of modern day politicians than with the fact that the number of MPs pursuing careers unconnected with Parliament has fallen considerably (Nolan, 1994a, p.27). Nevertheless, it is easy to draw the inference that a number of MPs undertake 'consultancies' for the purpose of supplementing their income and pursue policies on behalf of corporate clients with greater zeal than they would have done had they not been paid. In this connection the Committee drew attention to a second problem – that the Register of Members' Interests, valuable in its own way, had come to be regarded as an acceptable way for MPs to discharge their responsibilities to Parliament rather than, as was originally intended, merely provide a record of their interests (Nolan, 1994a, p.27). In particular, the

Committee drew attention to the problem of paid advocacy and the difficulty of separating it from paid advice. Whilst financial relationships between MPs and organizations which might wish to benefit from their expertise have always been regarded as acceptable, difficulties arise when that relationship is used primarily (if not solely) as a means of promoting particular interests. As the Committee pointed out, such relationships are not only unsatisfactory but breach the sprit of the 1947 resolution (Nolan, 1994a, pp.28-9).

The response of the Nolan Committee to these concerns was surprisingly cautious, especially in the light of its recognition that the activities of many MPs were of considerable public concern. Although it recommended that Members should be 'free to have paid outside interests unrelated to the work of Parliament' it decided that it was not practical to immediately ban the financial arrangements that so many MPs had reached with outside organizations, not least because 'the impact on the income of many MPs would have implications which could not be ignored'. Nonetheless, it particularly recommended that the practice of acting as 'general multi-client consultants' be prohibited (Nolan, 1994a, p.30). The Committee further decided that it was the responsibility of the House to hold Members accountable for their actions and thereby ruled out any attempt to use the law as a means of regulating MPs activities. The implication of this was that the problems were not so severe that they could not be dealt with by some clarification of the rules and the establishment of more certain procedures for dealing with breaches of those rules. Other particular recommendations thus included the appointment of a Parliamentary Commissioner for Standards and the drawing up of a code of conduct.

To some extent, therefore, the report was a disappointment. Whilst it clearly recognized that there was considerable public concern about the standards of conduct of MPs it felt unable to do more than suggest amendments (albeit extensive amendments) to existing procedures. The possibility that the procedures and processes adopted by the House were fundamentally flawed was not considered by the committee. Part of the reason for this, no doubt, was the very large remit of the Committee and its evident need to meet a number of public concerns very quickly. Another reason perhaps was the (necessarily) broad nature of its membership. Although two former Cabinet Ministers agreed to join the Committee along with a distinguished former Clerk and a well known Professor of Politics, it was never likely that the membership would be sufficiently radical to propose a fundamental review of the circumstances that had led to its appointment, or that it would ask whether the existing inadequate arrangements adopted by the House were so flawed that they needed complete rethinking rather than extensive adjustment. Had such a thought occurred to the Committee they would, no doubt, have succumbed to the prevailing ethos and concluded that such a review was a matter for Parliament itself and not one to be addressed by 'outsiders'.

The Code of Conduct has undoubtedly moved Parliament from a situation where the limited guidance available to MPs in respect of their ethical responsibilities was confusing and uncodified to one where they have substantial – possibly excessive – guidance. There can now be no excuse for a Member failing to understand the importance that Parliament attaches to adherence to appropriate ethical standards. Whilst this may be welcomed there is always a danger that too detailed a description of the responsibilities of Members will lead MPs to feel that they have to reveal every possible benefit that they might have received, from every possible source, to the benefit of nobody. It may also reinforce the problem noted on a number of occasions that MPs might feel that adherence to the requirements of the Register discharges their responsibilities to the House, instead of seeing it as a supplement to those responsibilities. Many of the complaints made to the Commissioner concern comparatively minor breaches of the rules, often the result of a misinterpretation or a simple oversight on the part of the offending Member. Although there is some value in ensuring that these inadvertent breaches are corrected, the process adds little to solving the problem of corrupt behaviour by MPs – indeed, perhaps it merely confirms that most MPs have no intention of acting in a way that might be considered corrupt.

The retiring report from the first Commissioner for Standards, published in 1998, argued that substantial progress had been made. The advocacy ban, first suggested by the Nolan Committee, had had a marked effect on the number of consultancies held by MPs and 'the main concerns about influence being bought and sold have been substantially reduced' (Select Committee on Standards and Privileges, 1997-98, Appendix, p.2). However, a number of problems remain. One is the continuing problem of the capacity of the Standards and Privileges Committee to reach decisions on some of the more complex issues that it examines. This was clearly an issue in the Hamilton affair where the Commissioner reached a balance of judgment based on the evidence available. In this regard the House has made only limited progress since the 1970s – much the same comments were made at the time of the report into the activities of Cordle, Maudling and Roberts (Doig, 1983). The complexities of the issues involved raise questions about both the capacity of the Commissioner and the Committee to undertake such inquiries and about the resources available to them. Sir Gordon Downey clearly felt that for routine breaches of the Code his staff was sufficient. But, as David Walker and David Hencke (1998, p.21) noted in a subsequent newspaper article, a limited staff restricts the nature of the cases that he is able to take on and prevents him from taking a more proactive approach to the problem of corruption. In particular, such a limited staff prevents any attempt to move a consideration of the ethical conduct of MPs beyond the narrow confines of conflicts of interest as a result of financial transactions.

A second problem relates to the procedures used to investigate individual cases. These currently comprise three stages involving the Commissioner establishing the facts and reaching a conclusion on breaches of rules, the Committee satisfying itself that the correct procedures were used and that conclusions are supported by evidence and, finally, the House itself which imposes such penalties as it sees fit. These fit a model of investigation where the Commissioner has limited powers, can only act in a quasi legal capacity and where his task is simply to investigate a case in order to establish the facts. By and large such a model appears to be acceptable both to the House in general and, with the exception of Neil Hamilton, to those who have been the subject of a complaint.

There are obvious reasons for keeping investigatory procedures outside the arena of the law and involving the police and the possibility of criminal proceedings only after the House has completed its inquiries. Nonetheless, the absence of rules about the conduct of enquiries leaves both the Commissioner and the Committee open to complaints that the procedures adopted do not meet the elementary requirements of natural justice. This is compounded by an accepted view that a Member may be found guilty of an offence based on a balance of probabilities rather than guilt beyond any reasonable doubt. The first Commissioner felt that the House was entitled to do this arguing, slightly tendentiously, that this was not a criminal case involving criminal sanctions. Hamilton, unsurprisingly, disagreed, arguing that the failure to observe the rules of natural justice meant that such findings were unsafe. Downey noted that the resolution of such a disagreement might mean the House considering the use of an external panel 'appointed by the House, on which a majority is apolitical' to act as an appellate board (Select Committee on Standards and Privileges, 1997-98, Appendix, p.3). He chose not to elaborate on the difficulties of choosing such a panel.

The third problem relates to the appropriate penalties to be exacted for breaches of the rules. Although there are four possible penalties of increasing severity, starting with a public censure, one MP likened these to the possibility of being executed publicly for shoplifting (H.C. Deb, 1998b). A further issue is that of fairness in the distribution of punishments – the Committee will do well to avoid the lingering suspicion from the judgment in the Cordle, Maudling and Roberts case that the popularity of the Members (or lack of it) was as much a factor in the penalties that were sought as the errors that each MP had committed. Downey noted a concern that the House had yet to establish an appropriate tariff for different grades of offences and expressed some concern that in at least one case the penalty meted out had been 'relatively severe' (Select Committee on Standards and Privileges, 1997-98, Appendix, p.4).

Conclusion

The need for the Nolan Committee, and the recommendations contained in its first report, points to the continuing weakness of Parliament's ability to regulate ethical behaviour both among its own members and among members of the government. It is perhaps significant that, in terms of the latter, the possibility of strengthening Parliament as a way of ensuring greater adherence to acceptable standards of behaviour seems not to have occurred to the Committee or to Members of the House. In terms of the behaviour of MPs, the House continues to try to rely on methods that do not challenge the evident probity of the majority of Members but, at the same time, provide little challenge to those tempted to act outside of appropriate conventions. Robert Sheldon's tribute on the occasion of the retirement of Sir Gordon Downey included the hope that the workload of Downey's (part time) successor would soon diminish as new standards were more widely recognized (H.C. Deb, 1998a). Whilst few would disagree with the optimism of his sentiments, the evidence of previous years seems to suggest the need for continuing, vigilant, control over existing standards which themselves may need to change in the light of changing circumstances.

Richard Chapman in an early but prescient response to the first report of the Nolan Committee noted that a code on its own would be insufficient; what was also needed was education and training for MPs as well as continuing public discussion about the standards to be expected from members of the House (Chapman, 1995, p.13). In this context, as in many others, transparency (in the form of a publicly available Register, and publication of reports by the Standards and Privileges Committee) is an effective means for ensuring that appropriate standards are adhered to. But the implications of Chapman's comments also make a more fundamental point. He might have been echoing Berlin's belief that it is only through a continuous process of trying to establish ideals that we are ever likely to ensure adherence to the standards we regard as appropriate for our public servants.

References

Berlin, I. (1998), 'The Pursuit of the Ideal', in Hardy, H. and Hausheer, R. (eds), *The Proper Study of Mankind*, London: Pimlico.

Chapman, Richard A. (1995), 'The First Nolan Report on Standards in Public Life', *Teaching Public Administration* Vol. XV, No 2, pp.1-14.

Doig, Alan (1979), 'Self – Discipline and the House of Commons: The Poulson Affair in a Parliamentary Perspective', *Parliamentary Affairs* Vol. 32, pp.248-67.

Doig, Alan (1983), 'Watergate, Poulson and the Reform of Standards of Conduct', *Parliamentary Affairs* Vol. 36, pp.316-33.

Doig, Alan (1998), '"Cash for Questions": Parliament's Response to the Offence that Dare Not Speak its Name', *Parliamentary Affairs* Vol. 51, pp.36-50.

H.C. Deb. (1947), 5s, Vol. 440, col 365, 15 July.

H.C. Deb. (1953), 5s, Vol. 510, col 2040, 5 February.

H.C. Deb. (1974), 5s, Vol. 874, cols 537-8 , 22 May.

H.C. Deb. (1975), 5s, Vol. 893, cols 735-45, 12 June.

H.C. Deb. (1998a), 6s, Vol. 319, col 808, 17 November.

H.C. Deb. (1998b), 6s, Vol. 319, col 820, 17 November.

Mancuso, Maureen (1993), 'The Ethical attitudes of British MPs: A Typology', *Parliamentary Affairs* Vol. 46, pp.179-91.

Nolan, Lord (1994a), *Standards in Public Life:* First Report of the Committee on Standards in Public Life, Cm. 2850-I, London: HMSO.

Nolan, Lord (1994b), *Standards in Public Life:* First Report of the Committee on Standards in Public Life, Cm. 2850-II, London: HMSO.

Ryle, Michael (1994), 'The Changing Commons', *Parliamentary Affairs* Vol. 47, pp.647-68.

Select Committee on Members' Interests (Declaration) (1969 -70), HC 57, London: HMSO.

Select Committee on the Conduct of a Member of the House, Session 1976-77, HC 490, London: HMSO.

Select Committee on Members' Interests, Session 1989-90, HC 135, London: HMSO.

Select Committee on Standards and Privileges, First Report, Session 1996-97, HC 88, London: The Stationery Office.

Select Committee on Standards and Privileges, Nineteenth Report, Session 1997-98, HC 1147, London: The Stationery Office.

Walker, D. and Hencke, D. (1998), *The Guardian*, 18 November.

4 The Ethics of Equal Opportunities

Susan Corby

This chapter looks at the ethics of equal opportunities in the UK public service from two perspectives: the state in its role as employer and the state in its role as government. Equal opportunities is used as shorthand terminology for efforts to achieve equality of opportunity in respect of gender, ethnic origin and disability, though the terminology can be extended to cover age, sexual orientation, and religious affiliation. Inevitably, however, this chapter concentrates on gender and ethnic origin as these areas of equal opportunities have been the subject of public discussion and public policy for a much longer period of time than other areas.

There are three main arguments in this chapter. First, equal opportunities was only seen primarily as an ethical issue for a short time, essentially from the 1960s to the early 1980s. In the first half of the twentieth century government considered that it was legitimate to discriminate against women and ethnic minorities and from the mid 1980s, equal opportunities has mainly been justified on business grounds, not ethical grounds. The second argument is that equal opportunities is threatened by delegation and decentralization in the civil service and local authorities, yet the equality dimension has largely been ignored in discussions about the ethical implications of public service restructuring. The third argument is that equal opportunities is undermined by a key ethical value in public service: selection and promotion on merit. The conclusions place these arguments in a wider context because the ethics of equal opportunities illustrate many key issues in the debates about public service ethics.

An ethical issue?

Discrimination legitimate

The Organization for Economic Co-operation and Development (OECD, 1996) looking at the public service cross-nationally, says that ethos is 'the sum of ideals which define an overall culture' and ethics are 'the rules that translate characteristic ideals or ethos into everyday practice'.

Ethical standards are not, however, absolute. Thus in the first half of this century, the dominant ideology held that it was legitimate to discriminate against women (though the women's movement dates back to the nineteenth century), and discrimination against ethnic minorities was disregarded. Thus it was not until 1928 that women obtained the vote on the same terms as men (i.e. from age 21). When the Sex Disqualification (Removal) Act 1919 was passed, a proviso was inserted to allow restrictions to be placed on the mode of admission of women into the civil service and their terms and conditions of service, which essentially were inferior to their male colleagues. Treasury regulations of 1921 required women civil servants to be single or widowed and it was lawful to reserve to men particular appointments in the civil service which were based abroad (Fredman and Morris, 1989). In the early 1920s a few local authorities paid women the same as men for the same work but a case was brought against the London Borough of Poplar, alleging that an equal pay regime was a misuse of the rates. The House of Lords held that Poplar's payment systems were unlawful as they were guided by 'eccentric principles of socialistic philanthropy, or by a feminist ambition to secure the equality of the sexes'.[1]

During the second world war the number of women in civilian employment rose and equal pay became an issue. A royal commission was established but its majority report, issued in 1946, supported continued inequality. Women were held to be less reliable, efficient or adaptable and lower pay was socially desirable as a stimulus to marriage. 'Given employer hostility to equal pay, trade union equivocation and a lack of leadership from the Labour government, the royal commission's view prevailed' (Pope, 1991, p.56).

Equality is ethical

Although the number of women in employment fell after the war, the figures for 1946 represented an increase of 15 per cent over those for 1939 (Pope, 1991) and the state began to act as employer. In 1946 it abolished the marriage bar for the home civil service, though not until 1972 for the foreign service (Hart, 1998). In 1955 it introduced equal pay for men and women into the civil service on a phased basis, as did local government for its employees, including teachers. In 1970, the government set up a committee, chaired by Mrs E. M. Kemp-Jones, to make recommendations to enable women to combine a career in the civil service with their family responsibilities. Its recommendations were virtually unprecedented elsewhere in Britain at that juncture. They included the provision of part-time work and a civil service workplace nursery, as well as relatively generous maternity leave (Civil Service Department, 1971). A joint management/union group, set up in 1980 to review progress, produced a report (Management and Personnel Office, 1982) which became the basis for a programme of action on women in the civil service.

The government's stance was a mixture of pragmatism (a desire to retain trained staff) and to be a good employer. The civil service unions too, who first established an equal pay committee in 1927, mixed pragmatism (males not wishing to be undercut by women providing cheaper labour) and social justice principles (Mortimer and Ellis, 1980).

The concentration on discrimination against women broadened to encompass ethnic minorities after an influx from the late 1950s of economic migrants, mainly from the West Indies, Pakistan and India. The campaign for the removal of racial discrimination, however, was less influenced by pragmatic considerations than the campaign for the removal of gender discrimination. The former 'was not based on the trade unions, but rather on organizations of ethnic minorities and sympathetic liberals and the Labour Party and other left wing organizations' (Hepple and Fredman, 1986, p.171). Accordingly, the Labour government introduced the Race Relations Acts 1965 and 1968 on social justice grounds. These Acts did not provide individuals with a right to litigate. Instead they had to go to the Race Relations Board whose main duty was to conciliate, but they were a start.

The importance of key ministers embracing a social justice perspective cannot be overestimated. For instance Barbara Castle, when Employment Secretary, claimed that the Equal Pay Act 1970 was enacted largely because of her determination to overcome what she called 'the macho-male chauvinists in the Treasury' (Castle, 1993, p.409). Similarly Roy Jenkins when Home Secretary, after seconding a human rights lawyer, Anthony Lester, as a political adviser, sponsored what became the Sex Discrimination Act 1975 and the Race Relations Act 1976. These Acts provided individuals with the right to go to an employment tribunal, extended the concept of discrimination from direct discrimination to indirect discrimination (a practice which is seemingly fair but is discriminatory in operation), and established the Equal Opportunities Commission and Commission for Racial Equality with strategic enforcement roles.

Meanwhile, during the 1970s and early 1980s many metropolitan authorities were proactive on equality, especially left-wing authorities such as Camden, Islington and Lambeth, as well as the Greater London Council (GLC), until its abolition in 1986. Both in their role as employer and in their role as government, these local authorities devoted much attention to fairness and justice, considering equal opportunities an integral part of this ethical stance, not only in respect of women and ethnic minorities, but also gays and lesbians. The GLC, led by Ken Livingstone, was at the forefront of the drive to equality, setting up a range of political and organizational structures to support its policies. In addition, it (and its sister organization, the Inner London Education Authority), copied the practice of contract compliance from the USA federal government. In 1983 the GLC made compliance with equal opportunity procedures and practices a condition of securing a contract to provide goods and services. It established a contract compliance equal opportunities unit to review the practices of contractors seeking retention on an approved list, thus encouraging companies to adopt an ethical stance out of self-interest. A study (Institute of Personnel Management, 1987) found that the GLC's unit had some success, resulting in significant numbers of companies changing their employment procedures and practices and the GLC's approach being copied by 19 other local authorities. The Conservative government, however, implemented the Local Government Act 1988 which outlawed contract compliance with regard to sex and circumscribed it in respect of race.

The business case

In the economic/political context of the 1980s and 1990s, arguments for equal opportunities based on moral obligations and social justice gave way to arguments based on business need. These arguments dovetailed with the emphasis in the 1980s on enterprise in a competitive global economy. In the public services they also dovetailed with the new right theories of bringing market disciplines into governmental activities, with the emphasis on efficiency and with the new public management (Corby and White, 1999).

It is important to stress that this chapter is merely saying that there was a shift in the dominant rationale and mobilizing vocabulary during the

1980s (Dickens, 1999). It is not suggesting that one can pinpoint a specific time when there was a marked change, nor that there can be only one rationale for equality at any one time. The social justice case for equality, especially gender equality as noted above, was often tempered by pragmatism. Similarly, from the 1980s although business case arguments dominated, social justice arguments were sometimes made. For instance the Cabinet Office, reporting in 1993 on the progress made under its programme to achieve equal opportunities for ethnic minority civil servants puts forward two rationales: organizational effectiveness and social justice (Cabinet Office, 1993).

The business case for equality centres on competition in the labour market. Organizations, it is argued, can secure higher quality employees if they recruit and select on the basis of merit, not stereotype; recruit from non-traditional sources such as women returners or ethnic minorities; provide family friendly measures to aid retention; and train and promote those in the lower grades where often women and ethnic minorities disproportionately cluster. Another strand of the business case focuses on organizational effectiveness. Organizations make better decisions if managers are diverse and have different perspectives because of their gender and ethnicity and reflect their customers' gender and ethnic mix. Although business case arguments are to be found now throughout the public and private sectors, their prevalence in the public sector represents a clear break with the past. The private sector has always been profit oriented and focused on business needs, while until the 1980s the ethical case provided the predominant rationale in public service.

In theory, these business case arguments, based on self-interest, are likely to be persuasive, offering a way to get equality identified as a strategic issue and trigger action. In practice, however, as Linda Dickens (1994) points out, the business case argument is contingent and partial and can lead away from equality, as well as towards it. For instance, where organizations experience labour market pressures they might opt for contracting out rather than recruiting from non-traditional sources, or opt for a higher rate of labour turnover rather than establishing a workplace nursery.

This chapter, however, does not focus on the pros and cons of the business case argument for equality. Rather it is concerned with noting the shift of the justification for equality from one primarily based on ethics and social justice to one based on the business case and added value. This new justification is most clearly seen in Opportunity 2000, a campaign to increase the quality and quantity of women's employment opportunities which is 'firmly built on the business case'. Opportunity 2000 says that its members:

are convinced that the business case for attracting, retaining and developing women will continue to be compelling well into the next century and see this as a key component of business excellence and global competitiveness (Opportunity 2000, undated).

Launched in 1991, Opportunity 2000 had 61 founding members including four civil service departments: Cabinet Office, Employment Department Group, HM Customs and Excise and Inland Revenue. In addition the Department of Health signed up on behalf of the National Health Service. At the end of 1998 there were 335 members. These included 19 local authorities and 32 civil service departments/agencies. A companion organization, Race for Opportunity, was established in 1995. Three years later, 16 of its 83 member organizations were civil service departments/agencies or local authorities (Race for Opportunity, 1998).

Business case arguments, however, do not only emanate from these campaigns. They also emanate from government and importantly have not been abandoned despite the change in the political party in power as a result of the 1997 general election. For instance, the Inland Revenue sponsored a research project focusing on how equal opportunities for the organization's employees adds value to the business and particularly resulted in improved customer service (Cabinet Office, undated). The then Trade and Industry Secretary, Peter Mandelson, said that an organizational focus on ethnic minorities is not 'linked to social altruism but to hard commercial return value' (Race for Opportunity, 1998, p.1). The White Paper, *Fairness at Work* (Department of Trade and Industry, 1998), when proposing family friendly legislation, used competitiveness and business effectiveness as the rationale.

The demise of the social justice case can also be seen in legislation. In the 1970s British equality legislation was far in advance of European Community (EC) law. Since the 1980s, however, this has changed. The UK government has seemingly become less concerned about furthering equality through legislation and more concerned that business can operate without legislative restrictions. Thus it has only legislated where it has been necessary to comply with EC requirements, for instance the amendments to the Equal Pay Act and the Sex Discrimination Act in 1983 and 1986 respectively and the parental leave provisions in the Employment Relations Act 1999. Similarly, the government did not institute the progressive Fair Employment Act (FEA) 1989 in Northern Ireland because of ethical considerations. Many large US corporations, after lobbying from Irish-Americans, refused to invest unless there was new legislation to further equality of opportunity for Catholics in Northern Ireland (McCormack and O'Hara, 1990).

Organizational restructuring and equality

The second argument is that devolution and decentralization are detrimental to progress on equality and that discussions on the ethical implications of organizational restructuring in the public services have centred on such issues as public accountability and the division of responsibilities between ministers and public servants. Rarely, however, have equal opportunities been included in such ethical considerations.

As readers know, unified bureaucracies in UK public services have been broken up into semi-autonomous units: executive agencies in the civil service, direct service organizations in local authorities, locally managed schools in education and self-governing trusts in the National Health Service. The effect on equality of these looser structures has been detrimental as the centre has been disempowered and can no longer drive policies forward. It can set a framework, disseminate good practice and act as a forum for the exchange of information but it cannot directly control. The Cabinet Office, for instance, does not carry out equality monitoring itself and although the civil service management code requires departments/agencies to monitor staff's gender, ethnicity and disability, they do not always do so comprehensively or adequately. Indeed, the Cabinet Office has expressed its concern as it is not able to assess which approaches promote equal opportunities and which get in the way. It says that departments 'report that they collect such data, but have provided little evidence to suggest that they have analysed the data, or where they have, have acted on the results of the analysis' (Cabinet Office, undated, p.10). Yet although the Cabinet Office says that it wants to improve the situation, its proposed remedy, revising the guidance on equal opportunities monitoring, is unlikely to be effective.

Allied with this organizational restructuring is delegation to the line. This increased delegation of authority is aimed at encouraging managers to manage, i.e. to be less risk averse and it has been argued that line managers' enhanced powers in such traditional personnel management areas as recruitment and promotion are favourable to equality. As the report of the advisory panel on equal opportunities in the senior civil service said, line managers traditionally considered 'personnel responsibilities in general and equal opportunities in particular to be someone else's problem. The new approach reinforces the responsibilities of line managers' (Cabinet Office, 1995a, p.25).

The research evidence, however, is less sanguine. For instance, a report on civil service promotion procedures found that many line managers were unaware of the potential for discrimination on grounds of gender, ethnicity and disability in staff appraisal reports and that there were departmental variations in the provision of training for line managers and in briefings for promotion board members and chairs (Stewart, 1993). Updating this research, the author points out that most of the recent changes in promotion procedures have resulted in greater delegation to line managers, which will allow even greater variations (Stewart, 1996). Similarly, research for the Equal Opportunities Commission found that managers of direct service organizations, the semi-autonomous units within local authorities, appeared to have a poor understanding of equal opportunities and that compulsory competitive tendering had had a more adverse impact on women than men in terms of numbers employed, hours worked and pay levels (Escott and Whitfield, 1995).

This delegation of responsibility to line managers is taking place at the same time as cost pressures on the public services increase. This has a harmful effect on equality for four reasons. First, central equality resources are being cut back and there is less support for line managers. For instance, at Manchester City Council, separate equality units for race, gender and disability were first merged and then abolished; and in 1996, according to the Council of Civil Service Unions, the equality unit in the Cabinet Office was reduced with a loss of a third of its staff. Second, cost reductions have led to lower staffing levels and organizational delayering. As women and ethnic minorities are concentrated at the base of departments/agencies or local authorities and at the lower levels in each occupational hierarchy, a reduction in promotion opportunities means that there is a decreased likelihood of changing the organization's gender and race profile. Also, organizational delayering often results in heavier workloads and longer working hours for those still in post and as a result many women have 'to make a stark choice between their careers and their families' (Coyle, 1995, p.60). Third, funding restrictions have encouraged short-termism, leading particularly to a decrease in equal opportunities training, according to Mary Coussey, who looked at two civil service agencies and two local authorities. She found that line managers, concerned to meet their financial targets, saw reductions in equal opportunities training as a relatively easy option (Coussey, 1997). Fourth, cost pressures are leading to economies on staff costs. For instance some local authorities, such as Camden and Islington, have cut maternity benefits and leave for dependants (Incomes Data Services, 1997).

An ethical conflict

The third argument in this chapter is that the conventional ethics of the civil service, which entail the principles of recruitment, selection and promotion on merit (see Chapter 7 for an account of the establishment of these principles), and the ethics of equal opportunities at best sit uneasily together and at worst are incompatible. These tensions, however, seem not to be appreciated. Thus the OECD says:

> Human resource policies promote ethics by ensuring fair and equitable treatment of employees ... Recruitment and promotion by merit reflects fairness. These processes can also meet equity criteria by ensuring that all social groups are represented in a public service (OECD, 1996, p.40).

Similarly, in the UK, the Permanent Secretary of the Office of Public Service has said in a foreword to a progress report on equal opportunities in the civil service that 'equality of opportunity for all is one of the foundations on which the civil service is based' (Cabinet Office, undated, p.2), a comment incidentally representing a misconceived view of history – see above. The report goes on to say: 'It is a fundamental principle that recruitment to the civil service is by fair and open competition and that selection is on merit' (Cabinet Office, undated, p.26). To take another example, John Major's administration re-emphasized the government's commitment to ensuring equality of opportunity and, in the same document said: 'The principle of selection and promotion on merit must represent the bedrock of a [politically impartial] Civil Service' (Cabinet Office, 1995b, p.3).

Admittedly, on its face, selection and promotion on merit go hand in hand with the civil service's equal opportunity programmes which revolve around removing discrimination. Such discrimination distorts the operation of the labour market but recruitment, selection and promotion based on fair procedures, it is assumed, will enable the best person to win and will generate a random distribution of ethnic minorities and women within the occupational hierarchy. As Nick Jewson and David Mason point out, however, this is a liberal concept of equal opportunities (Jewson and Mason, 1986). It concentrates on the rules of the game and leads to an emphasis on training to instruct employees in the formal procedures, to circumvent neglect and manipulation and to increase employees' understanding of other cultures and gender differences. To promote equal competition, liberals seek to remove obstacles to the operation of the labour market, so they adopt family-friendly measures at the workplace, advertising campaigns to reassure candidates from disadvantaged groups that their applications will be judged on their merits, and what is in British law called 'positive action' – training open only to disadvantaged groups such as women-into-management courses and outreach work encouraging disadvantaged groups to apply. This is starting gate equality in that it brings disadvantaged groups to the start of the 'race' on an equal footing with other competitors; but the race can only be won by the fastest. Selection and promotion is on merit.

In contrast, radicals argue that the evaluation of 'ability' and 'talent' is not politically or morally neutral. Those in positions of power define desirable knowledge and skills and the liberal concept of the meritocratic rise of the talented reinforces social inequalities. Accordingly, radicals would argue that it is legitimate to intervene in the workplace to ensure a fair distribution of rewards, for instance to waive entry or promotion requirements for women and ethnic minorities. Equality is achieved when there is equality of outcomes and the removal of discrimination and starting gate equality will not produce equality of outcomes because the 'race' will not be won by the disadvantaged, even when they have been the subject of remedial measures when adult.

The civil service employs liberal approaches to further equal opportunities and insists that recruitment and selection is on merit but paradoxically measures progress on equality by equality of outcome, a radical measure. Not surprisingly, this conflation and confusion leads to disappointing results. Thus as mentioned above, the civil service adopted a programme of action for women in 1984, a liberal programme, but it regards statistical advances as 'key indicators of progress' (Cabinet Office, undated). In 1984, when the programme was launched, women comprised 6 per cent of those with responsibilities equivalent to what is now called the senior civil service. The comparable figure in April 1998 was 16 per cent, an improvement certainly, but a slow one. In 1998 only 1.6 per cent of staff at senior civil service level were ethnic minority staff, compared to 1.4 per cent in 1989, the first year civil service ethnicity data was available (Government Statistical Service, 1999). The Civil Service Commissioners, who are charged with the responsibility for maintaining the principle of selection on merit on the basis of fair and open competition, show disappointment when they say:

> While we are confident that our selection procedures at all stages are demonstrably fair and objective, we would wish to see more applications for senior civil service jobs from ethnic minority candidates and more achieving success (Civil Service Commissioners, 1998, p.11).

The government's stance on equality on grounds of race and sex is different from its stance on equality on grounds of religious affiliation in Northern Ireland. Under the Sex Discrimination Act and the Race Relations Act, quotas are outlawed and only limited so-called positive action is allowed, essentially training for disadvantaged groups and outreach work. In contrast, in Northern Ireland (after pressure from USA corporations – see above), the government recognized that liberal measures would not necessarily yield significant outcomes and that radical approaches towards equality would have to be adopted under what was termed 'affirmative action'. Accordingly the FEA defines affirmative action in the following terms:

> In this Act 'affirmative action' means action designed to secure fair participation in employment by members of the Protestant, or members of the Roman Catholic, community in Northern Ireland by means including:
> (a) the adoption of practices encouraging such participation ...

Although fair participation is not defined in the Act, it is argued that it must mean equality of outcome, ie overall Protestants and Catholics are employed at all levels in proportions approximating to their number in the population and that any practice aimed at achieving fair participation, including tempering the merit principle, is lawful (McCrudden, 1992). More recently, the Patten report on the future of the Royal Ulster Constabulary recommends recruitment quotas, i.e. that recruits to the Northern Ireland police force should be drawn on a 50:50 basis from the Catholic and Protestant communities (Independent Commission on Policing for Northern Ireland, 1999).

The tempering of the merit principle on grounds of gender is also creeping into European Union law which takes priority over UK law. The European Court of Justice (ECJ) in a case centring on the civil service law of the German regional government of North Rhine-Westphalia,[2] held that it is not contrary to the Equal Treatment Directive for qualified women to be given preference for promotion where there are fewer women than men at the level of the relevant post. Although their decision is not clear and unambiguous the ECJ says:

> As the Land and several governments have pointed out, it appears that even where male and female candidates are equally qualified, male candidates tend to be promoted in preference to female candidates, particularly because of prejudices and stereotypes concerning the roles and capacities of women in working life.

In addition, the 1997 Treaty of Amsterdam provides that:

> With a view to ensuring full equality in practice between men and women in working life, the principle of equal treatment shall not prevent any member state from maintaining or adopting measures providing for specific advantages to make it easier for the under-represented sex to pursue a vocational activity or to prevent or compensate for disadvantages in professional careers.

This will allow, but not require, member states to adopt radical measures to promote equality and to temper the merit principle and, for instance, would allow all women shortlists for candidates to be Members of Parliament, a practice which the Labour Party tried before the 1997 general election until an employment tribunal held that the practice was unlawful.[3]

The British civil service, however, so far has given no signs of even recognizing that the ethics of equality and the traditional ethics of the civil service may not be compatible. Thus it does not seem to have started to discuss whether the merit principle should be tempered on grounds of gender and ethnicity (unlike the public service in the USA).

The wider context

The ethics of equal opportunities illustrate key issues in public service ethics generally. This chapter first suggested that equality was only seen as an ethical issue for a short time, the 1960s to the early 1980s. Before then it was considered legitimate to discriminate and since then equality measures have largely been justified by business need and not on social justice grounds. But ethical standards are not absolute in public service and, as Richard Chapman points out, 'what is acceptable in one place or at one time may differ from what is acceptable in another place or a different time' (Chapman, 1993, p.1).

Secondly, this chapter argued that equal opportunities may be undermined by the wider public policy context of delegation and decentralization in the public services. This illustrates Lawrence Pratchett's point in Chapter 8 that ethical decision making is shaped by the institutional context. It also exemplifies the point that public service restructuring, undertaken with the aim of improving managerial efficiency by bringing in market disciplines or proxies for them, may have ethically adverse results. As the OECD says: 'governments may have to decide if there is an implicit trade-off between ethics and efficiency and where the appropriate balance lies' (OECD, 1996, p.22). This is illustrated by compulsory competitive tendering which has had a more adverse impact on women than men. (Martin Painter, looking at the Australian experience in Chapter 11, focuses on other ethical implications of contracting out.)

Thirdly, the chapter has argued that equal opportunities is threatened by a key ethical value in public service, recruitment and promotion on merit, but again this conflict of core principles is not uncommon. Two public service standards may be equally desirable but when taken together may conflict. For instance Lawrence Pratchett in Chapter 8 points to the potential conflict between openness in public administration and accountability of the civil service to the government of the day.

The chapter also discussed the liberal and radical approaches to equal opportunities, the former focusing on process and the latter on outcomes. Both John Major's and Tony Blair's administrations have placed great stress on the measurement of outcomes for the public services but this has not always gone hand in hand with the necessary measures to achieve such outcomes, for instance recruitment quotas in the case of equal opportunities. Whether the focus is on process or on outcomes is a central debate in public service ethics and is particularly salient in the context of the Human Rights Act 1998. Judicial review of administrative actions centres on process: illegality, irrationality or procedural impropriety[4] but, as George Szablowski explains in Chapter 5, s.6 of the Human Rights Act centres on acts of public authorities, i.e. outcomes. Also, the liberal and radical approaches to equality provide different views of what is in the public interest: should the civil service be seeking starting gate equality or equality of outcome? The problem of defining the public interest is an important theme in public service ethics as Barry O'Toole demonstrates in Chapter 6 and he gives the example of the Iran/Iraq war when one department thought that the public interest was best served by selling as much equipment as possible and another department thought that the public interest was best served by not arming a potential enemy.

In short, the ethics of equal opportunities can be considered in their own terms but they can also be seen as a microcosm for ethics in public service. They effectively are a case study of how public service ethics are shaped by wider public policy objectives but these objectives, and underlying ethical values, vary over time. Moreover, objectives, although equally commendable, may conflict, for instance the objective of bringing market disciplines into the public services and the objective of ensuring that greater numbers of ethnic minorities and women hold senior positions in public administration, or objectives relating to process and objectives relating to outcome. To pretend that there will not continue to be ethical problems is disingenuous, but both greater transparency and a consideration of the wider ramifications of public policy objectives could lead to a greater awareness of the ethical implications. Prime Minister Tony Blair has argued for integration and 'joined up' government (Cabinet Office, 1999). This should not just focus on public policy and the delivery of public services, it should extend to underlying values.

Notes

1. *Roberts v Hopwood* [1925] AC 578.
2. *Marschall v Land Nordrhein-Westfalen* [1998] IRLR 39, ECJ. This effectively overrules a previous ECJ decision, *Kalanke v Freie Hansestadt Bremen* [1995] IRLR 660, that such positive action was contrary to the Equal Treatment Directive.
3. *Jepson and Dyas-Elliot v The Labour Party and others* [1996] IRLR 116.
4. *Council of Civil Service Unions v Minister of the Civil Service* [1984] 3 All ER 935 HL.

References

Cabinet Office (undated), *Equal opportunities in the civil service 1995-97: a progress report*, London: The Cabinet Office.
Cabinet Office (1993), *Equal opportunities in the civil service for people of ethnic minority origin: third progress report 1992-1993*, London: HMSO.
Cabinet Office (1995a), *Advisory panel on equal opportunities in the senior civil service*, London: Cabinet Office.
Cabinet Office (1995b), *The Civil Service: taking forward continuity and change*, Cm. 2748, London: HMSO.
Cabinet Office (1999), *Modernising government*, Cm. 4310, London: The Cabinet Office.
Castle, Barbara (1993), *Fighting all the way*, London: Pan Books.
Chapman, Richard A. (ed.) (1993), *Ethics in Public Service*, Edinburgh: Edinburgh University Press.
Civil Service Commissioners (1998), *Annual report 1997-98*, London: Office of the Civil Service Commissioners.
Civil Service Department (1971), *The Employment of Women in the Civil Service: a report of a committee chaired by Mrs Kemp-Jones*, London: HMSO.

Corby, Susan and White, Geoff (eds) (1999), *Employee relations in the public services: themes and issues,* London: Routledge.
Coussey, Mary (1997), 'Public sector study' in *Decentralisation and devolution: the impact on equal opportunities,* Ware, Herts: Wainwright Trust.
Coyle, Angela (1995), *Women and organizational change,* Manchester: Equal Opportunities Commission.
Department of Trade and Industry (1998), *Fairness at work,* Cm. 3968, London: The Stationery Office.
Dickens, Linda (1994), 'The business case for equality: is the carrot better than the stick?' *Employee Relations* Vol.16, No. 8, pp.5-18.
Dickens, Linda (1999), 'Beyond the business case: a three pronged approach to equality action', *Human Resource Management Journal,* Vol. 9, No. 1, pp.9-19.
Escott, Karen and Whitfield, Dexter (1995), *The gender impact of CCT in local government,* Manchester: Equal Opportunities Commission.
Fredman, Sandra and Morris, Gillian S. (1989), *The state as employer,* London: Mansell.
Government Statistical Service (1999), *Equal Opportunities in the Civil Service: Data Summary 1998,* London: Cabinet Office.
Hart, Jenifer (1998), *Ask me no more,* London: Peter Halban.
Hepple, Bob and Fredman, Sandra (1986), *Labour Law and Industrial Relations in Great Britain,* London: Kluwer.
Incomes Data Services (1997), *Pay in the public services: review of 1996, prospects for 1997,* London: Incomes Data Services.
Independent Commission on Policing for Northern Ireland (1999), *A new beginning: policing in Northern Ireland,* report of Commission chaired by Christopher Patten.
Institute of Personnel Management (1987), *Contract compliance: the UK experience,* London: Institute of Personnel Management.
Jewson, Nick and Mason, David (1986), 'The theory and practice of equal opportunities policies: liberal and radical approaches', *Sociological Review* Vol. 34, No. 2, pp.307-34.
Management and Personnel Office (1982), *Equal opportunities for women in the civil service: a report by the joint review group on employment opportunities for women in the civil service,* London: HMSO.
McCormack Vincent and O'Hara, Joe (1990), *Enduring Inequality: religious discrimination in employment in Northern Ireland,* London: National Council for Civil Liberties.
McCrudden, Christopher (1992), 'Affirmative action and fair participation: interpreting the Fair Employment Act 1989', *Industrial Law Journal* Vol. 21, No. 3, pp.170-98.

Mortimer, James E. and Ellis, Valerie A. (1980), *A professional union: the evolution of the Institution of Professional Civil Servants*, London: Allen and Unwin.

Opportunity 2000 (undated), *About the campaign*, London: Business in the Community.

Organisation for Economic Co-operation and Development (OECD) (1996), 'Ethics in the Public Service: current issues and practice', *Public Management Occasional Papers* No. 14, Paris: OECD.

Pope, R. (1991), *War and society in Britain 1899-1948*, Harlow, Essex: Longman.

Race for Opportunity (1998), *Newsletter*, November.

Stewart, Marie (1993), *Equal opportunities and promotion: a report to the Cabinet Office*, unpublished, London: Taylor-Stewart Associates.

Stewart, Marie (1996), *Equal opportunities in promotion procedures: a report to the Cabinet Office*, unpublished, London: Taylor-Stewart Associates.

5 Courts, Parliament, and Public Authorities under the British Human Rights Act 1998

George J. Szablowski

Introduction

In the *Brind* case, decided in 1991, the House of Lords held that public authorities (including ministers), acting in the exercise of administrative discretion, were free to violate human rights guaranteed in the European Convention on Human Rights (ECHR) because the 'treaty, not having been incorporated in English law, cannot be a source of rights and obligations' (Lord Ackner in *R. v. Secretary of State for the Home Department*, 1991). In 'Administrative Discretion and the Protection of Human Rights' (Szablowski, 1993) it was argued that, if statutory incorporation of the ECHR was politically impossible at the time, the protection of Convention rights in Britain should become the professional responsibility of all civil servants and such responsibility should be explicitly recognized in their respective codes of ethics.

The new Civil Service Code did in fact place ministers and civil servants under a duty to comply with 'international human rights treaties to which the United Kingdom is party' (Constitution Unit, 1996, p.27). This well-intentioned general measure represented an important step in the right direction. Its significance, however, has been now totally overshadowed by the Human Rights Act 1998 (HRA) which provides (for the first time and without precedent in the history of British public administration) that 'it is unlawful for a public authority to act in a way which is incompatible with a Convention right' (Section 6(1)).

The HRA forms part of a package of constitutional bills recently introduced before Parliament by the Labour Government and described by Tony Blair as 'the biggest programme of change to democracy ever proposed' (Hazell, 1999, p.1). It is expected that this programme of reform, when implemented, will 'transform the political landscape and reshape the British state in ways that are not fully understood' (Hazell, 1999, Foreword). In the field of human rights, we may witness an entirely novel structure of institutional conflict between courts, Parliament, and public authorities: United Kingdom courts as guardians and enforcers of Convention rights, the UK Parliament as maker and protector of offending (incompatible) legislation, and UK public authorities as perpetrators of unlawful acts. It is the intention of the Government to implement the HRA gradually and selectively by bringing its provisions into force 'on such day as the Secretary of State may by order appoint; and different days may be appointed for different purposes' (HRA, section 22(3)). Section 19 which requires ministers to make 'statements of compatibility' with respect to bills introduced in the House of Commons has been already brought into force.

The Constitution Unit's Report on Human Rights Legislation contemplates that, before the Act takes effect, it may be necessary to provide guidance to public bodies and law enforcement agencies, to undertake a programme of public education, and to offer additional training and guidance for judges 'both in terms of the rationale for human rights and the practicalities of their protection' (Constitution Unit, 1996, pp.93-4). It is the government's intention to render the new human rights protection regime fully operational in October 2000 (Constitution Unit, 1999, September, p.6).

Some critics question the readiness of the legal professionals (lawyers and judges) to perform effectively the new intellectual tasks demanded by the HRA. 'English lawyers receive less by way of higher education than do their counterparts anywhere else. It is hard to see how a three year university education can possibly prepare the next generation of lawyers with the intellectual tools necessary to enable the full potential of the Human Rights Act to be realised. This is even more true of the ability to research, understand, and present social science data which may become of increasing relevance in Convention litigation' (Leigh and Lustgarten, 1999, p.63).

In this chapter, the key provisions of the HRA as a human rights protection instrument and as a future battleground for contending institutional and individual interests are examined. New institutional roles and relationships between the courts, Parliament, and the public authorities will be shaped as those claiming violations of Convention rights will take their claims, first, before UK courts and, then, before the European Court of Human Rights in Strasbourg. How will the new human rights regime function in Britain? Will it deliver the Government's promises: to realize 'the biggest change to democracy ever proposed', and (more modestly), to decrease the number of cases taken each year from Britain to Strasbourg, and to cut the litigation delays and expenses?

Courts and Parliament

The HRA treats public authorities very differently from Parliament and primary legislation. It is important, for our purposes, to understand this difference in legislative treatment and its consequences. Broadly speaking, sections 3, 4 and 5 of the Act give new powers and responsibilities to the courts to interpret primary and subordinate legislation 'in a way which is compatible with Convention rights' and to make declarations of incompatibility when necessary. Sections 6, 7, 8 and 9 deal with public authorities and impose on them legal restrictions and sanctions which they have not faced before. These include:

a) the prohibition (subject to important exceptions) to act in a way that is incompatible with Convention rights; this prohibition extends to administrative decisions and to subordinate legislation (regulations) passed or adopted under delegated authority;
b) the obligation to submit to civil court proceedings when unlawful acts (i.e. acts incompatible with Convention rights) are committed; and
c) the obligation to comply with court orders that are 'just and appropriate' including orders quashing unlawful administrative decisions or regulations, and/or awarding damages against the responsible public authorities.

These civil restrictions and sanctions do not apply to either House of Parliament nor to 'persons exercising functions in connection with proceedings in Parliament', even if a higher UK court declares an act of Parliament (or its provision) to be incompatible with a Convention right. They do apply, however, to all public authorities defined very broadly to include all individuals and institutions (including courts) performing public functions (HRA, section 6).

Clearly, the HRA establishes a double standard for the domestic enforcement of the Convention rights in Britain. Public authorities must not breach substantive Convention rights incorporated into UK law. If they do, they face judicial review. Parliament, on the other hand, is subject to a different standard. Higher courts (in England and Wales or Northern Ireland: the High Court or the Court of Appeal; in Scotland: the High

Court of Justiciary sitting in appeal; and the House of Lords (HRA, 1998, section 4(5))) are given the power to declare primary legislation incompatible with Convention rights. They are not permitted, however, to strike down such legislation as invalid. Instead, the offending provisions remain in force, and it is up to the government of the day to decide whether the incompatible law should be amended and the incompatibility removed. Section 10 of the Act permits (but does not require) a minister of the Crown to take 'fast-track remedial action' for this purpose. Presumably, a minister acting pursuant to this section qualifies as a 'person exercising functions in connection with proceedings in Parliament' and is therefore exempt from potential liability under section 6.

Ian Leigh and Laurence Lustgarten in their original and exhaustive analysis of the HRA suggest that the Act was deftly devised to 'protect human rights through the courts without infringing upon the fundamental principle (or sacred dogma) of parliamentary supremacy'. They write:

> At the most optimistic, this is treading a line of anorexic fineness; to critics ... it is an attempt to square a circle. The ingenious solution embodied in the Act is to give the courts the power to declare that an Act of Parliament is contrary to the Convention, but not to negate, annul, hold illegal or even to 'disapply' it (Leigh and Lustgarten, 1999, p.48).

The double standard produces two sets of consequences. In the domestic arena, it establishes a new kind of dichotomy between public administration and government policy expressed in primary legislation. The scope and autonomy of the former is curtailed by 'higher values', i.e. human rights; the scope and autonomy of the latter remains unaffected unless in a specific case and for 'compelling reasons' the government decides to take 'remedial action' under section 10. According to Professor Paul Craig 'the expectation is that a judicial declaration of incompatibility will render it difficult for Parliament to resist modification of the offending provisions. Whether this proves to be the case remains to be seen' (Craig, 1999, p.70). The real question, of course, is how the government of the day will decide on the basis of its own policy priorities and objectives. Moreover, 'fast-track' remedial orders of incompatible legislation may be part of a deft constitutional design, but, as Leigh and Lustgarten aptly point out, they are 'fundamentally inconsistent with the idea of vindicating individual *rights* ... a litigant who has in a formal sense won a case is left empty-handed' (Leigh and Lustgarten, 1999, p.51).

The Home Office White Paper attempts to justify this dichotomy on the basis of the 'importance which the Government attaches to Parliamentary sovereignty'. The White Paper claims that 'a provision enabling the courts to set aside Acts of Parliament would confer on the judiciary a general power over the decisions of Parliament and would draw the judiciary into serious conflict with Parliament' (Home Office, 1997, p.10).

This statement is difficult to reconcile with the government's declared objective to modernize British politics. It, also, misrepresents the relationship between government and Parliament, and the reality of substantive judicial review. This is not the place to engage in a discussion of the doctrine of parliamentary sovereignty, which many constitutional scholars regard as a 'vision' or an 'orthodoxy' based on 'questionable ... to say the least ... empirical and normative assumptions' (Craig, 1999, p.68). However, from the perspective of human rights enforcement, it is important to dispel certain misconceptions about judicial review and about the power of the courts to strike down offending primary legislation.

Substantive judicial review does not threaten Parliament's competence or its capacity to make laws for the following reasons:

1. Judicial examination of the relationship between a protected human right and an allegedly infringing legislative provision is narrow, issue-specific, and done in the context of the particular facts of the case; consequently, this type of inquiry does not even come close to the exercise of a 'general power over the decisions of Parliament'.
2. The process of arriving at, and taking, the decision to set aside a particular legislative provision is 'principled' that is, it is informed and guided by rules of interpretation and by precedents developed by the courts and intended to distinguish this process as much as possible from political decision-making which is free from such constraints.
3. Broadly based and protracted policy conflicts between the judiciary and Parliament are unlikely because the courts are typically reactive/remedial institutions lacking a coherent political agenda, and the resources to pursue such an agenda consistently. This is not to say that specific judicial decisions protecting human rights have no significant impact on issues of public policy. Such impact, however, is legitimate because rights set out in a constitutional document (whether entrenched or not) are meant to trump infringing public policy unless the government can justify it as a reasonable and proportionate limitation (Hiebert, 1999).
4. Judicial review based on the supremacy of EC law over domestic law already permits UK courts to question the validity of legislation passed by Parliament. However, the EC law must have direct effect in the UK,

and it will prevail only to the extent of a clear conflict between it and the UK law in question. Again, the principles of interpretation, the precedents, and the narrow scope of review make a real threat to Parliament's general power to make laws unlikely (Chalmers, 1998, pp.277-81 and 366-92).

Canadian experience confirms that judicial review available under the Canadian Charter of Rights and Freedoms does not impede the processes of governance and law making (Greene et al, 1998, especially Chapters 1 and 9). However, it does create a forum for public discourse about the role of the courts in policy-making.

Canadian courts have the power to set aside offending primary and subordinate legislation as well as administrative and policy decisions of federal, provincial and municipal governments (*Operation Dismantle v. R.* 1985), but, they use this power with care and only pursuant to established principles, rules, and doctrines intended to guide the process of Charter interpretation and enforcement. Before they strike down a prima facie infringing legislative provision, they must examine the alleged violation in the context of 'reasonable limits prescribed by law' which permit governments to justify the infringement as necessary in a free and democratic society.

The Canadian Supreme Court has developed a modified 'margin of appreciation' approach to section 1 of the Charter which is known as the 'justification and reasonable limits clause'. It includes a 'proportionality test' very similar to the principle of proportionality applied by the European Court of Human Rights. Pursuant to this approach, the Canadian Court will rarely question the judgment of the government on, either the importance of the law or its objective. It will focus, instead, on the question whether 'the law has impaired the Charter right no more than is necessary to accomplish the objective' (Hogg, 1998, p.711). Thus, governments can significantly maximize their chances of success under section 1 by designing their legislation to meet the crucial criterion of 'least drastic means' and by presenting appropriate evidence before the courts to show that the offending law does not, in fact, impair Charter rights more than is necessary to accomplish the intended and legitimate policy objective.

In addition, the Canadian Charter also contains a 'notwithstanding' clause which permits legislative override of certain rights and freedoms for a period of five years without any required justification (section 33). Although this clause has been rarely invoked since 1982, there is a growing recognition of its potential usefulness and validity as a 'balancing' measure in the on-going 'dialogue' between the legislatures and the courts.

In a recent study, Professor Janet L. Hiebert examined the relationship between courts and Parliament in the context of three social policy issues and came to the following conclusion:

> Institutional disagreements should not be thought of as a disadvantage to democratic politics. The Charter introduces a dynamic force into the policy process that requires more attention be paid to whether and how policies undermine important rights. Judicial review and the prospects of nullifying legislation that does not comply with the judiciary's interpretation of the Charter, enhance the pressure to comply with constitutional values. This increased focus on rights need not result in frequent or destabilizing conflicts. This is the genius of the Charter's contribution to the Canadian polity (Hiebert, 1999, p.32).

In the international arena under the European Convention, the double standard adopted in the HRA creates potentially serious problems and opens the door to challenges before the European Court of Human Rights and, possibly, before the European Court of Justice. A member state's obligation to secure for everyone within its jurisdiction the rights and freedoms set out in the Convention (article 1) applies in the same manner, equally and without distinction, to the state's legislative, executive, administrative and judicial acts. The Convention case law does not extend to member states a greater 'margin of appreciation' for violations resulting from their incompatible primary legislation, nor does the Convention grant a privileged status to the doctrine of parliamentary sovereignty claimed by the UK government (Home Office, 1997, p.10). Professor A. W. Bradley called this doctrine 'a massive obstacle' to the protection of human rights in Britain (Bradley, 1989, p.44).

It is, to say the least, disturbing when a Labour Government, intent upon constitutional reform and modernization, uses this ambiguous and increasingly questionable doctrine as an excuse for its unwillingness to 'bring home' rights fully and without equivocation.Without a substantive judicial review of primary legislation, the incorporation of the ECHR into British law is incomplete. It fails to satisfy both the letter and the spirit of the European Convention, and it fails to take into account the recently enacted provisions of the Treaty of Amsterdam regarding fundamental rights. These provisions impose an express obligation on the member states to respect Convention rights which now form part of the EC legal order (Chalmers, 1998, pp.290-318, and Duff, 1997, pp.3-11).

More precisely, article 1 of the Convention imposes on each member state the duty of securing to everyone the specified rights and freedoms; and article 13 requires that everyone whose rights are violated 'shall have an effective remedy before a national authority' (significantly, these two articles have been omitted from schedule 1 of the Human Rights Act and, consequently, are not incorporated into UK law). There is a considerable body of ECHR case law on the interpretation and meaning of these provisions (Janis et al, 1995, pp.428-67). The general trend of the European Court's jurisprudence is to grant to member states a wide margin of appreciation in the choice of 'effective remedy'. Thus, 'national authority' does not need to be judicial. An aggregate of remedies provided under domestic law may satisfy the requirements of article 13, even if a single remedy does not; and there is no 'given manner' for ensuring effective implementation of article 13, and no legal requirement to incorporate the Convention into domestic law (Janis et al, 1995, p.437).

As a matter of fact, the Convention has been incorporated into the domestic laws of practically all member states. There is, also, a growing view that the past interpretation of articles 1 and 13 is unsatisfactory and unsustainable. It reflects a degree of reliance on the margin of appreciation doctrine which is inconsistent with the emerging and appropriate role of the Strasbourg Court as set out in Protocol No. 11. The Protocol, which has been in effect and binding on all member states since November 1998, restructures the control machinery of the Convention system 'in order to maintain and improve the efficiency of its protection of human rights and fundamental freedoms' (Council of Europe, 1994, Protocol No. 11, Preamble). Significantly, the clauses giving member states the options of accepting the jurisdiction of the Court or the right of individual petition have been dropped. Under the new system, member states, by their ratification of Protocol No. 11, automatically grant the right of individual petition to their citizens and residents, recognize the jurisdiction of the Court and are bound by its judgments. This change in the Convention system strengthens the autonomous status and the legitimacy of the Strasbourg Court *vis-à-vis* the member states and their governments.

Consequently, it should not be surprising if, in the future, the Court decides to alter its interpretation of articles 1 and 13 by requiring the states to provide in their domestic laws a standard judicial 'effective remedy' for the enforcement of Convention rights. Subject to the diversity of national court systems and variations in domestic constitutional traditions and practices, a degree of procedural/remedial standardization is likely to be acceptable to member-states. Such a measure would be consistent with the developing convergence between European Community law and European Human Rights law. The European Court of Justice, for instance, has already recognized its jurisdiction to protect fundamental human rights in the interpretation of EC law and in the course of judicial review of EU administrative decisions and practices (Chalmers, 1998, pp.304-19).

Pursuant to Schedule 1 of the HRA, the substantive rights and freedoms set out in the Convention and in its first and sixth protocols are made part of British law, while procedural and institutional provisions of the Convention are left out. This probably means that the rules governing the process before the European Court, its organization, and its final judgments remain in the realm of international law only and may not be directly enforceable by British courts. Section 2 of the Act, however, imposes a duty on the courts to 'take into account' judgments of the European Court of Human Rights 'relevant to the proceedings'. This may open the door for the courts to examine the procedure for optional remedial action (section 10 of the Act) as an 'effective remedy' under article 13 of the Convention. Would a UK higher court declare section 10 to be incompatible with effective protection and enforcement of Convention rights?

Although article 13 of the Convention has not been incorporated into UK law, the obligation to protect Convention rights is now embodied in Community law which has direct application in the UK (Treaty on European Union, article 6(2)). In addition, the Amsterdam Treaty makes the 'respect for human rights and fundamental freedoms' a formal condition of membership in the European Union (Treaty on European Union, article 49). These Treaty provisions have 'direct effect' in the UK and, thus, they take precedence over potentially conflicting domestic law such as section 10 of the Human Rights Act. A UK court may have no choice but to rule on the validity of this section in the context of the Community law obligation to respect and to enforce Convention rights (*Amministrazione delle Finanze Stato v. Simmenthal*, 1978). Craig quotes the following statement of the House of Lords uttered in *Factortame (No. 2)*:

> Some public comments on the decision of the Court of Justice, affirming the jurisdiction of the courts of the member states to override national legislation if necessary to enable interim relief to be granted in protection of rights under Community law, have suggested that this was a novel and dangerous invasion by a Community institution of the sovereignty of the United Kingdom Parliament. But such comments are based on a misconception ... Whatever limitation on its sovereignty Parliament accepted when it enacted the European Communities Act 1972 was entirely voluntary. Under the terms of the 1972 Act it has always been clear that it was a duty of a United

Kingdom court, when delivering final judgement, to override any rule of national law found to be in conflict with any directly enforceable rule of Community law (Hazell, 1999, p.69).

In conclusion, the Government's decision to exclude primary legislation from domestic judicial review under the HRA was unwise. Moreover, there is good reason to believe that it will prove to be embarrassing and ineffective. Worst of all, it is unnecessary because it purports to protect the British system of government from a danger that does not exist.

Courts and public authorities

On first reading, sections 6, 7, and 8 of the Human Rights Act provide far reaching and effective remedies against violations of Convention rights. Acts of public authorities, if shown to be incompatible with Convention rights, are unlawful; persons directly affected by such acts ('victims') can bring proceedings against them; and courts are empowered to grant 'such relief or remedy, or make such order' that is 'just and appropriate' (HRA, 1998, section 8(1)). This broad range of remedies includes damages and orders quashing the offending acts.

When we examine the language of these sections more closely, however, the initial impression of far reaching and effective remedies begins to fade. The definition of a 'public authority' appears to be broad and includes any person or institution performing 'functions of a public nature', presumably, whether these functions are administrative, executive, legislative or judicial. However, if the functions of an 'authority' are of a public nature and the offending act *itself* is held to be private, such act will not be unlawful under section 6 and there will be no remedy (HRA, 1998, section 6(5)). This is the first escape clause which public authorities can use in defence of claims under the Act. Its effectiveness will depend on the judicial interpretation of 'private' versus 'public' acts of public authorities.

Acts of Parliament and those of any person working in connection with proceedings in Parliament are specifically excluded, but not the decisions of the House of Lords sitting in its judicial capacity. Curiously, the new Scottish Parliament and the National Assembly for Wales, as well as the new institutions in Northern Ireland, are public authorities under the Act and thus subject to section 6.

The Home Office in its White Paper tells us that the term 'public authorities' includes 'companies responsible for areas of activity which were previously within public sector such as privatized utilities, to the extent that they are exercising public functions' (Home Office, 1997, p.8). However, there is nothing in the HRA about privatized 'authorities', and it is not clear what public functions they may still be performing. It can be expected that, if proceedings are instituted against such companies under the Act, they will be defended rather vigorously. Nicholas Bamforth in his examination of the application of the HRA to private bodies concludes that 'horizontal effect would have to be brought about through statutory amendment' (Bamforth, 1999, p.18).

Potentially, the widest escape clauses (and those that are most damaging to the protection of Convention rights) are contained in subsection 2 (a) and (b) of section 6 of the Act. They exempt from judicial review any public authority which can demonstrate to the satisfaction of a court that:

a) it was forced by primary legislation to act the way it did ('it could not have acted differently') or
b) it was merely giving effect to a provision of primary legislation, *itself* incompatible with Convention rights, which cannot be interpreted otherwise.

Craig appears to be convinced that section 6 (2) does not present a danger to human rights enforcement under the HRA because the courts are likely to interpret it in a restrictive manner beneficial to individuals, on the ground that it impinges on their fundamental rights (Craig, 1999, pp.74-5). Thus, he states, 'the court will often deny the public authority's defence (based on section 6 (2)) by rejecting the argument that the public authority could not, for example, have acted differently' (Craig, 1999, p.75). The essential assumption here is that section 6 (2) impinges on or denies human rights; but, a different interpretation is equally plausible.

Section 6 (2) deals with certain acts of public authorities and the application of section 6 (1) to them. It specifies the conditions under which these acts will be neither incompatible with Convention rights nor unlawful (although, under (b) the enabling primary legislation may be incompatible). It permits public authorities to use these conditions as defences to claims against them brought under section 6. Surely, public authorities, as defendants in civil proceedings, are entitled to plead provisions of the Act as statutory defences, and to insist that these should not be rendered illusory by a restrictive interpretation, even if such defences may narrow the scope of the application of the Act (which Parliament clearly intended) and, only indirectly and cumulatively, may have the effect of limiting the range of human rights protection under the Act.

Thus, section 6 (2) may not infringe directly any of the Convention rights listed in schedule 1. Rather, its purpose and effect appear to be to exclude certain categories of claims based on acts of public authorities which, by statutory definition, are not unlawful because they cannot be separated from the enabling primary legislation.

This purpose and effect is consistent with the more general exclusion in the Act of all claims based on primary legislation. As a matter of principle, human rights victims are denied recourse against acts of Parliament even if they are flagrantly incompatible with Convention rights. Section 6(2) extends the application of this principle to public authorities. If this interpretation is correct, the courts need not, and must not, construe section 6 (2) in a restrictive manner. On the contrary, they should give the language employed its full meaning and permit the defendants to take fair advantage of the available defences, without rendering them impotent or illusory.

Section 6 (1) imposes a duty on the court to determine whether a specific act of a public authority is incompatible with a Convention right. 'Incompatibility' appears to be a new concept carefully selected by the designers of the HRA. It is significant that the Act, as a human rights enforcement measure, does not speak of 'violation' or 'infringement' of Convention rights, and does not require proof of infringement before the court can grant the remedies set out in section 8. It is only 'incompatibility' between acts and rights that matters. Will the courts hear evidence or only arguments on the question of incompatibility? The Act contemplates incompatibility of primary and subordinate legislation, and incompatibility of the acts of public authorities, but it does not state that incompatibility is equivalent to violation, nor that it results, or may result, in violation or infringement.

What is the difference between incompatibility and inconsistency? The Canadian Constitution Act 1982 provides in section 52 (1) that 'any law that is inconsistent with the provisions of the Constitution is, to the extent of the inconsistency, of no force or effect'. This provision is seen as a general principle of Constitutional supremacy and the source of substantive judicial review. In the course of Charter analysis, however, the courts rely on section 24 (1) of the Charter itself which speaks expressly of infringement or denial of rights, and requires that infringement be established before any remedies can be awarded. Sections 13, 34, and 41 of the ECHR, speak also of 'violations' of the protected rights and freedoms which give the European Court the power to grant 'just satisfaction'. Thus, it would appear that the use of 'incompatibility' in the HRA may be similar to the use of 'infringement' or 'violation' in the ECHR and in the

Canadian Charter; the objective is to establish a standard for civil liability; but why did the British drafters avoid the terminology so well known and generally recognized in human rights legislation and in existing international and national case law?

Is it possible that the ECHR (including Protocol No. 11) and the HRA (including the schedules) create two separate but related regimes of human rights enforcement? (Early indications are that implementation of the HRA in Scotland may lead to the development of a distinctive Scottish human rights regime (Monitor, 1999, September, p.9)). It can be argued that British courts directly involved in the latter regime need not, perhaps should not, import from the other regime concepts, doctrines, rules, and ideas unless they are directly relevant for the administration and enforcement of the HRA, and also 'relevant to the proceedings' before them (HRA, 1998, section 2). The British regime is concerned with 'incompatibility' and 'unlawfulness' (which applies only to public authorities); it is not concerned with 'violations' of rights which is the domain of the other regime. If this is how the relationship between the ECHR and the British Act is to be structured, then it is open for the British courts to develop their own rules and doctrines for the interpretation of the domestic human rights legislation, to avoid 'unsuitable' convergence with the European system, and to maintain and protect the distinctiveness of their own regime. In practical terms, however, the HRA protection will have to be at least as extensive as the ECHR protection, or litigants will simply go to Strasbourg and win there after losing in the UK courts.

The intention here is to underline the significance of the approach adopted by the designers of the HRA, and the choices they have made in the selection of concepts and terms which appear to signify a measure of intended divergence from (instead of convergence with) the ECHR (and, indirectly, the Canadian) system of human rights enforcement. This measured divergence is most prominent in the area of primary legislation; but it may also have a real impact on claims against public authorities.

All is in the hands of British judges and lawyers who will initially (and probably for some time) produce a variety of different interpretations of the HRA until the House of Lords eventually steps in with a clear line of binding precedent. The Act offers great opportunities for professional disagreement about the meaning and effect of many of its provisions. What the designers and drafters intended is one thing, what the courts (with the help of litigation lawyers) will ultimately decide may be very different.

There is little doubt that public authorities will face the brunt of litigation under the HRA. They can always settle without actually admitting liability and agree on a remedy acceptable to the victim; but it is a fair guess that in most cases they will choose to use the provisions of the Act to defend themselves. The HRA is written in such a way that litigation is made a promising enterprise for both plaintiffs and defendants, and of course for the lawyers who will advise and represent them. In anticipation of future claims to be made against them, public authorities will do well to prepare for all eventualities.

The first strategy will require the development of 'in-house' personnel trained in the fields of human rights as well as law and competent to use the HRA as a 'litigation preventive strategy'. Such strategy may require rewriting of subordinate legislation (regulations), re-fashioning of internal rules of conduct and procedures, and behavioural changes aiming to limit the exposure to human rights claims under the Act. The second strategy will focus on the fullest and most effective utilization of the escape clauses and other provisions of the HRA. Since there is hardly any UK precedent on this subject, knowledge of the ECHR case law will be crucial. With regard to the critical issue of 'incompatibility', judges and lawyers will face an entirely novel situation. New procedural and evidenciary ground-rules for the litigants will have to be worked out. Will evidence be admissible to prove (and to rebut) 'incompatibility'? Or, is 'incompatibility' strictly a question of law to be argued by lawyers? Should 'incompatibility' be seen as tantamount to 'infringement', thus opening the door to a wider reliance on the ECHR and other human rights judicial precedents and experience? There is little doubt that imaginative and persuasive interpretation of the HRA will become a highly valued professional enterprise, sought-after by British public authorities of every description.

The HRA will become the source of new human rights litigation practice in Britain. As such, it is likely to generate increasing professional activity leading to an increasing volume of claims lodged by victims against public authorities over time. Although for the first time British judges will hear and decide cases which would have been taken in the past to the Strasbourg Court, it is very doubtful that the actual number of ECHR based lawsuits originating from Britain will decrease. Good litigation lawyers will not stop their efforts on behalf of human rights victims just because all domestic recourses have been exhausted. They will find grounds to go to the ultimate judicial authority and they will advise their clients accordingly.

Here is a list of eleven most obvious circumstances where claims initially brought against public authorities under sections 6, 7, and 8 of the HRA will have to be taken to the European Court of Human Rights in Strasbourg, unless they are settled or dropped:

1. When the trial court rules that the defendant is not a 'public authority' because its functions are held to be not of a public nature under section 6 (3), and an appeal is denied, or final appeal is unsuccessful.
2. When the trial court rules that the defendant is not a 'public authority' under section 6 (5) because the offending act (or omission) is held to be private, and an appeal to a higher court is denied, or final appeal is unsuccessful.
3. When the trial court rules that the plaintiff is not a victim of the unlawful act under section 7 (1) and (7), and an appeal to a higher court is denied, or final appeal is unsuccessful.
4. When the trial court rules that the proceedings against the public authority have been brought after the end of the period of one year following the date on which the act complained of took place, and the court refuses to extend this period on equitable grounds under section 7 (5), and an appeal to a higher court is denied, or final appeal is unsuccessful.
5. When the trial court rules that the offending act (or omission) is not incompatible with a Convention right under section 6 (1), and an appeal to a higher court is denied, or final appeal is unsuccessful.
6. When the trial court rules that the offending act (or omission) is not unlawful because the public authority could not have acted differently pursuant to the relevant provisions of primary legislation under section 6 (2) (a), and an appeal to a higher court is denied, or final appeal is unsuccessful.
7. When the trial court rules that the offending act (or omission) is not unlawful because the public authority merely gave effect to primary legislation which, according to the court, cannot be read in a way which is compatible with the Convention rights under section 6 (2) (b), and an appeal to a higher court is denied, or final appeal is unsuccessful.
8. When the trial court rules that the offending act (or omission) is incompatible with a Convention right but it fails to grant any remedy to the plaintiff under section 8 (1), and an appeal to a higher court is denied, or final appeal is unsuccessful.
9. When the trial court, in determining whether to award damages or the amount of the award, fails to take into account the principles applied by the European Court of Human Rights in relation to the award of compensation under article 41 of the Convention.
10. When the trial court renders final judgment in favour of the plaintiff and an appeal is denied to the public authority or its final appeal is unsuccessful.
11. When the trial court renders final judgment in favour of the public

authority and an appeal is denied to the claimant or his/her final appeal is unsuccessful.

Conclusion

Clearly, the incorporation of the ECHR into UK law is an event of great constitutional and political significance. It should end the UK's unreasonable isolation from the other member states of the Council of Europe which share 'written constitutions, fundamental rights, and comprehensive systems of public law' (Lester, 1989, p.368). Yet, there are elements in the HRA which suggest that full convergence between UK law and the UK judiciary, on the one hand, and the European regime of human rights protection and the European Court of Human Rights, on the other, may not be soon forthcoming. These elements appear to represent the designers' intention to mark the HRA with a significant degree of distinctiveness thus making full reciprocity between the HRA regime and the ECHR regime more difficult. This conclusion is supported specifically by the following provisions:

1. Introduction of 'incompatibility' as the key operating concept in the HRA in place of the generally recognized concepts of 'violation' and 'infringement' used in the ECHR.
2. Exclusion of primary legislation from judicial review.
3. Optional rather than mandatory 'remedial action' by a minister of the Crown with respect to legislation incompatible with Convention rights.
4. Omission from schedule 1 of significant parts of the European Convention, and especially articles 1 and 13, which are thus unincorporated into UK law.
5. The statement in the HRA that judgments of the European Court of Human Rights must be merely 'taken into account' by UK courts rather than followed as precedents (section 2 (1)).
6. A questionable remark in the Home Office White Paper that 'UK judges do not deal in the same concepts as the European Court of Human Rights (which) limits the extent to which their judgments can be drawn upon and followed' presumably by European courts (Home Office, 1997, p.7).

The issue of convergence is critical in international and national human rights litigation and enforcement. Academic scholars and other researchers recognise the reality and the need for conceptual, doctrinal, and procedural 'coming together' in the practice of law-making, law-interpretation and application, and in the practice of judging. High professional standards are universal and increased convergence of practices across national boundaries makes good common sense (Greene *et al*, 1998, Chapters 1, 5, and 9). A good example of a 'converging' approach to human rights is the current search for 'horizontality' in the application of existing national and international regimes by British scholars through comparative analyses of the HRA, the Canadian Charter, the ECHR, and other relevant jurisdictions (Eg. Hunt, 1998; Leigh, 1999; Bamforth, 1999).

Murray Hunt expresses most directly the view about the needed convergence in legal culture and judicial function between the national and international regimes of human rights adjudication:

> The (UK) courts will have to carry out a highly structured exercise in judicial reasoning identical to that carried out by the Court in Strasbourg. They will have to decide whether the interest for which protection is sought is within the scope of a Convention right, whether there has been an interference with that right, whether that interference is prescribed by law, whether it serves a legitimate aim and whether the extent of the interference is proportionate to the aim pursued ... With this expansion of the legitimate judicial role, it is to be hoped that the courts will embrace a more explicit acknowledgment of the irreducible political content of (human rights) adjudication (Hunt, 1999, pp.17-18).

References

Amministrazione delle Finanze Stato v. Simmenthal (1978), Case 106/77, E.C.R. 629.
Bamforth, Nicholas (1999), 'The Application of the Human Rights Act 1998 to Public Authorities and Private Bodies', unpublished manuscript.
Bradley, Anthony, W. (1989), 'The Sovereignty of Parliament – in Perpetuity?', in Jeffrey Jowell and Dawn Oliver (eds), *The Changing Constitution*, 2nd edn, Oxford: Clarendon Press.
Chalmers, Damian (1998), *European Union Law. Volume One*, Aldershot: Ashgate Publishing.
Chalmers, Damian and Szyszczak, Erika (1998), *European Union Law. Volume Two*, Aldershot: Ashgate Publishing.
Chapman, Richard A. (ed.) (1993), *Ethics in Public Service*, Edinburgh: Edinburgh University Press.

Constitution Act, 1982 including Canadian Charter of Rights and Freedoms (1982), Appendix III in Peter W. Hogg, *Constitutional Law of Canada* (fourth edition), Toronto: Carswell.

Constitution Unit (1996), *Human Rights Legislation*, London: University College.

Constitution Unit (1999), *Monitor – The Constitution Unit Bulletin*, Issues: 6 (March), 7 (June), and 8 (September), London: University College.

Council of Europe (1950), Convention for the Protection of Human Rights and Fundamental Freedoms, as amended by Protocols.

Council of Europe (1994), Protocol No. 11 to the European Convention on Human Rights and Fundamental Freedoms.

Craig, Paul (1999), 'Constitutionalism, Regulation and Review' in Robert Hazell (ed.) *Constitutional Futures: A History of the Next Ten Years*, Oxford: Oxford University Press.

Duff, Andrew (1997), *The Treaty of Amsterdam*, London: Federal Trust/Sweet & Maxwell.

Greene, Ian, Baar, Carl, McCormick, Peter, Szablowski, George and Thomas, Martin (1998), *Final Appeal: Decision-Making in Canadian Courts of Appeal*, Toronto: James Lorimer.

Hazell, Robert (ed.) (1999), *Constitutional Futures: A History of the Next Ten Years*, Oxford: Oxford University Press.

Hiebert, Janet L. (1999), 'Wrestling with Rights: Judges, Parliament and the Making of Social Policy', *Choices*, Montreal: Institute for Research in Public Policy, Vol. 5, No. 3, July 1999.

Hogg, Peter W. (1998), *Constitutional Law of Canada* (fourth edition), Toronto: Carswell.

Home Office (1997), *Rights Brought Home: The Human Rights Bill*, Cm. 3782, London: Stationery Office.

House of Commons Library (1998a), Research Paper 98/24 (13 February) 'The Human Rights Bill'.

House of Commons Library (1998b), Research Paper 98/27 (13 February) 'The Human Rights Bill: Some Constitutional and Legislative Aspects.'

Human Rights Act (1998), London: Stationery Office.

Hunt, Murray (1997), *Using Human Rights Law in English Courts*, Oxford: Hart Publishing.

Hunt, Murray (1998), 'The "Horizontal Effect" of the Human Rights Act', *Public Law* Autumn pp.423-43.

Hunt, Murray (1999), 'The Human Rights Act and Legal Culture: the Judiciary and the Legal Profession', unpublished manuscript.

Irvine of Lairg, Lord (1997), 'Constitutional Reform and a Bill of Rights', *EHRLR*, pp.483-9.

Irvine of Lairg, Lord (1998), 'The Development of Human Rights in Britain under the Incorporated Convention on Human Rights', *Public Law* Summer pp.221-36.
Janis, Mark Kay, Richard and Bradley, Anthony (1995), *European Human Rights Law: Text and Materials,* Oxford: Oxford University Press.
Laws, Sir John (1998), 'The Limitations of Human Rights', *Public Law* Summer pp.254-65.
Leigh, Ian (1999), 'Horizontal Rights, the Human Rights Act and Privacy: Lessons from the Commonwealth?', *International and Comparative Law Quarterly* Vol. 48, pp.57-87.
Leigh, Ian and Lustgarten, Laurence (1999), 'Making Rights Real – the Courts, Remedies and the Human Rights Act', *Cambridge Law Journal* Vol. 48, pp.509-45.
Lester, Anthony (1989), 'The constitution: decline and renewal' in Jeffrey Jowell and Dawn Oliver (eds.), *The Changing Constitution,* 2nd edn. Oxford: Clarendon.
Operation Dismantle v. R. (1985) 1 S.C.R. 441.
Pannick, David (1998), 'Principles of Interpretation of Convention Rights under the HRA and the Discretionary Area of Judgment', *Public Law* pp.545-51.
R. v. Secretary of State for the Home Department ex parte Brind (1991), 1 A.C. 696.
Szablowski, George J. (1993), 'Administrative Discretion and the Protection of Human Rights' in Richard A. Chapman (ed.) *Ethics in Public Service,* Edinburgh: Edinburgh University Press.
Treaty on European Union (1991), as amended following the ratification of the Treaty of Amsterdam.
Wade, Sir John (1998), 'Human Rights and the Judiciary', *EHRLR,* pp.520-33.

6 The Public Interest: A Political and Administrative Convenience?

Barry J. O'Toole

'The Public Interest' is a phrase redolent with the authority which attaches to the State. Sceptics, however, may see it as simply a phrase used by those in positions of state authority to legitimize their actions; and by those not holding such positions, but who wish to affect public policy, as a means of lending weight to their proposals. Others may view it as a concept which is essentially ethical in nature, and which is central to ideas about democracy in modern western societies. It is not, however, a modern concept. Indeed, as with directly related ideas about 'public duty', 'the public interest' is as old as philosophy itself. Thus, just as public duty was central to Plato's views on government in his *Republic*, so the public interest, or more accurately, 'the common interest', was central to those of Aristotle on *Politics* (and both were certainly aware of the perversions of each idea in the actual world). Its pedigree is long and honourable, and philosophers from all epochs have dealt with it, at least implicitly, in their writings, including St Thomas Aquinas and more latterly the idealists of the nineteenth and twentieth centuries, including Harold J. Laski, whose views are to form part of the basis of this discussion.

The purpose of this chapter is to consider the meanings of the concept, explore its manifestations in the world as it actually is, and raise questions about whether the sceptical or the philosophical view is of more value in understanding the actual work of politicians, officials and others in the political process. The approach is normative, the thoughts of various thinkers from different traditions are explained and contrasted and examples taken from the actual world are examined. The two exponents of the public interest dealt with here are Aristotle (with some comments from Aquinas) and Laski; and two writers who deny the existence of any such phenomenon, and may be described as being from the 'sceptical school', are Arthur F. Bentley and David B. Truman, both early 'group theorists'.

These two latter have been chosen for two reasons: first, because their work forms the foundation upon which contemporary so-called 'network theorists' and students of 'governance' have developed ideas of policy communities etc.; and secondly, because they were explicit in denying the existence of what Bentley described as 'the social whole', and thus by implication any objective public interest. The question is whether the public interest is a concept which promotes ethical behaviour or is simply a term used for political or administrative expedience.

Philosophical considerations on 'The Public Interest'

Sir Ernest Barker, whose 1946 translation is the basis of this discussion, is clear on the central place of ideas about the public or common interest in Aristotle's *Politics:* 'The common interest ... is not only or mainly economic: it is an interest in the attainment of a *good* (rather than a comfortable) life: and it requires for its satisfaction those institutions, such as a system of justice, which are necessary for such a life. It is this common interest in the attainment of a good life which is the chief end served by the state' (Aristotle, 1946 edition, note on p.111). In Aristotle's own words, 'Those constitutions which consider the common interest are *right* constitutions, judged by the standards of absolute justice. The constitutions which consider only the personal interests of the rulers are all wrong constitutions or *perversions* of the right forms' (Book III c.vi s.10).

Of course, Aristotle was concerned with the ideal state, or rather when discussing perversions of the right forms of constitutions appears to have been harking back to what might now be described as a 'golden age' of communities in which equal citizens took it as their duty to serve the community in turns, where 'the office of ruler [was] primarily intended for the ruled' and in which 'each assumed that others would take over the duty of considering his benefit, just as he had himself considered the interests of others' (III vi 10). Such a state was, in Aristotle's view, a 'natural system'. However, the contemporary situation was different: 'Moved by the profits to be derived from office and the handling of public property, men want to hold office continually...' (III vi 11). To Aristotle, this actual state of affairs was *unnatural* because it undermined the common interest: for him people are or ought to be 'drawn together by a common interest ... The good life is the chief end, both for the community as a whole and for each of us as an individual ...' (III vi 3, 4). The duty of the rulers in the 'right' form of constitution is always to act in the common interest and promote the 'good' life. The legislator should understand 'that what is "right" should be understood as what is "equally right"; and what is "equally right" is what is for the benefit of the whole state and for the common good of its citizens' (III xiii 11-12).

In his comments on Aristotle, Aquinas, primarily taken here from the *Summa Theologica*, is even more emphatic about the 'common good'. With Aristotle, Aquinas believed that 'man is naturally a social animal' (D'Entreves, 1954, p.105); and because of this he is also a political animal. He accepted that there 'could be no social life for many living together unless one of their number were set in authority to care for the common good' (p.105). The wise and the righteous would have command over the rest and make the laws. In addition, since 'every part bears the same relation to its whole as the imperfect to the perfect, and since one man is a part of that perfect whole which is the community, it follows that the law must have as its proper object the well-being of the whole community' (p.111). Indeed, 'Law, strictly understood, has as its first and principal object the ordering of the common good' (p.111). The law is 'nothing other than a rational ordering of things which concern the common good' (p.113). Moreover, society cannot be in a healthy state unless the citizens, or at least 'such of them as are called to take up the direction of affairs', are virtuous (p.119).

Both Aristotle and Aquinas were, of course, concerned with the ideal, or if actual, with small states. In societies with which they would have been familiar it would still theoretically be possible for a large proportion of the citizens to take in turn the responsibilities of office, and perhaps be constrained in the ways Aristotle outlined to act in the common interest. Over time, however, societies have become larger and more complex and the phenomenon of 'the state' as we understand it now, and loosely defined, has emerged. The modern state, as with other large organizations in the world as we perceive it, is elitist: it consists of those institutions which, subject to certain constraints, set the parameters, legal and to some extent moral, within which the rest of society operates, and it is staffed by those who regard themselves, and are regarded by others, as being the 'leaders' of society. In 1921 James Bryce alluded to this in his *Modern Democracies:*

> In all assemblies and groups and organised bodies of men, from a nation down to the committee of a club, direction and decisions rest in the hands of a small percentage, less and less in proportion to the larger and larger size of the body, till in a great population it becomes an infinitesimally small proportion of the whole. This is and always has been true of all forms of government, though in different degrees (1921, Vol II, p.542).

Rather than concerning himself with the *polis*, the state as he understood it, it is about these elites of the modern state which Aristotle would almost certainly write if he were living now. Harold Laski, because he did write about the state and the elites of the state, is used here as a modern exemplar of idealism, though, of course, other idealists also considered such matters (see O'Toole, 1990). He was as clear about the idea of the promotion of the common interest in his 1925 work *The Grammar of Politics* as Aristotle was in the *Politics* and Aquinas was in his writings. 'The State', Laski writes, 'is ... a fellowship of men aiming at the enrichment of the common life' (p.37). Individual citizens of the state have certain rights, inherent in them as members of society, counterbalanced by certain duties. In Laski's words, 'I am given rights that I may enrich the common life' (pp.39-40). Further, 'I judge the state, as a fundamental instrument of society, by the manner in which it seeks to secure for me the substance of those rights' (p.39). Indeed, '... if those rights fail of realisation, I am entitled to examine the State upon the hypothesis that its will is directed to ends other than the common good' (p.40). In other words, the state 'does not possess power without conditions. It possesses power because it has duties. It exists to enable men, at least potentially, to realise the best that is in themselves ... The State ... is subject to a moral test of adequacy' (pp.27-8).

Of course, it is not the state, but the individuals who work in the corridors of power, who constitute the elites of the state, which are the actual moral agents. As Laski puts it:

> the effective source of State action is the small number of men whose decisions are legally binding upon the community. They are at once the trustees and the governors of the whole. It is their business to glean the needs of society and to translate those needs into terms of effective statutes. The purpose of the State finds its personification in them (p.26).

He goes on: 'A working theory of the State must be conceived in administrative terms. Its will is the decision arrived at by a small number of men to whom is confided the legal power of making decisions' (p.35).

Clearly, this is an over-simplification. Society is much more complex than this characterization of the state allows. If it were simply that the holders of state power were able to glean clearly what the best interests of society are, then we would not have debates about what the public interest is, and Laski recognised this problem: 'The will of the state .. is the will which is adopted out of the conflict of the myriad wills which contend with each other for the mastery of social forces...' (p.35). More importantly, there are problems associated with personal or group interests which may interfere with the judgment of those who are charged with the determination of the public interest, problems of a much greater magnitude than Aristotle alluded to in the *Politics*. It is, however, to the myriad wills that this chapter next turns.

The Myriad Wills: The public interest simply as one amongst many interests

Writing only a few years before Laski, Bentley, the founding father of the group approach to the study of government, published his seminal work *The Process of Government* (1908). In it he took quite a different view of the state from that of Laski and other idealists. Bentley believed that there is no such thing as 'the social whole'. He derived this proposition from his view of nations as comprising a myriad of groups. He says that: 'Every classification of the elements of a population must involve the analysis of the population into groups' (p.206). There is 'a limitless criss-cross of groups' (p.208). These groups all have an 'interest'. Indeed, for Bentley, 'An interest ... is the equivalent of a group ... There exists only one thing, that is, so many men bound together in or along the path of a certain activity' (p.211). Furthermore, 'What we actually find in this world, what we can observe and study, is interested men, nothing more and nothing less' (p.212). Indeed, the political process cannot be studied without first the processes underlying groups being studied. His assertion is that political groups (such as organs of the state or political parties) are built out of or upon other groups. They are 'highly differentiated ... reflecting or representing other groups, which latter can easily, and ... for most purposes properly, be regarded as being more fundamental to society' (p.209).

Furthermore, there is no such thing as 'the public interest', except as the interests of the groups which form political organizations. Bentley is quite clear. 'We are often told', he opines:

> that social interests or social welfare demands this thing or that thing; that this custom or that institution has survived because it furthers the welfare of society ... I think I am justified in asserting positively that no such group as 'the social whole' enters into the interpretation in any form whatever (p.220).

He argues that it might be possible in the case of two nations at war to treat each nation as 'a separate group', 'but it is clear that under such circumstances neither nation is "the social whole"; it takes two together to make the society whose processes we are at the time studying' (p.220).

In domestic policy terms Bentley is even more clear: 'we should never be justified in treating the interests of the whole nation as decisive. There are always some parts of the nation to be found arrayed against other parts' (p.220). He continues:

> Usually we shall find, on testing 'the social whole', that it is merely the group tendency or demand represented by the man who talks of it, erected into the pretence of a universal demand of the society; and thereby, indeed, giving the lie to its own claims; for if it were such a comprehensive all-embracing interest of the society as a whole it would be an established condition, and not at all a subject of discussion by the man who calls it an interest of society as a whole (p.220).

Giving various examples, ranging from housing conditions to corporate murder, Bentley satisfies himself that the idea of 'the social whole', and thereby a public or national interest should be abandoned:

> under any society in which we are called upon to study [political questions], we shall never find a group interest of the society as a whole. We shall always find that the political interests and activities of any given group – and there are no political phenomena except group phenomena – are directed against the activities of men ... in other groups, political or other. The phenomena of political life ... will always divide the society ... along lines which are very real. ... The society itself is nothing other than the complex of groups that compose it (p.222).

The Government is simply one such group: it is 'a differentiated, representative group, or set of groups, performing specified governing functions for the underlying groups of the population' (pp.260-1). As a group, of course, the governing body also has its own interest. This is not, however, the public interest; nor is it 'as prominent as it is made out to be'; it is rather and simply 'the class activities of the persons who are most prominent in, or who make up, the governing body' (p.290). Government as an activity may simply be 'considered as the adjustment or balance of interests' (p.264). To Bentley, 'All phenomena of government are phenomena of groups pressing one another, forming one another, and pushing out new groups and group representatives (the organs or agencies of government) to mediate the adjustments' (p.269).

Truman, a writer in the same tradition as Bentley, also deals with what we might label in short hand as 'the public interest', and essentially comes to the same conclusion. He considers the question as a means of heading off criticism of the group approach, the particular criticism being that the group explanation of the political process 'inevitably must ignore some greater unity designated as society or the state' (1951, p.59):

> Many of those who place particular emphasis on this difficulty assume ... that there is an interest of the nation as a whole, universally and invariably held as standing apart from and superior to those of the various groups included within it. This assumption is close to the popular dogmas of democratic government based on the familiar notion that if only people are free and have access to 'the facts', they will all want the same thing in any political situation. It is no derogation of democratic preferences to state that such an assertion flies in the face of all that we know about the behavior of men (p.50).

The conclusion thus is that 'in developing a group interpretation of politics ... we do not need to account for a totally inclusive interest, because one does not exist' (p.51). In reaching this conclusion, however, Truman accepts that he does not 'completely dispose of the difficulty raised by those who insist that a group interpretation must omit "the state"' (p.51). Indeed, he accepts that groups are inevitably drawn towards government because they have 'since the Renaissance, especially national governments, ... become the most inclusive power concentrations in Western society ...' (p.106). Nevertheless:

> Within limits ... organized interest groups, gravitating towards responsive points of decision, may play one segment of the structure against another as circumstances and strategic considerations permit. The total pattern of government over a period of time thus presents a protean complex of criss-crossing relationships that change in strength and direction with alterations in the power and standing of interests, organized and unorganized (p.508).

The question from the perspective of this chapter is this: is this characterization simply the same as Laski's view of the world as it actually is, that: 'The will of the State ... is the will which is adopted out of the conflict of the myriad wills which contend with each other for the mastery of social forces' (Laski, 1925, p.35)? Is the will of the state just one of these myriad wills? Or is it, to pervert Truman's phrase, 'standing apart from and superior to' the others of those myriad wills? In the first case, clearly, there is no such thing as the public interest, and Laski, in separating out the actual from the ideal, might simply be viewed as having accepted that the sceptics' opinion of the public interest is substantiated. In the second, the protection and promotion of the public interest may well be the state's *raison d'être*. This, of course, begs the question thus far only alluded to or answered by implication: what is the public interest?

The public interest in the actual world

Phrases such as 'the public interest', 'the national interest', 'the common good' or even 'the General Will', all have in common the idea that there are 'long term, core objectives of the state ... [and] fundamental, immutable interests of all the citizens' held collectively (see Wyllie, 1998, p.1472). There are at least three basic problems associated with such terms, however: first, that it is difficult to decide what those objectives and interests are; secondly, that modern societies are complex and pluralistic in nature, with thousands of groups with competing objectives and interests, some, if not most, of which will conflict with the collective objectives and interests; and thirdly, that the groups and interests in society will claim that the national or public interest is with them, and that what they seek will promote and protect it. These problems induce a sense of scepticism about the use of such phrases; and this is fortified by the widespread perception that those in positions of state authority, who *formally* make decisions about what the public interest is, appear to be guided by their intuition, even if they are genuinely concerned with it (see Wyllie, 1998, pp.1472-3).

Such scepticism, and the problems which create the conditions in which it grows, should not, however, be taken to imply that the public interest does not, or should not, exist. Indeed, it could be argued that the state exists primarily for the purposes of promoting and protecting the public interest, however defined. This is certainly one interpretation that can be put on the writings of Aristotle or Laski, as well as other political philosophers. They would all accept, that what is here termed public interest stands apart from and is superior to the varied interests of the myriad wills. In other words, for these and other political philosophers, there is indeed a 'social whole' and it is the duty of the state to ensure that its interests, the fundamental and immutable interests which collectively form the public interest, are served and protected. This view is, of course, an ideal. However, it is not an ideal in just the Platonic sense but also an ideal in the sense of being an aspiration for those charged with public office. Aristotle's 'good life' is the equivalent of Laski's 'full and rich existence'. It is a state of being (in the real as distinct from the actual world) in which individuals have 'realised the best that is in themselves' (Laski, 1925, pp.27-8), or have 'realised themselves as moral beings' (T.H. Green, quoted in Laski at p.39). In the actual world, the public or common interest is that the state attempts to create the conditions in which this morality can be aspired to. As Laski puts it:

> I have, as a citizen, a claim upon society to realise my best self in common with others ... I have, that is, rights which are inherent in me as a member of society; and I judge the State as a fundamental instrument of society, by the manner in which it seeks to secure for me the substance of those rights ... Rights, in this sense, are the groundwork of the State. They are the quality which gives to the exercise of its power a moral penumbra (pp.39-40).

The substance of those rights is, of course, that anyone in common with others can achieve the 'full and rich existence' (p.40), or Aristotle's 'common good'.

There is one special problem associated with the concept of the public interest and its manifestations in the actual world to which all of the illustrious thinkers referred to here have turned their attention, and to which unfortunately none has produced a completely convincing solution. The problem is this: that it is difficult to accept that those charged with formulating and defending the public interest will not in fact promote their own interests, or at least the interests of those with whom they have most of their dealings. This is not a problem for Bentley or the other 'group' theorists, because they do not accept the existence of the 'social whole' in the first place. They simply accept that state organs and agencies have their own varied interests, which they will pursue in competition with other interests; and that those who hold positions in those organs and agencies will have other interests which they will pursue in the same way. It is simply a fact. For political philosophers, however, the problem is of a different order. To them, public officials *ought* not to behave in this way. This is where the 'real' and the 'actual' worlds clash, as it were. Whilst the idealist might argue that politicians and officials *ought* to behave in certain ways, in the everyday world in which they operate there are obstacles to them actually behaving in those ways. These may be related to limits on knowledge or ability (cf. Simon, 1955) or to the fact that politicians and officials are merely corruptible and self-interested, as all humans are. This can be illustrated from two recent examples: the first being the brouhaha surrounding the so-called 'Arms to Iraq Affair' as revealed in the Scott Report; the second being the controversy surrounding the resignation of the European Commission in 1999.

The Iran Iraq war, which broke out on 22 September 1980 and which lasted eight years, presented the British government with significant policy problems, both in terms of diplomacy and also in terms of trade, particularly the sales of arms and defence related equipment to the combatants. The declared policy was that the British government would do nothing that might prolong or exacerbate hostilities, and that, in line with this policy, it would not issue licences for the export of lethal weapons to either Iran or Iraq. Guidelines were drawn up to allow the implementation of this policy. The three departments involved, however, had different perspectives on the policy, and thus confusion arose as to how the guidelines might be implemented. In addition, the guidelines were amended to take into consideration events in the Middle East. Nevertheless, some generalizations can be made about how the various actors involved viewed the problems. The Department of Trade and Industry, which was responsible for issuing export licenses, naturally thought that it was in the public interest to sell as many pieces of equipment as possible to whoever would buy them. Its view was, thus, that the policy be implemented liberally. This was a view shared, though only up to a point, by the Ministry of Defence, with the proviso that it is always possible that dangerous equipment may be used against British troops in the future. The Foreign Office was concerned about relations with the various powers in the Middle East. The water was muddied by the fact that British public opinion was affected by various events connected with the combatants, for example the use by Iraq of chemical weapons against its own Kurdish populations; Iraq's execution of Fazad Bazoft, an investigative reporter for a British newspaper; and the Iranian *Fatwah* against Salman Rushdie, the British author of the controversial novel, *The Satanic Verses*. In addition, the senior personalities involved at the ministerial and official levels in the British administration also had differing interpretations of the policy. Fundamentally, however, there were two types of interpretation of the policy. The first was that the public interest would best be served by selling as much equipment as possible to whoever wanted it, because this was good for British manufacturing industry; the second was that the public interest would best be served by selling as little equipment as possible to anyone on the grounds that it might sour relations with allies and might indeed arm a potential enemy.

It is beyond the purview of this chapter to examine the details of the Arms to Iraq Affair or, indeed, of the Scott Report. The report was commissioned because it became clear, in consequence of a failed attempt to prosecute one of the companies which had been involved in the sales of defence related equipment to the combatants, that the government had not been consistent in the application of its own policy, and that ministers may have misled Parliament and the public. In essence, the report revealed that the constitutional conventions which are said to govern the activities of ministers and officials in British central government were constantly being undermined and that Parliament and the public were indeed being misled, throughout the period under review. This had happened because ministers and officials had not told Parliament and MPs about what Scott believed to be significant changes in policy (related to changes in the guidelines), or at least had only told them when it was politically and administratively expedient to do so. The ministers and officials involved argued that their actions had been governed by 'the public interest'. Scott shows, however, that, because the various departments involved had different policy objectives, and because Middle East politics is so sensitive and complex, ministers and officials contrived to present policies in such a way that the true nature of the effects of those policies was not always apparent. Notwithstanding that the ministers and officials involved consistently argued throughout their evidence to the Scott Inquiry that they believed they were acting in the public interest, the report makes clear that the Inquiry believed that ministers and officials acted out of embarrassment and the fear that some of their actions might offend the sensitivities of the British electorate, and out of a desire not to offend any of the countries involved in Middle East politics, not just Iran and Iraq, but in particular Saudi Arabia and the United States. The Scott Report is very clear on this:

> The obligation of Ministers to be forthcoming with information in answer to PQs about their departments' activities lies at the heart of the important constitutional principle of Ministerial Accountability. The public interest in a full discharge of this obligation should be a constant heavy weight in the balance. Throughout the period that the Inquiry has had to examine there is to be found a consistent undervaluing by the Government of the public interest that full information should be made available to Parliament. *In circumstances where disclosure might be politically or administratively inconvenient, the balance struck by Government comes down, time and time again, against full disclosure* (emphasis added, Scott, 1996, para. D.1.165).

It seems clear from reading the Scott Report that while the ministers and officials involved may genuinely have believed that their actions were governed by a sense of duty to the public interest, *de facto* they were protecting their own interests. The problems may have been exacerbated by confusion surrounding the policy, and by the differing perspectives on the public interest of the individuals and departments involved. Nevertheless, Scott's view was clear: the actions of ministers and officials were guided by political and administrative convenience. Moreover, because of the overriding principle that, in a democracy, accountability of the governors is of fundamental importance, and because they sought to prevent disclosure of information which would have allowed Parliament and the public to hold them to account, they were actually undermining the public interest.

The second example from the actual world is taken from a report into the activities of the Commission of the European Union (Committee of Independent Experts, 1999). The report led to the resignation of the Commission, essentially because the Committee of Independent Experts found that individual Commissioners acted in their own personal interests and because the Commission as a whole did not act 'responsibly' or in the public interest. The details of the report need not be dealt with here, but some of its findings are valuable as practical observations on what acting in the public interest actually means. The Committee believed that 'there exists a common core of "minimum standards", in addition to rules laid in black and white' which should guide the Commission, individual Commissioners and other individuals employed by the Commission in their administrative activities (para. 1.5.2). These are defined in the report as:

> acting in the general interest of the Community and in complete *independence*, which requires that decisions are taken solely in terms of the public interest ... [and] behaving with *integrity* and discretion and ... in accordance with the principles of accountability and *openness* ... [meaning that] when decisions are taken the reasons for them are made known, the processes by which they were taken are transparent and any personal conflicting interests are honestly and publicly acknowledged (para. 1.5.4).

Essentially, the Committee of Independent Experts believed that this 'common core of "minimum standards"' had been breached, in two fundamental respects. The first was that there had been mismanagement, by which is meant 'serious or persistent infringements of the principles of sound administration' (para. 1.4.3). The second was that there had been a lack of responsibility on the part of individual Commissioners and of the

Commission as a whole. By responsibility the Committee meant 'ethical responsibility, that is responsibility for not behaving in accordance with proper standards in public life' (para. 1.6.2). What they found was that

> it is becoming increasingly difficult to find anyone who has even the slightest sense of responsibility. However, that sense of responsibility is essential. It must be demonstrated, first and foremost, by the Commissioners individually and by the Commission as a body. The temptation to deprive the concept of responsibility of all substance is a dangerous one. That concept is the ultimate manifestation of democracy (para. 9.4.25).

Such sentiments echoed those of Sir Richard Scott in his report on the activities of ministers and officials in British central government. Clearly, both reports locate ideas about the public interest within wider considerations about democracy.

The public interest: a political and administrative convenience?

In compiling its report about the European Commission, the Committee of Independent Experts drew heavily on the First Report of the British Committee on Standards in Public Life (Nolan, 1995). That report is probably most famous for stating clearly what the 'Seven Principles of Public Life' are: Selflessness, Integrity, Objectivity, Accountability, Openness, Honesty and Leadership (p.14). The first of these principles, selflessness, means that 'Holders of public office should take their decisions solely in terms of the public interest' (p.14). These words, and the general tenor of the report, echo those of the Scott Inquiry and of the Committee of Independent Experts. They also sit very easily with the second *a priori* assumption about the public interest made at the beginning of this chapter, that it is a concept which is essentially ethical in nature and is central to ideas about democracy in modern societies. Aristotle himself could have used the exact phrase; Aquinas would have agreed, as would Laski and the other idealists of more recent times. However, they are words which *do not* sit easily with the first *a priori* assumption about the public interest, the sceptical view of it as a 'hurrah' phrase used by those in authority to legitimize their actions, a view expressed eloquently by Bentley and Truman. Which is the more apt view?

The view of the group theorists about how society actually works, of course, is compatible with some of the fundamental problems associated with the public interest – the most fundamental of which is that the state consists of elites, and these elites, in the actual world, are likely to have their own interests and to pursue them, either knowingly or subconsciously. This particular problem is both related to and exacerbated by other basic problems of the public interest. In considerable part these are definitional problems and problems associated with how it is to be determined and by whom. The problems derive from the pluralistic nature of modern societies, from the complexities of government and from the fact that government itself is not a machine. Indeed, it is made up of individuals who have their own ideas about what is right or wrong, about their duty in relation to their official work, and ultimately about what the public interest is (O'Toole, 1997, p.130). Nevertheless, these problems should not be used simply to deny the existence of the public interest. It might be useful to make a distinction between the overall public interest, which it is the duty of the state to protect and promote, and a public interest as perceived by the multitudes of public servants, be they politicians or officials, which it is their individual duty to protect and promote. This latter, of course, does raise questions about how these individuals perceive, or make decisions about, the public interest in specific circumstances; and it might be part of the overall public interest that a society possesses public servants who are trained and/or socialized into what Rousseau would refer to as *unnatural* behaviour. In other words, public servants should behave as Plato would have his guardians behave and be taught to set aside their own individual and collective personal interests. In a democracy, of course, this is extremely difficult. Politicians cannot really be expected to set aside their personal ambitions, even though such ambition may be closely linked with a genuine desire to do good and to use political power for the benefit of society. Yet it is politicians who, in a democracy, are both *formally* and to some extent *practically* the arbiters of what the public interest is. Officials are not elected, and therefore lack the main source of legitimacy in a democracy. Their legitimacy derives from bureaucratic, hierarchical and technical forms of authority, which are meant to be put at the disposal of those who have been elected. Yet government is so complex and time-consuming that it is unreasonable to expect politicians to be present when every decision which might affect the public interest is made. Should citizens simply accept that officials will act in a disinterested way?

The Association of First Division Civil Servants (FDA), which is the professional association of senior civil servants in the United Kingdom, has been concerned with such matters for some considerable time. It is fair to say, indeed, that it has addressed the question of professional ethics on every occasion it has given evidence to royal commissions and other public inquiries since its foundation in 1919 (see O'Toole, 1989). However, the first time it considered these questions explicitly, if internally, was in 1970, when, shaken by its own perception that the professional standing and standards of the civil service were being questioned by politicians and public alike, it set up a committee on professional standards. The points raised in the report of that committee, and in the debate at the FDA's Annual General meeting which led to its establishment, are as salient now as when the committee undertook its work, and worthy of examination in the light of the questions raised in this chapter.

It was at the 1969 annual general meeting that the anxiety of members of the association about professional standards manifested itself publicly. This was reflected in the following motion passed by that meeting:

> To call attention to the need to define the professional standards expected from public servants in the light of their constitutional role and developments in government administration, and to ask the Executive Committee to play its part in stimulating discussion of this question ... (FDA, 1970, para. 1)

The resolution was moved by Mr D.H. Morrell of the Home Office in a speech which is regarded by many as one of the most moving ever made at an annual general meeting. In it he argued fiercely that civil servants are not amateurs:

> We are professionals. Ever since the great reforms of the last century we have exhibited the two primary characteristics of a true profession. We profess an ethic regulating our work; and we possess knowledge and know-how specific to that work. Our ethic is simply stated. We stand committed to neutrality of process. We profess that public power is not to be used to further the private purposes of those to whom it is entrusted. It is to be used solely for the furtherance of public purposes as defined by constitutional process.

The difficulty lay in the practical application of this 'principle of universal validity'. In particular Morrell recognized the difficulties involved in evolving a set of procedural rules such that officials who were applying them, people who were 'not in themselves value-neutral – because they are human beings with needs and aspirations', could, by accepting them, contribute to the process of determining and administering public policies. In the light of these observations he suggested:

that our professional commitment to neutrality of process needs to be worked out afresh in rules of procedure which will liberate, and make available for the public good, the immense store of human sensitivity and creativity which I believe to be imprisoned by an outmoded myth of personal objectivity (First Division Association, 1969).

The response of the Executive Committee was to establish the Sub-Committee on Professional Standards in the Public Service.

There was, 'no question of the FDA committing itself to a specific point of view' (First Division Association, 1971). Nevertheless, some of the contributions made then by senior civil servants to the committee, and some of the comments in the report about the public interest remain valuable as insights about what the public interest might be, and how it might be worked out in the world as it actually is.

What then were the issues which the committee considered? First it seemed sensible to state what the responsibilities of civil servants were. Their primary duty was to the minister and to the ministerial office which they (civil servants) were concerned to maintain (First Division Association, 1970, para.9). Secondly they had a *de facto* duty towards their official superiors (para. 10). Thirdly, they arguably had a duty to the administration as a whole – however, 'with executive powers vested in their official head, the system is biased in favour of the interests of the part where they may conflict with the interests of the whole' (para. 11). In other words, practical loyalty was usually to the minister and not to the government as a whole. More debatable than these three duties was whether civil servants had still wider responsibilities, for example to Parliament and to the democratic system (para. 12); and whether they 'should be conscious of ... [the democratic process] and of the rights and desires of the individuals who make up the community' (para. 13).

The views of the committee on these matters were not unanimous. One view *not* shared by the majority was that:

> any discussion of professional standards for civil servants must be based on the proposition that civil servants have a duty only towards the government whom they serve and that this duty is only fully discharged by loyal, truthful and objective service to Ministers .... Ministers would be answerable for their policies to Parliament and the electorate and civil servants would be debarred from altering, applying or presenting government policy so as to take account of anything other than the wishes of the government (para. 30).

This was regarded by the committee as 'a restricted view' and might lead civil servants 'in certain circumstances [to] find it difficult to act in a manner which was honourable, truthful and in accordance with their conscience'. For example:

> they might believe the government's policy to be against the public interest, unfair, or simply irrelevant to the real facts. They might be reluctant to defend government policy when, in their opinion, the arguments against it were stronger and more in accordance with the facts than the arguments for it. They might find it hard, in presenting government policy, to present all the facts in perspective (para. 31).

The majority view of the committee was that the duty to the minister and duty to wider institutions were not mutually exclusive and that in all conceivable circumstances the primacy of duty to the minister was beyond all dispute: to suppose that was to oversimplify the civil servant's position (para. 34). 'The majority of us feel', read the report, 'that the possibility of conflict between Ministers' wishes and professional standards must be faced, and that making the departmental minister the final judge in all circumstances does not provide a sufficient practical guide to solving such problems' (para. 37).

Within this majority there were several strands of opinion. One was that civil servants had, indeed, a duty to the 'public interest'. Despite the many problems in defining what the public interest was some of the committee felt that the civil service:

> should recognise a professional task of ascertaining objectively what is the public interest in a particular context. Individual responsibility would be an important component and formative element in this ethic: the erosion of anonymity should be accepted as one consequence, and management by objectives adopted widely so as to ensure that responsibility was not diffused. New methods of consultation on policy such as Green Papers would lead to a wider agreement on the aims of departments and thus provide more objective criteria of the public interest (para. 39).

Another view was that action should be taken to preserve the integrity of the civil service against threats arising from 'tendentious briefing, the corruption of power, and inattention to the true interests of the people'. This action would involve a new charter or 'contract of service to the people', laying down a code of conduct which neither senior officials nor ministers might overrule. It would forbid censorship of facts or opinions, insist on merit rather than conformity as the criterion for promotion, and institute machinery in which there was staff participation to deal with discipline and grievances (para. 41). Despite these radical strands of opinion, the committee went no further than to suggest further discussions which would involve interested people inside and outside government service.

Many of the suggestions made to the Sub-Committee on Professional Standards have indeed come to pass in the United Kingdom, including, for example, a code of conduct for civil servants and strengthened guidance for ministers, as well as an increasing openness in government, the decline of the principle of anonymity for civil servants and, of course, greater use of business management techniques in public administration. The problem is, however, that the perception of declining standards remains and is growing. Indeed, it could be argued that some of these changes have themselves exacerbated the situation. In particular, the increasing 'marketization' of the civil service and the tendency to performance measurement and performance related rewards have to some extent undermined the selflessness which was previously the hallmark of public service. These tendencies themselves have led to anxiety about the behaviour and attitudes of public servants and created the conditions in which it was thought desirable to introduce codes of ethics. Such anxieties were aggravated in the United Kingdom by numerous public scandals, most notoriously the so-called 'Arms to Iraq Affair' discussed above; and the findings of the Scott Report into that affair. These and other reports, including that of the Report of the Committee of Independent Experts for the European Union, confirm that there are severe problems associated with expecting that public officials will always behave in ways conducive to the promotion and protection of the public interest. However, the Scott Report in particular indicates that the presence of politicians is certainly no guarantee that the public interest will be the uppermost consideration in the making of decisions (notwithstanding that they may genuinely believe that they are acting in such a way as to protect or promote it). The reports provide ample evidence of the problems which might be encountered both in relation to politicians and to officials. Those findings seem compatible with common-sense intuition about human nature. Nevertheless, the reports discussed here suggest strongly that there is a public interest, and they do not come into the group theorist's camp. They express a certain scepticism that public servants will always act in the public interest; but they do not come to the conclusion that the public interest does not exist.

Both Scott and the EU report point to two simple and linked reasons: first, the institutions they investigated exist within a democratic framework; and secondly, the public interest lies in ensuring that public servants behave responsibly and can be held to account. In other words, the public interest, at least in the modern liberal political systems, is about ensuring the maintenance and sound operation of democratic principles. Such principles, some of which are not modern, and which, indeed, can be traced back to Aristotle, entail and require that *the interests of every citizen are accounted for*. This seems to be incompatible with the views of the group theorists, notably of Bentley, part of the basis of whose work was that 'There are always some parts of the nation to be found arrayed against other parts' (Bentley, 1908, p.220). The first duty of government is to ensure that there are no clashes between the various interests in society which might weaken the democratic system – a theoretical possibility in the Bentley view. The second duty of government is to ensure that those whose interests are not represented by groups, i.e. those Truman refers to as 'unorganized interests' (see Truman, 1951, pp.509-14) are not marginalized. Why? Because democracy is not simply about the *rights* of the many; it is also about the *duties* owed by the many to the few, especially in the protection of the recognized rights of minorities.

The question remains, of course, how can such high minded principles be put into effect? Here again we can look to Aristotle who, in Barker's words, insisted that the good life 'requires for its satisfaction those institutions, such as a system of justice, which are necessary for such a life' (Aristotle, 1946 edition, note on p.111). In other words, and in modern terms, the public interest is about maintaining the democratic system, and requires for its purpose a system of *responsible* public institutions staffed by public servants whose duty it is to promote and protect the interests of all. The late Victorians seem to have understood this, at least in their own elitist terms. With a combination of political pragmatism and high-mindedness, they recreated the public service ideal, and sought to establish responsible institutions through the reform of various of the parts of the government machine. In particular, they attempted to ensure that those recruited to established positions in the public service would be of a character such that they would, indeed, seek to put the public interest before their own personal interests (see Richard Chapman's comments in Chapter 7). These ideas have informed public service in the UK throughout most of the twentieth century. At the end of that century we seem to be in danger of forgetting the wisdom of much that the Victorians had to offer.

As we approach the new millenium it is as important, perhaps even more important given the greater role of democracy now, that the institutions of the state should still be staffed by persons who will attempt to set aside their own interests and act in the public interest. Yet recent and proposed reforms undermine such possibilities. Indeed, they create the conditions where personal and group interests can flourish. The public interest, which stands above and is superior to the interests of the myriad wills, for it protects those wills from each other, and allows those not able to exercise their will to have a voice in the affairs of the 'social whole', is thereby damaged. The 'good life', which exists when all in society are allowed the full and rich existence an enlightened state can provide, can never be fully achieved unless public servants are encouraged to put aside their own interests. There was never a 'golden age' of perfect public service. The danger is, however, that in the twenty-first century there will not be many who will be able to have as their epitaph that which is inscribed on the memorial to Prince Albert in Kensington, that each of their lives was 'a life devoted to the public good'. The public service will be the poorer for it; the public interest will be undermined by it.

References

Aristotle (1946 edition), *Politics*, Edited and Translated by Sir Ernest Barker, Oxford: Oxford University Press.
Bentley, Arthur F. (1908, 1955 edition), *The Process of Government*, Evanston, Illinois: The Principia Press.
Bryce, James (1921), *Modern Democracies*, New York: Macmillan.
Committee of Independent Experts (1999), *First Report on Allegations regarding Fraud, Mismanagement and Nepotism in the European Commission (15 March)*, Internet: http://www.europarl.eu.int/experts.
D'Entreves, A.P. (ed.) (1954), *Aquinas, Selected Political Writings (Translated by J.G. Dawson)*, Oxford: Basil Blackwell.
First Division Association (1969), *Minutes of the Annual General Meeting held on 10 May*, FDA file reference I80367.
First Division Association (1970), *Report of the Sub-Committee on Professional Standards in Public Service*, FDA file reference A00082.
First Division Association (1971), *Monthly Notes* (April).
Laski, H.J. (1925), *The Grammar of Politics*, London: George Allen & Unwin.
Nolan, Lord (1995), *First Report of the Committee on Standards in Public Life*, Cm. 2850-I, London: HMSO.
O'Toole, Barry J. (1989), *Private Gain and Public Service: the Association of First Division Civil Servants*, London: Routledge.

O'Toole, Barry J. (1990), 'T.H. Green and the Ethics of Senior officials in British Central Government', *Public Administration* Vol. 68, pp.337-52.

O'Toole, Barry J. (1997), 'Ethics in Government', *Parliamentary Affairs* Vol. 50, No.1, January, pp.130-42.

Scott, Sir Richard (1996), *Report of the Inquiry into the Export of Defence Equipment and Dual-Use Goods to Iraq and Related Prosecutions* HC 115, London: HMSO.

Truman, David B. (1951), *The Governmental Process: Political Interests and Public Opinion*, New York: Alfred A. Knopf.

Wyllie, James (1998), 'National Interest', in *International Encyclopaedia of Public Policy and Administration* Vol. 3, pp.1472-4, Boulder, Colorado: Westview Press.

7 Setting Standards in a New Organization: The Case of the British Civil Service Commission

Richard A. Chapman

The Civil Service Commission, the central department for the selection and certification of qualified staff, was created in Britain in 1855 and abolished in 1991. In its early years it quickly established itself as a significant institution for making central government administration more efficient and for eliminating the corruption which resulted in large part from patronage in the appointment of officials. It was a pioneering institution because, as Dorman B. Eaton, Chairman of the Civil Service Commission in the United States, wrote in 1880, no nation had previously tried competitive examinations for staff recruitment on a large scale (Eaton, 1880, p.201). The Civil Service Commission became a powerful factor in the development of a unified civil service in the United Kingdom – a unified service that became known for its high standards of propriety because of the adoption of publicly known and widely respected rules and procedures, and through the development of an administrative culture which built upon expectations of personal integrity in the public interest. It played a vital role in the practice of public administration through the introduction and refinement of new methods of examination and assessment, and by pioneering research into methods of assessment, mainly using its own records. In short, the creation and development of the Civil Service Commission provided the central thrust and bedrock for the promotion of what is now referred to as the 'public service ethos'.

The purpose of this chapter is to consider how the Civil Service Commission became established and achieved its success, and to assess its contribution to the high standards for which the British civil service became justly proud. The chapter reviews the basis for its authority, explains how it went about its work in the early years of its life and, in particular, considers how it operated within the system of government by setting standards for itself and by exercising influence and persuasion on others. During the first half century of its existence it became a widely respected institution with operations on a very considerable scale. Indeed, it may be argued that it became the backbone of the British civil service – a unified service that effectively dates from 1855 to 1991.

The foundation of the Civil Service Commission: the legal and philosophical bases for its authority

To the surprise of many public administration practitioners and scholars in other countries, there is no 'Civil Service Act' in the United Kingdom. Other countries nearly all have a basic and comprehensive document, often enshrined in law, which lays down both the structure of the civil service and the relations of civil servants with ministers and among themselves, and also indicates procedures and the standards of behaviour that are required of officials. Even at the end of the twentieth century no such document exists in the United Kingdom, though there is now a Civil Service Code that is sometimes thought to be an appropriate substitute for anything more comprehensive, and which is to be found as an annex to a government White Paper published in 1995 (Prime Minister, 1995). From time to time there are requests and/or proposals for a Civil Service Act, but there has been no determined move in this direction.

Instead of an act or acts of Parliament, most of the fundamental rules and procedures governing the civil service have, in the United Kingdom, been promulgated by executive decrees known as Orders in Council, and by rules of more specific and mundane sorts subordinate to such Orders. It is therefore hardly surprising that the originating authority to set up the Civil Service Commission, stating its terms of reference, is to be found in an Order in Council. The reason for this is that, although the Northcote/Trevelyan *Report on the Organisation of the Permanent Civil Service*, written in 1853, said that its recommendations could only be successfully carried into effect by an act of Parliament, and although a bill was officially prepared along the lines intended by Northcote and Trevelyan,[1] it appears to have been the judgment of politicians that they would not be likely at that time to get such an act passed. Their judgment seems to have been well founded because, when the provisions of the Order in Council of 21 May 1855 were discussed in Parliament on 10 July of that year, there were significant reservations by Lord Palmerston about reforming at greater speed.[2] In any case, it could be argued that the authority of the

Crown, expressed through Orders in Council, was the most appropriate means for regulating the organization and procedures of the Queen's public servants.

The Order in Council of 21 May 1855 was specific and concise. Its first major provision was to appoint three Commissioners: Sir Edward Ryan, Assistant Comptroller of the Exchequer; John George Shaw Lefevre, Clerk Assistant to the House of Lords; and Edward Romilly, Chairman of the Board of Audit. Its second major provision was to outline their duties. Any men who were to be appointed in any department of the civil service, before being admitted on probation, were now required to be issued with a certificate of qualification from the Commissioners, and it was the duty of the Commissioners: to ascertain that the candidate was within the limits of age prescribed for the position; to ascertain that he was free from physical defect or disease; to ascertain that his character qualified him for appointment; and to ascertain that he possessed the necessary knowledge and ability for his official duties. These details became of crucial significance when the Superannuation Act of 1859 stated that no person could be considered as serving in the permanent civil service unless he had been admitted with a certificate from the Civil Service Commissioners. The provision for superannuation allowances therefore reinforced the importance of certification.

Whilst the role of the Civil Service Commission and the significance of certification became important for individual civil servants, for the purpose of this chapter it is at least as important to draw attention to the intellectual basis for the Commission, because this established its approach to its work. The intellectual basis is to be found in two major reports – though they, in turn, depend on other reports which preceded them. The two major reports are Lord Macaulay's Report on the Indian Civil Service and the Report by Sir Stafford Northcote and Sir Charles Trevelyan on the Organisation of the Permanent Civil Service.

It was from the Indian Civil Service (ICS) that the term 'civil service' originated – for the employees of the East India Company were referred to as its civil servants to distinguish them from its army, navy and ecclesiastical employees, and slowly the technical phrase of the Anglo-Indian became adopted for home use. The ICS had its own training college, from 1809 it was at Haileybury, that produced men who realized, according to the college prospectus of 1806, that in the ICS there were traditions to be kept up and handed over, 'a political faith to be cherished, and a code of public and private honour to be maintained' (Tout, 1916, pp.35-6). From 1853, when the last Charter Act of the East India Company abolished recruitment through nomination by directors, members of the ICS were recruited by open competitive examination, conducted to ensure the selection of candidates with thorough, not merely superficial, knowledge. Lord Macaulay was Chairman of the Committee to advise on the best method of introducing open competition, which it did in its report published in 1855. The essential feature of the philosophy of the Macaulay Report was soon accepted for other fields as well. The Report said: 'We believe that men who have been engaged up to twenty-one or twenty-two in studies which have no immediate connection with the business of any profession, and of which the effect is merely to open, to invigorate, and to enrich the mind, will generally be found, in the business of every profession, superior to men who have, at eighteen or nineteen, devoted themselves to the special studies of their calling' (Macaulay, 1855, pp.7-8).

The *Report on the Organisation of the Permanent Civil Service*, by Northcote and Trevelyan, was an impressively concise document of some twenty pages, though it was the culmination of a series of inquiries into public offices in the 1840s and 1850s. The Report suggested that the best method of recruiting good civil servants, and of making the most of them in their employment, was to train young men, carefully selected by examination, and whose permanent appointment would be confirmed only after the satisfactory completion of a short period of probation. In order to ensure that the examinations could be carried out in an effective and consistent manner throughout the service, the Report recommended that a Central Board of Examiners should be established, and said that the examination should be a competitive literary examination (plus an inquiry into the age, health and moral fitness of the candidates). The Civil Service Commission was therefore intended to be a centralizing and, by implication, unifying feature, to compensate for what Northcote and Trevelyan critically referred to as the 'fragmentary character' of the civil service they examined.

The Queen's Speech at the opening of Parliament in January 1854 included the phrase: 'I shall direct a Plan to be laid before you, which will have for its Object to improve the system of Admission, and thereby to increase the Efficiency of the (Civil) Service'.[3] In the event, it was not an act of Parliament but, as already explained, an Order in Council, which set up the Civil Service Commission, and instead of the Commissioners holding office during their good behaviour, as provided for in the draft bill, the Order in Council gave them appointments to be held only during the pleasure of Her Majesty.[4] Earl Grey had already argued, during the debate on the Queen's Speech, that 'much may ... be done by the authority of the Crown',[5] and Sir George Cornewall Lewis, who supported the procedure, argued that the setting up of a board of examiners 'would necessarily entail some expense, and however small this might be, it would necessitate an annual vote which would give the House of Commons a practical veto upon the system once in every session' (quoted in Hughes, 1954, pp.38, 45). The British civil service, as a unified and meritocratic organization, therefore effectively had its origins in 1855: indeed, this was the date taken for its beginning by the Tomlin Royal Commission on the Civil Service (Tomlin, 1931, para. 29).

Getting the Civil Service Commission established within the civil service

After the Northcote/Trevelyan Report was published, Trevelyan sent copies of it to a large number of people whose comments were likely to be valued. This had two results. One was to stimulate yet more suggestions about how to introduce the proposed arrangements. The other was to strengthen the body of opinion favourable to the new arrangements: it was a process of inverse consensus, a process of consulting and informing as many people as possible in order to build up a significant body of support (Chapman, 1968, pp.9-10). Among the responses three, as examples, are mentioned here. John Stuart Mill wrote that the recommendations had been called 'in Parliament and elsewhere, a scheme for taking patronage from the Crown and its officers, and giving it to a body of examiners ... But the conferring of certificates of eligibility by the Board of Examiners would not be patronage, but a judicial act ...'. Edwin Chadwick wrote: 'On the examination of the causes of the frequent superiority of private enterprise, will be found principles of action, as conditions of success, which in the Civil Service are wanting. One of the first principles is unity of direction, and of individual interest and responsibility'. John Wood, Chairman of the Board of Inland Revenue, wrote: 'It is essential that the examination should be undertaken by a tribunal so constituted as to secure confidence in its competency and impartiality'.[6]

The 1855 Order in Council appointed the first three Civil Service Commissioners. The Chairman was Sir Edward Ryan, Assistant Comptroller of the Exchequer, ex-Chief Justice of Bengal, and a friend of Macaulay. The official records do not show how or why the Commissioners were selected, or who else may have been considered for appointment, though it is clear that their names were decided by politicians in association with the Treasury, at that time the key department in British central government. It should also be noted that, at that time, Trevelyan was Assistant Secretary (i.e. the most senior official) at the Treasury. He was educated for four terms at Haileybury before spending a number of years in India where he met Macaulay; and he later married Macaulay's sister Hannah. Northcote was an ex-civil servant in the Board of Trade, who gave up his official career for personal and domestic reasons, and became a Member of Parliament, later Chancellor of the Exchequer.

In the early days of the Commission, its duties were mainly to administer test examinations to candidates who had been nominated, and to administer limited competitions. Recruitment of staff to the Commission itself, however, was by open competition from its beginning, and the Home Office and Board of Works also adopted open competition as early as 1857. It was only after the Order in Council of 4 June 1870 that open competitions became obligatory. The important point, bearing in mind that open competition was intended to be the rule, is that in carrying out this policy, the Civil Service Commission was itself administering the philosophy and practice laid down in the Macaulay and Northcote/Trevelyan Reports. From the outset, the Treasury also had an important role to play. The 1855 Order in Council said that the Commissioners' power to appoint assistant examiners and others was 'subject to the Approval of the Commissioners of Her Majesty's Treasury', and the Treasury was also to be responsible for the estimates of the Commission.

As there was no unified civil service in the mid-nineteenth century, the Commissioners had first to agree, with the authorities of each department individually, the details of the rules applicable to the various posts for which they were to examine. Although the formal authority came from the Orders in Council, the powers of the Commissioners were essentially dependent on the requirement for their certificates, which were issued not to the individuals but to the employing departments. Everything else, involving much detailed administrative work, which rapidly escalated in volume, was largely a matter of negotiation and influence. Success in the early years of the Commission was therefore dependent on establishing a position of respect and authority within the various offices of central government.

The Commission acquired this respect and authority by accumulating experience from consulting departments, as well as from conducting examinations. It was soon able to comment authoritatively on the performance of candidates and to make suggestions to departments deciding upon their own requirements. It did this partly through its contacts with individual departments but, in addition, through its annual reports, which were published. These reports were an important factor in attracting attention to its work, for stimulating discussion about its experience and, almost certainly, for enhancing its reputation and authority. Most of the annual reports published in the nineteenth century were major documents of several hundred pages: for example, the first annual report was 361 pages,[7] and the sixth report was 570 pages.[8]

The Commissioners also had to establish their independence. This, in the first instance, was done by ensuring that the Commissioners were appointed by Order in Council – a practice which continues to the present day. Their staff, however, were civil servants, appointed according to the rules applicable from time to time, though the Commissioners led the way by introducing open competition for most of their own staff from the creation of the Commission in 1855. As the Commission grew in reputation, and the volume of its work increased, the toehold of control by the Treasury (in 1855 limited to Treasury approval of the appointment of examiners and others, and to responsibility for the estimates), was extended. For example, the Order in Council of 4 June 1870 laid down that the rules applicable to posts in each department, were to be settled 'subject to the approval of the Commissioners of Her Majesty's Treasury, by the Civil Service Commissioners and the chief authorities of the Department'. The 1870 Order in Council also required the Treasury to approve all the regulations for competitive examinations, their frequency, and the scale of fees from candidates.

In some respects the Commissioners were able to establish their independence quickly, with the help of useful cases to create precedents. A significant case of this sort occurred in 1857. C.G. Barrington wrote from Downing Street on 6 July to say that Lord Palmerston had asked to see the examination papers for 'three gentlemen who lately competed for the Clerkship in the Treasury'. In his reply, of 8 July, J.G. Maitland sent a copy of the Table of Marks but refused to release the scripts. Barrington, on 21 July, wrote that 'as Head of the government Lord Palmerston deems it his duty to inform himself as to any matter connected with the Administration of the affairs of the country' and 'he again requests to see ... the examination papers'. This brought a personal reply from Lefevre, one of the Commissioners, explaining that the efficacy of the Commission would be 'totally destroyed' if 'any interference on the part of the Government were to take place with respect to our judgment in individual cases'. As Barrington had also said, however, that Palmerston wished to disclaim any intention of querying the cases of individual candidates, and had specified that his request was so as to be informed 'as to the manner in which our system of Examination is carried on' (and had also drawn attention to the controversy associated with the nature of the questions being asked in the examinations), then the Commissioners transmitted for Palmerston's 'own information' the examination papers, 'including the questions proposed, the answers given, and the reports of the examiners'. The point was nevertheless made, and a precedent was established that ministers, including the Prime Minister and First Lord of the Treasury, could not interfere in the judgments of the Commissioners.[9]

Setting standards and applying them

Having established its authority, independence and reputation, the Civil Service Commission was in a strong position to push for high standards of public service, both within the Commission and in the wider civil service. In addition, it had encouragement from the social and political environment (particularly from the world of education) to aim for the highest standards, to apply them rigorously, and to let it be abundantly seen that high standards in public service were expected, indeed demanded, and were being applied. Politicians, the press, and academics followed the Commission's work in its early years and, where appropriate, sought to advance their own conceptions of the public interest in relation to its activities.

There was widespread concern that the highest possible standards should be applied in the administration of literary examinations. An example which drew the Commissioners' attention to this expectation was a memorandum, sent on 14 April 1859 from the British Consulate in Shanghai to the Foreign Office in London, and forwarded to the Secretary of the Civil Service Commission on the direction of the Foreign Secretary, the Earl of Malmesbury. The memorandum, dated 13 April 1859, was written by Thomas T. Meadows. It was about an Imperial Edict reported in the *Peking Gazette* on the 18th March, and illustrated the importance attached in China to the integrity of public service examinations as the basis of its system of public administration. The memorandum outlined the press report:

> Pih-tseum, one of the four principal ministers of state, officers similar to our prime minister, with the secretaries of the foreign, colonial and home affairs, having been found guilty of conniving at the substitution of a set of essays for the degree of Ken-jin (the second counting from below), he was condemned to decapitation by a specially constituted court, composed of Imperial princes, ranking next to the Emperor himself, of members of the Cabinet, of high officers of the Imperial household, and of presidents of the boards. The Emperor having summoned into his presence the members of this court, confirmed their sentence, and though 'unable to restrain his tears',

ordered the minister to be immediately decapitated, appointing the president of the criminal board with another officer to witness the execution.
The edict speaks of three other officers being condemned to death, in connexion with the case, and common report says that 12 in all have been executed, and that many others who were convicted of negligence, though not of cognizance, have been cashiered (Civil Service Commissioners, 1860, pp.122-3).

In Victorian Britain the expectations for high standards, and the sentences on individuals who themselves slipped from the highest standards, were not as extreme as in Imperial China. Nevertheless, expectations were high, as was concern about inefficiencies and corruption in the public services, and penalties were sometimes severe. An example from consultations with the Foreign Office illustrates this. When the Commissioners were considering the requirements of departments and setting standards for the examinations, the Foreign Office explained their requirements: 'The Foreign Office requires of the Clerks great sacrifices of time, of comfort, and of amusement, and that they should take such an interest in the Office as to consider its credit and reputation as their own'.[10]

An example of an individual case comparable in terms of the severity that could be expected in Britain to the Chinese example mentioned above, and which contributed to the internal precedents developed by the Commissioners into rules of practice akin to case law, occurred in 1887. Arthur Mowbray Berkeley, the second son of Colonel, later Major-General, F.G. Berkeley, was sixteen when he was convicted, on his own confession, of copying from his neighbour during the Preliminary Sandhurst Examination. Representations were made by his headmaster, Rev J.M. Eustace of the Oxford Military College, and by Douglas Jones who wrote on behalf of the Field Marshal Commanding in Chief, to ask whether Berkeley could be 'put back twelve months, as a sufficient punishment' instead of being barred from being a candidate at *any* future public examination. The matter was considered at a meeting of the three Commissioners: the Earl of Strafford, Sir George Dasent and Theodore Walrond, but they felt they could not abandon 'the principle that candidates guilty of such offences should be held ineligible for admission to any future examination'. A carefully worded but very firm letter was sent to the Army pointing out how serious would be any deviation from their rule. The consequences would, in their opinion, have to include a publicly announced modification to rules already approved by His Royal Highness the Field Marshal Commanding in Chief, it would create a difference between the rules for entrance into the Army and the rules for entrance to the civil service, and 'the Army Examinations conducted by the Commissioners are just as broadly distinguished by their public character from examinations held at Educational Institutions as the examinations held by the Commissioners for Civil appointments ...'.[11] In the event, no relaxation of the rule was allowed. When it came to the needs of the Army during the First World War, however, recruitment conditions had changed. Berkeley, who had joined the staff of the Assam Bengal Railway in 1893, and was its Chief Engineer from 1906 to 1914, served in the First World War in France and Mesopotamia, rising to the rank of Lieutenant Colonel in the Royal Engineers; he was mentioned in despatches and became a Companion of the Order of the Indian Empire.

Such attitudes were also expected of the examiners, and great emphasis was put on them serving the public interest too. As far as the India Office was concerned, it made clear that the pensions of professors at Haileybury were granted with the proviso that they would 'engage, if called upon to give their assistance, in the Examination of candidates for the Civil Service of India without remuneration'[12] – though travelling and other incidental expenses were later authorised if the professors were not resident in London or its immediate vicinity. Even into the twentieth century, the expectations of public service were reflected in the arrangements for paying fees and expenses to interviewers: 'The majority of our interviewers do tend to claim less rather than more of what is their legal right. This, it seems to me, is the quality of character we are entitled to expect from interviewers'.[13]

Especially in its early years, the Commission had to deal with a variety of attempted bribery and cheating connected with its examinations. Cases of fraudulently altering birth and baptismal certificates so that an otherwise ineligible candidate could compete were, it seems, not uncommon.[14] There was also occasional cheating in examinations, including personation;[15] there was even a case in Liverpool of a candidate for a position as clerk in the Stationery Office, Mr Frederick William Partington, fraudulently attempting to arrange a reference for himself from someone who had not employed him.[16] What is remarkable about many of these cases is that some of the individuals were extraordinarily naive. Sometimes they did not appear to appreciate that their behaviour was improper.[17] People generally had therefore to be educated in the standards to be expected by the Commission. The Commissioners contributed to this by issuing notices with examination timetables, outlining the rules for behaviour in examinations, with an explanation that disqualification would follow detection of impropriety; they fully explained their decisions to individuals concerned;

wherever possible they prosecuted or encouraged departments to prosecute for fraud; they publicized details of incidents in their annual reports and, above all, they adopted a rule that anyone caught cheating would be prevented, on grounds of character, from ever again becoming a candidate in a Civil Service Commission public examination.[18]

Nowhere were standards more rigorously expected than among the Civil Service Commission's own staff or others engaged on work for the Commission. Mrs Champion, in an attempt to get examination papers in advance to help her son who was a candidate for the Royal Military College, Sandhurst, tried to bribe someone on the staff of Messrs Harrison and Sons, the printers. This led to the Civil Service Commissioners persuading the Treasury to insert a clause into the bill that became the Official Secrets Act 1889, to prevent the disclosure of such information from firms engaged on work for government departments.[19] An Acting Sergeant in the Royal Irish Constabulary was found, by a Court of Inquiry, to have tampered with official examination marks and he was dismissed: he claimed to be innocent, but his case attracted considerable publicity in the *Irish Daily Independent*.[20] A salutary incident occurred in 1861. On Friday 5 July, Reginald H. Paynter, a Senior Clerk in the Record Department of the Civil Service Commission, left the office at 8.30 p.m. to go home, but he had a cold and fell asleep on the train, missing his home station, Weybridge, so that he continued to Southampton, where he arrived at 1.30 a.m. He immediately sent a telegram to Mr Horace Mann, the Registrar and Chief Clerk, in the hope that someone else in the office could take his place on duty for Saturday. He took the earliest train back to Weybridge, but did not arrive until 4.00 a.m., too tired to go to work that day. At about 1.30 p.m. on the Saturday, however, Mr Theodore Walrond, who was in charge of examinations at the Civil Service Commission, saw Paynter in Regent Street. Paynter said he had had to go to London on private business, and when asked for further information declined to give details because he reckoned he would in any case be losing a day's leave because of his absence on Saturday. The Commissioners, at their meeting on 12 July, recorded their disapprobation, found Paynter's explanation unsatisfactory, and also recorded that Paynter's attitude showed 'a want of personal courtesy towards the Registrar who was acting under the express directions of the Commissioners'. They directed that a copy of their Minute be not only given to Paynter but also circulated in the office. On 31 December 1861 the Commissioners accepted Paynter's resignation from his position at the Commission.[21]

Insights and lessons from experience?

The Civil Service Commission was the most important institutional invention for the reduction of corruption, and in the evolution of a unified civil service. It was established after a series of investigations had considered the administration of a significant number of government departments. The Northcote/Trevelyan Report, which specifically recommended the creation of a Board of Examiners was, in effect, a concluding essay which reflected upon the earlier enquiries and succinctly presented conclusions from their experience. The report itself, and especially its recommendations for open competition for the selection of staff, was debated in Parliament and in the country. It stimulated considerable support from politicians and from the informed public. Moreover, discussion and support for administrative reform was not a particularly partisan matter. It was of importance to both major parties in Parliament, though there were cross-party reservations as well; and it was a matter widely regarded as being 'in the public interest' – a concept already considered by Barry O'Toole in Chapter 5.

Once the general direction of reform measures for the civil service had been enunciated in the Northcote/Trevelyan Report, the route to implementation had to be chosen. Northcote and Trevelyan thought their objectives could only be successfully advanced through legislation – mainly, it seems, because they thought legislation would ensure permanence and prevent the proposed arrangements from being later abandoned (Northcote/Trevelyan Report, 1854, final paragraph). They recognised that the reforms they wished to see implemented would be resisted as a result of the long usage and powerful interests that were supporting the practices they criticized. It therefore seems to have been a consequence of political and administrative expediency that the Civil Service Commission was set up not by an act of Parliament but by the exercise of executive authority through an Order in Council – a procedure not similarly available in other countries, but constitutionally acceptable because of the flexibility of the British system of government. Furthermore, this procedure was consistent with, and could be indicated to emphasize, the growing regard people had for public servants not as the appointees of particular ministers or a particular government, but as the increasingly a-political and permanent servants of the state whose head was a monarch.

The main constitutional effect from creating the Civil Service Commission was to mark the beginning of a unified civil service, which over time developed its own standards and culture – its own ethos. By reviewing the Commission since its demise, and in the context of the widely recognized significance of its own standards and culture, it may be asked how those standards and culture became established. Early in its life the Commission itself wrestled with some of the issues which the Commissioners and others recognized as being important in this context. This is because the qualities and modes of behaviour that contribute to the administrative culture can only be usefully examined by looking at the experience and behaviour of individuals. In this context the recruitment of officials is particularly important as the first stage of that experience, and the recruitment procedures were concerned with much more than the factual knowledge possessed by candidates. Knowledge of intellectual matters was, of course, important, but it was also the means of reflecting what Macaulay and others recognised as the moral perspective of individuals. This moral perspective was clearly stated in Macaulay's Report on the ICS and further spelled out in the Third Report from the Civil Service Commissioners. Macaulay's Report had concluded that

> ... Early superiority in science and literature generally indicates the existence of some qualities which are securities against vice – industry, self-denial, a taste for pleasures not sensual, a laudable desire for honourable distinction, a still more laudable desire to obtain the approbation of friends and relations... the intellectual test which is about to be established will be found in practice to be also the best moral test which can be devised.

The Third Report of the Civil Service Commissioners elaborated on this by saying that superiority in science and literature

> ... implies, to some extent at least, the like superiority in some moral qualities, such as self-denial, regularity, perseverance and energy. We admit, nevertheless, that there are other moral qualities, such as 'judgment', 'discretion', 'moral courage', 'stability of purpose', 'fidelity', respecting which a certain conclusion cannot be drawn... (Civil Service Commissioners, 1858, p.xxiii).

The Commissioners argued that although these qualities were not measurable or comparable between candidates in intellectual examinations they could be assessed during probation and during promotion by merit. In the twentieth century the Commission followed the example of the armed forces and pioneered work which led to what became known as the Method II system of selection using the Civil Service Selection Board and the assistance of psychologists. In the nineteenth century, however, the Civil Service Commissioners demonstrated leadership qualities themselves by setting high standards for the Commission which they directed. It recruited its own staff at the outset by open competition; and it focused its attention on the less easily measurable qualities it wished to recognize through the rigorous use of probation. Not only should the best candidates be appointed, they should subsequently be assessed to ensure that the highest standards of public service were upheld. Thus the Commissioners were always very diligent in considering staff who reached the end of their period of probation. In particular, in 1902, they reviewed the pattern of cases failing probation and, for their own guidance, worked out a scheme for disallowance of increments on grounds of what they called 'moral default'. This ranged, for example, from carelessness, inaccuracy and unpunctuality (loss of increments for 2 years), through insubordination, stubbornness and unreliability (loss of increments for 4 years), through other categories up to character and conduct unsatisfactory in serious matters (removal from list).[22]

Part of the reasoning behind setting such high standards, and in penalizing any deviation from those high expectations, was that it was to be recognized as an honour to be a civil servant. Indeed, the privilege was, on occasion, reckoned to be so significant that it was reward enough, without remuneration. Consequently, the first Commissioners were unpaid. By 1862 the two Commissioners were Sir Edward Ryan, who was receiving £1,000 as Deputy Comptroller of the Exchequer, and Sir John Lefevre, who had been a member of Macaulay's Committee on the ICS, and was receiving a large salary of £2,500 a year as Clerk of Parliaments. Their duties in their paid positions continued, but their work as Civil Service Commissioners was onerous. In the early days they met daily, including Saturdays, to review certificates, testimonials and the examination papers of candidates, to approve drafts of letters, and to meet people. The volume of work was well illustrated by the number of candidates they examined and certificated and by their large correspondence, much of which was printed and/or reported in their annual reports.

Being unpaid and holding office 'at pleasure' was, however, recognized by them and by others as being a disadvantage – and, perhaps, even, a danger to the continuation of what the Commission was for. The Commissioners recognised that their 'functions were more analogous to those of judicial officers than to those of the great majority of civil servants'. They recognized the 'personal feeling which must from time to time influence friends and patrons, who will in many cases be persons of high official position'. Consequently, they argued that knowing 'that any pressure which may be exercised will be all on one side and that the tendency will therefore always be towards indulgence of individuals at the expense of the public, we cannot refrain from submitting a decided opinion that the offices which we hold should be tenable during good behaviour'.[23] In 1862 Treasury officials and ministers, including Gladstone, who was Chancellor of the Exchequer, recognized that the experience of six years had shown that the experiment of creating the Civil Service Commission had been 'eminently successful' and the time had arrived to treat it as a permanent institution. Moreover, they thought that 'the permanent continuance of services altogether gratuitous' was 'neither to be expected nor perhaps altogether desirable'. Therefore from 1862, when Lefevre retired, Sir Edward Ryan was designated First Commissioner, with a salary of £1,500 a year, though the services of the other two Commissioners, selected because they were 'Gentlemen of Eminence', were to be rendered gratuitously: they were Sir Edward Head and the Hon Edward Turner Boyd Twistleton.[24]

The important and widely respected role quickly achieved by the Commissioners was to a large extent a result of the industry and high standards set and publicized within the civil service by the Commissioners themselves. Their rules were applied with judicial precision and authority. Where their experiences and decisions on particular cases might be used as lessons for others they were publicized – in annual reports and in correspondence. In particular, corruption and fraud was, wherever possible, prosecuted and reported in the press: general standards were to be improved by lessons of bad examples made public. All this activity contributed to setting high standards and educating people about them, and also to maintaining and enhancing those standards. It was not long before the Civil Service Commission acquired other functions of personnel administration, normally associated with a central department. The Commissioners quickly became the guardians of the rules for admission to the civil service – while the Treasury was increasingly representing what it saw as the general interests of the service. Rarely did the Commissioners lose an opportunity to assert their role as they saw it, of promoting the efficiency of the civil service in the public interest. For example, R. Howell, of the Commission, wrote to the Board of Trade in 1903, when it was being somewhat difficult about the qualities it sought in particular clerks: 'A Clerk in the Second Division is a member of the State Service not a Departmental service and no arbitrary standards can be set up by any Department in relation to him', and in 1904 Stanley Leathes, then the Secretary to the Commission, wrote to the Secretary, Charity Commission:

'The selection of Second Division Clerks for assignment is not made by the Heads of Departments but by the Civil Service Commissioners ...'.[25] In addition, provisions were made which buttressed their position. The Commission was told when clerks were surplus to requirements: they could then be re-allocated to another department. Sometimes staff did not satisfy probation requirements but could successfully be reallocated by the Commission. Provision was made for successful candidates to choose the departments in which they would prefer to work, with preference being given according to their place in the examination list. The Commission also became increasingly consulted for advice when criteria were being considered for filling vacant positions. All of these developments buttressed the position of the Commission as a unifying authority within the civil service.

The present UK government, its predecessor, and the leaders of the civil service have, in recent years, emphasised that the British civil service is still a unified civil service, though it is not uniform. The essential values that bind it together include its impartial, a-political character; recruitment by fair and open means; promotion on merit; and its capacity loyally to serve the government of the day. It also has a set of characteristics and values which may be less easy to specify and measure, but which may nevertheless be important. These values are sometimes referred to, together, as the administrative culture. They include the quality of relationships among staff, how they work together and how they relate to citizens and organizations outside the civil service. Although the United Kingdom still has a number of Civil Service Commissioners (there are currently nine of them) all of whom are part-time, and there is an Office of the Civil Service Commissioners, as a result of the devolution of authority, recruitment is the responsibility of over 3,000 recruitment units. Indeed, some of the implications of this devolution are considered by Susan Corby in Chapter 7. Questions may now be asked about the administrative culture that holds the, arguably unified, civil service together. Is it important? What is it? What was it in the past, when the British civil service was so much admired? How did past standards become established? How can standards be maintained, added to, or changed? Useful lessons may, perhaps, be learned from administrative history, especially if re-engineering is to be on the agenda. The intention of this chapter has been to indicate that a fertile source for answers to some of these contemporary questions may be the experience of one of the most admired, but now past, institutions of British public service.

Notes

1. PRO/CSC8/4; PRO/T1/6362B.
2. Parl Deb, 3s, Vol 139, Cols 675-745, 10 July 1855.
3. Parl Deb, 3s, Vol 130, Col 4, 31 January 1854.
4. PRO/CSC8/4; PRO/T1/6362B.
5. Parl Deb, 3s, Vol 130, Col 62, 31 January 1855.
6. PP, 1854-55, Vol XX.
7. PP, 1856, Vol XXII.
8. PP, 1861, Vol XIX.
9. PRO/CSC2/35.
10. PRO/CSC2/5, Hammond to Mann, 25 June 1855.
11. PRO/CSC3/155.
12. PRO/CSC2/8, enclosure to a letter dated 12 May 1855.
13. PRO/CSC3/354, comments by CM, dated 11 August 1949.
14. PRO/CSC3/269.
15. PRO/CSC3/213.
16. PRO/CSC3/351.
17. PRO/CSC3/87.
18. PRO/CSC3/70; PRO/CSC3/87; PRO/CSC3/144.
19. PRO/CSC3/207.
20. PRO/CSC3/334.
21. PRO/CSC8/3.
22. PRO/CSC8/7.
23. PRO/T1/6362B, Civil Service Commissioners to Chancellor of the Exchequer, 1 January 1862.
24. PRO/T1/6362B, Memorandum 14 July 1862.
25. PRO/CSC3/257.

References

Chapman, Richard A. (1968), *Decision Making*, London:Routledge and Kegan Paul.

Civil Service Commissioners (1858), *Third Report of Her Majesty's Civil Service Commissionerss: together with appendices*, PP.1857-58, Vol. XXV, pp.1-380, London: HMSO.

Civil Service Commissioners (1860), *Fifth Report of Her Majesty's Civil Service Commissioners: together with appendices*, PP.1860, Vol. XXIV, pp.305-532, London: HMSO.

Eaton, Dorman B. (1880), *Civil Service in Great Britain*, New York: Harper and Brothers.

Hughes, Edward (1954), 'Civil Service Reform 1853-5', *Public Administration* Vol. 32, pp.17-51.

Macaulay, T.B, and others (1855), *The Indian Civil Service, Report to the Right Hon. Sir Charles Wood*, London: W. Thacker and Co.

Northcote/Trevelyan (1854), *Report on the Organisation of the Permanent Civil Service*, PP. 1854, Vol. XXVII, pp.1-31, London: HMSO.

Prime Minister (1995), *The Civil Service: Taking Forward Continuity and Change*, Cm. 2748, London: HMSO.

Tomlin, Lord (1931), *Royal Commission on the Civil Service, Report*, Cmd. 3099, London: HMSO.

Tout, T.F. (1916), *The English Civil Service in the Fourteenth Century*, Manchester University Press, Manchester.

8 The Inherently Unethical Nature of Public Service Ethics

Lawrence Pratchett

The existence of a public service ethic – a core set of principles which prescribe the minimum standards and guide the behaviour of all those involved in public life – is a widely held and much cherished belief in western democracies. The notion of such ethics is a fundamental feature of public administration, providing for continuity and consensus of values across a wide range of otherwise disparate professions and organisations. These ethics have an institutional status, providing the substance which holds government together. To challenge this belief, therefore, is to challenge one of the central pillars of modern democracy. Yet this chapter maintains that the ethical principles of public service are inherently unethical precisely because they are institutionalized structures of values which shape and constrain behaviour. Four propositions form the core of this argument:

1. Ethical principles in public service are inherently vague and ambiguous. It is only when they are placed in particular political or organizational contexts that they have any meaning.
2. The diversity of agencies and organizations which proliferate in the modern world of public service compromise the ability of either government or society to define meaningful standards which transcend organizational boundaries. The consequence is that ethical standards often provide only the lowest common denominator between organizations rather than shared ideals of public life.
3. Ethical dilemmas in public life are essentially concerned with achieving a balance between competing or conflicting values. The ethical public servant, therefore, is someone who is able to weigh up and make sense of these competing values within a clear framework of moral values.
4. Political institutions appear to provide a moral framework for ethical

decision-making. However, the nature of political institutions results in the application of codes and conventions for ethical practice which act as surrogates for true ethical behaviour. Consequently, the public servant's responsibility for ethical behaviour is abrogated by his or her existence within political institutions.

The chapter will explore each of these propositions in more detail, before concluding with an analysis of the implications of this argument for modern public administration.

The ambiguity of public service ethics

Achieving a comprehensive and transferable definition of ethics which has meaning in both contemporary structures of public administration, and potentially evolving patterns of public service, is a complex and somewhat impossible task. As N. Dale Wright and Stanford S. McConkie argue:

> We make declarations as to the modes of behavior that ought to be expected of, and followed by, our disciples without equivalent consideration of the means for transmitting the expectation from generation to generation. In our individual self-confidence, each remains unsure that his or her personal value commitments are shared by colleagues as the basis for the renovation of administrative theory and practice (Wright and McConkie, 1988, p.2).

Indeed, they observe the absence of any consensus among academics or public administrators over the precise nature of ethics and their meaning in particular cases, although they do recognise that there is some agreement over the general principles which underpin public life. What emerges from most discussions of public service ethics, therefore, is a high level of consensus over the fundamental values which can be expected of public servants (whether elected representatives or appointed officers) but also a high level of ambiguity over the meaning of such values in particular contexts. For this reason Alan Lawton argues that 'virtue' among public service managers is a key feature which mediates between abstract values and defined principles on the one hand, and ethical behaviour in specific contexts on the other. Thus, he envisages a flow of moral behaviour which originates in the fundamental values held across society, and culminates in ethical practice (Lawton, 1998, p.48):

VALUE → PRINCIPLE → VIRTUE → PRACTICE

In this respect it is the existence of virtue among individual managers which is the key to ensuring that abstract principles are translated into ethical practice – ethical practice which meets with society's normative expectations. The difficulty with this argument is that virtue appears to be an intuitive characteristic. Unchecked intuition itself may lead to ambiguity in the way that individuals translate principles into practice.

Despite an absence of knowledge about how broad values and principles are translated into practice, public administration abounds with examples of ethical principles. While the Nolan Committee's 'seven principles of public life' are probably the best example of such principles in Britain (Nolan, 1995), this approach is far from unique. The public management branch of the Organization for Economic Co-operation and Development (OECD) has attempted to develop a 'checklist' for reviewing 'ethics regimes', again concentrating upon the ability of governments to ensure that such principles underpin public service (OECD, 1996). While the OECD recognises political, cultural and constitutional differences in each of its member states it is implicit in its development of such a checklist that it sees a core set of values as underpinning public service in all modern democracies. There is, therefore, some common ground across nations over the fundamental values which form the basis of public service. These can even be articulated into core principles, centred around such notions as the impartial and accountable bureaucrat and the open and honest politician (Montanheiro, 1998). Where these can be clearly stated and understood across organizations then there is little ambiguity over them. The ambiguity emerges in relation to their interpretation in particular organizational and institutional contexts, especially when core principles conflict with, or contradict, one another.

The other feature of this ambiguity concerns the range of issues which emerge as a result of it. In charting the rise of administrative ethics as a field of academic study in the United States over the last century, Terry L. Cooper observes how the emphasis shifted from an early focus on administrative efficiency in the late nineteenth century, through concern over the neutrality of public servants and equity in public service delivery, to more recent attention on virtue among public servants and its relevance to broader notions of citizenship and democracy (Cooper, 1994). The consequence is that public service ethics can mean anything from a focus on eradicating corrupt practices to the observing of exemplary standards of behaviour; from a structure of legal codes and practices to a systemic set of moral values; and from a broad set of responsibilities to a specific system of accountability. Rather than helping to clarify the meaning of ethics, such a broad application of the concept inevitably compounds its inherent ambiguity.

The argument here is not that the underlying values of modern public service are ambiguous. Indeed, the normative framework from which current conceptions of public service derive is relatively explicit and unequivocal. Furthermore, the rise of new structures and processes in public management, coupled with recent scandals in various parts of the public sector have served to focus greater attention on the underlying ethos of public service and the extent to which recent experiences challenge or change these values (Greenaway, 1995; Pratchett and Wingfield, 1996). Rather, the argument here is that public service ethics are ambiguous despite the clarity which has been given to the core values of public administration. The limits of public administrators to understand the processes through which core values and principles are translated into ethical practice, when combined with the broad range of issues which currently present ethical challenges, leads to a high level of ambiguity at the point at which ethical decisions have to be taken. This ambiguity, of course, does not necessarily lead to inherently unethical behaviour on the part of individual public servants, but it does leave the door open for possible shortcomings in the way in which fundamental principles are translated into practice in particular contexts.

The diversity of agencies and organizations in modern governance

In traditional structures of public administration the potential contexts in which ethical dilemmas could occur were restricted to a limited number of organizations, most (if not all) of which were bound by a similar and narrow set of legal and constitutional arrangements. Even so, the range of ethical dilemmas which presented themselves to individual public servants within these limited number of organizations was impressively large. The emergence of new patterns and structures of governance has greatly increased the number of organizational contexts in which ethical dilemmas can occur. Governance as a concept remains an essentially contested area of political science (Rhodes, 1996; Stoker, 1997). It is apparent, however, that at its most simple 'governance' refers to the existence of a multiplicity of agencies which extend across conventional public/private sector boundaries, and which are collectively important for the development and delivery of public policies. Discussions of governance, therefore, acknowledge the importance of various organizations in the policy process, including those which may operate on a wholly commercial basis. The significance of governance for public service ethics is more than simply the number of new agencies and organizations which now potentially fall within the broad sphere of public administration, although the proliferation of agencies, arms-length organizations and contracted-out services has been a central feature of the new mode of governance. More than this, it also highlights the diversity of actors which now populate the public sector, many of whom have different motivations and values from the traditional public servant, and view the work of public service in very different ways. In many respects these new actors have greatly enhanced public service by introducing new approaches and methods of managing organizations and greater levels of efficiency and productivity in the delivery of public services. These new actors, however, have also introduced new ethical dilemmas for public service and called into question the extent to which existing ethical regimes are sustainable (Fortin and Van Hassel, 1998).

The consequence of the fragmentation, decentralization and contractualization which emerges as a product of the new modes of governance, is a greater diversity of organizations and agencies involved in public services, leading to a much greater variety of contexts in which ethical dilemmas may develop. This is compounded by the fact that a much greater variety of actors with very different backgrounds are now confronted by the ethical dilemmas of public service. Such diversity of both actors, and the contexts in which they find themselves, calls into question the extent to which it is possible to design standards of behaviour which can have common meaning across such a diverse range of settings. The recent attempts by the Nolan committee, the OECD and other national or international agencies, to define the core principles of public life provide a starting point for understanding the high ideals which are expected to transcend time and place. In their quest to develop a universally applicable set of core principles, however, these attempts highlight the limits to which such universality is possible. What emerges is not so much a core set of principles which provide the moral foundations for public service in a range of countries, institutions and organizations, but a set of basic values which provide the lowest common denominator across a complex set of heterogeneous locations. The fact that these principles are subject to interpretation in different contexts leads to the conclusion that they can mean different things to different people: different political, professional and organizational imperatives may place different emphasis upon both the meaning of individual principles, and the relative importance of each principle to one another. Once such interpretations are accepted it is difficult not to conclude that these are any more than the lowest common denominator across functionally and organizationally differentiated public servants. Such a conclusion means that the definition of core principles in public service does not advance either the understanding or the practice of ethics very far. If these core principles are really only the lowest common denominator across a multiplicity of very different organizational and operational contexts, then they provide only a very weak frame of reference for public service, notwithstanding the difficulties noted earlier of translating such principles into ethical practice.

The growing diversity of organizational locations in which issues of public service ethics arise further calls into question the ability of individual public servants to reach ethically correct decisions. Moreover, they also call into question the extent to which ethical standards have universal application. Such doubts, however, do not make public service ethics inherently unethical. To further this argument it is necessary to explore in more detail the different values which form the basis of ethical behaviour in public service and the ways in which these require deliberate balancing of competing principles on the part of individual public servants.

The ethical public servant: balancing competing values

Even if it is possible to identify the core principles which constitute the lowest common denominator for ethical standards in public organizations, such principles ignore the fact that different individuals bring different sets of values to bear in weighing up the relative importance of each. Richard A. Chapman argues that these values are of fundamental importance:

> The personal values of public servants are the most important element in public service ethics. These values have a variety of sources which include the family background and early socialisation of officials; their education; their choice of career and selection at recruitment stage; training and socialisation after recruitment; the continuing changing values in society; influence from the political environment; the embodiment of some of the values and other factors in constitutions, codes and rules; and the requirements of national (and sometimes international) law (Chapman, 1993, p.168).

In developing an analysis of the way in which public sector values are changing, M. Van Wart identifies five major sources of values which have relevance here: individual, professional, organizational, legal and public interest values. Probably the most widely recognized of these are *individual values* which are concerned with the special levels of integrity expected of public servants:

> Integrity for public servants brings an unusually weighty responsibility ... because acceptance of public employment implies active acceptance of civic principles that society generally endorses. Public administrators are expected to have 'civic integrity', which means an appreciation of the Constitution and the laws of the land and a respect for the political-legal system. Without honor for the general system of authoritative decisionmaking and an appreciation for its underlying legitimacy, public officials could view the laws as nuisances to be overlooked or skirted when no one is paying attention (Van Wart, 1998, pp.8-9).

While Van Wart assumes a degree of universal consensus over the notion of civic integrity, however, it does not take much imagination to envisage instances in which different individuals will bring different preferences to bear in particular contexts and still consider themselves to be behaving with integrity – that is, with honesty, consistency, coherence and reciprocity. For example, magistrates courts are frequently criticised for their inconsistent treatment of minor offences, with some courts imposing much harsher sentences on offenders than others. In these instances it is not that different courts have differing levels of integrity. Rather, the problem is one of different individual notions of what constitutes integrity, especially when issues of integrity are blurred by other personal values such as concerns with social justice or differing perceptions of the seriousness of particular crimes.

The other sources of values share similar ambiguities: different professionals may give greater emphasis to different values; different organizations may favour different approaches to public life; the legal context of different agencies may lead to different patterns of accountability; and different political, social and educational backgrounds may lead individuals to perceive the public interest in very different ways. The point here is that while it is possible to be relatively clear about the normative preferences for each of these values, all remain essentially contested concepts which are open to interpretation. Furthermore, there is no necessary coherence or consistent balance between each of these value sources. Professional values may well conflict with legal requirements to undertake particular tasks. Organizational imperatives may not necessarily fit with the beliefs or value preferences of individuals. For Van Wart it is the conflicts between competing value sources which lie at the heart of ethical dilemmas in public service:

> Much more challenging and relevant to most administrators are the situations in which they must discharge a vague law, balance rival public interest groups, sort out the appropriate organizational interests from organizational ego, consider a higher but costly professional standard, and not overstate or abandon personal interests. For the most part, the really tough administrative decisions are those involving two or more legitimate value sources competing for consideration (Van Wart, 1998, p.23).

These conflicts give rise to more than simply the classic ethical dichotomy between means and ends: that is, between deontological considerations of ethics as 'due process' compared with teleological concerns with ethical ideals. More than this, they also emphasise the equal legitimacy of a variety of value sources in ethical decision-making - values which may well contradict one another in particular contexts, but which nonetheless have equal legitimacy in informing ethical decisions.

The consequence of this for public servants is that they, as individuals, become the prime focus for ethical decision-making. From this perspective the practise of public service ethics is not an organizational issue, it is an essentially individual activity, concerned with the weighing and balancing of competing values and imperatives in order to arrive at the most ethically suitable decision, however that is normatively defined. Two simple but important propositions follow. First, public servants must understand the nature of their individual responsibility in taking decisions - in Cooper's (1982) words, they must become 'responsible administrators'. Second, organizations must facilitate administrative discretion in such a way as to ensure that the 'responsible administrator' has the opportunity to behave responsibly. In other words, public servants need to be able to understand and balance all of the competing values and preferences which may inform a particular decision - and organizations should afford all possible opportunity to public servants for the careful articulation and balancing of these competing values. Only then can decisions be deemed to be ethical either in terms of process or outcome. Despite appearances, this is not an argument for greater administrative discretion, for as John A. Rohr (1989) observes, claims by public servants to exercise discretion are tantamount to claims to govern. It is, however, an acknowledgement of reality. The unique context of every ethical dilemma requires individuals to have both the moral and intellectual capacity, and the operational ability, to balance competing imperatives in order to reach ethical decisions. Again, an acknowledgement of this position does not lead to inherently unethical practices among public servants. It simply shifts the onus and responsibility for public service ethics on to individuals. The ethical public servant, therefore, is one who can show that all values have been carefully weighed before a final decision is made.

The institutional basis of ethical decision-making

If individuals are to be held responsible for their own ethical decisions, then the organizational and institutional pressures which may shape their understanding of particular contexts need to be taken into consideration. The literature on new institutionalism (Lowndes, 1996) provides a useful frame of reference for developing this understanding. New institutionalist approaches draw attention to the informal norms and customs which transcend individual organizations. These institutions are broad structures of power which shape behaviour in particular contexts. In this respect the shared values which are deemed to comprise the public service ethos can be seen as a culture which shapes and structures the behaviour of public servants (Pratchett and Wingfield, 1996). The new institutionalism is not one theoretical premise but a range of different academic approaches linked by the simple but important belief that the way in which political life is organized makes a difference (Blom-Hansen, 1997). Thus, in developing a political science approach to new institutionalist analysis, March and Olsen (1984, 1989) explicitly reject much of the reductionist, utilitarian, functionalist and instrumentalist concerns of extant political studies in favour of an approach which emphasises the relative autonomy of social and political institutions, and which focuses as much upon symbolic processes as it does upon efficient outcomes. While much of March and Olsen's work has been criticised as being confused and ambiguous (see for example Sjöblom, 1993; Jordan, 1990), its interpretation of informal norms and rules as providing a political context for behaviour remains important, especially in relation to the study of ethics and ethical behaviour in public life. In many respects, of course, this focus on informal institutions is not new. Analysis of the British constitution has always been as much concerned with informal customs and practice as it has been with legal constraints and requirements. However, as an emerging analytical framework the new institutionalism is useful in highlighting three features of informal institutions which are of particular relevance to the argument being developed here: those of simplification, symbolism and order.

Simplification refers to the way in which political institutions simplify otherwise complex situations for individuals, providing them with a set of rules as to what may be deemed appropriate behaviour. Consequently, existence within political institutions imposes duties and obligations upon actors, restricting the scope for personal choice and shaping decisions through a 'logic of appropriateness'. As March and Olsen (1984, p.741) put it 'in contrast to theories that assume action is choice based on individual values and expectations, theories of political structure assume action is the fulfilment of duties and obligations'. Insofar as public servants inevitably exist within political institutions, so their actions are shaped by a logic of appropriateness – by a sense of ethical duties and obligations which provide a frame of reference for behaviour.

Symbolism refers to the way in which institutions are rich in processes which confirm that decisions have been taken in the way in which they are supposed to be taken. In other words, by following institutionally recognized processes, the public servant is reassured that events have happened the way they should. Indeed, March and Olsen observe that in many institutional contexts political rituals provide actors with an innate pleasure and conclude that 'the processes of politics may be more central than their outcomes' (1984, p.742). Within political institutions actors look for symbols to confirm that events are occurring in the way that they are supposed to. For public servants this suggests that ethical decisions are ones which can be seen to have been reached through 'due process' in accordance with accepted norms, codes and customs. This corresponds with the widely held belief that the appearance of ethical behaviour is as important as its practice (Van Wart 1998).

Finally, *order* refers to the way in which institutions provide for coherent and consistent structure in a potentially complex and multi-dimensional political world. By simplifying complexity and providing symbols of 'due process' institutions help individuals to make sense of the world. Consequently, institutions give the appearance of order – a sense of historical and temporal progression in which events have evolved according to sets of norms and rules. This sense of institutional order provides for continuity in processes, giving institutional meaning to otherwise disparate and unrelated events. For public servants, therefore, prescribed ethical frameworks provide the sense of institutional order which enable them to make sense of otherwise complex and unrelated ethical dilemmas, offering a set of rules, norms, conventions and symbols which justify decisions as inherently ethical.

So far, the new institutionalism has been offered as a framework which adds to ethical behaviour, especially as it provides for a way of understanding the political structures which order values and preferences, which simplify complex issues, and which generate a set of rituals and symbols that confirm ethical practice. But it is precisely because institutions provide such norms and customs that they make the current practice of public service ethics inherently unethical. In short, institutions routinize behaviour and substitute personal responsibility for ethical decisions with a set of institutional standards and practices. Individual public servants look to existing symbols for guidance in resolving ethical dilemmas, rather than examining the moral assumptions which underpin such symbols, and feel reassured by the notion of order which it imposes upon outcomes. In so doing, the individual's moral responsibility for weighing and balancing competing values as the basis of ethical decision-making is abrogated by norms and conventions which may be rooted in some notion of ethical behaviour, but which nonetheless contravene a fundamental principle of ethics in that they reduce ethical decisions to simplified rituals and symbols. Ethical decisions taken within the context of institutions are shaped by the precedents and practices of previous decisions. Consequently, the emphasis is more upon consistency and order than it is upon understanding the complex interplay of competing values and the unique circumstances of each individual ethical dilemma. Indeed, it is not uncommon to hear public servants justifying actions on the basis of precedent and the need to demonstrate consistency. While institutions may have the appearance of offering an ethical framework to guide the behaviour of individual public servants, therefore, they also absolve those same public servants from moral and ethical responsibility for their behaviour. Individuals become more concerned with following customs and practices than they are with achieving ethical outcomes. Institutions make public service ethics inherently unethical.

In order to substantiate this argument it is useful to briefly reflect upon one such institution in political life: that of professionalism in public services. In analysing the ethical basis of accountancy Gowthorpe and Blake (1998) note the way in which institutional practices have over-emphasised accounting processes in place of any awareness of the ethical consequences of individual decisions. Yet the way in which accountants perform their functions can have important implications both at the micro-level of individual organizations and at the macro-economic level – witness the creative accounting practices which emerged in local government during the 1980s as a way of circumventing the Thatcher government's attempt to control local authority spending. The importance of Gowthorpe and Blake's argument – one which they claim is relevant to most professions – is that accountants perceive themselves to operate within a clear ethical framework: a framework which has clearly defined standards and practices set by professional bodies which provide a frame of reference for all decisions. However, the practice of accountancy varies considerably across organizations, and Gowthorpe and Blake accuse accountants of operating in grey areas using dubious accountancy practices in order to achieve desired organizational preferences (see also Blake, Amat and Dowds, 1998, in the same volume). In effect, their argument is that a narrowly defined set of institutional ethics acts as a surrogate for real ethical practice in accountancy, liberating accountants from moral and ethical responsibility for their actions. As long as the correct processes have been followed the accountant believes that ethical obligations have been fulfilled. More than simply being a narrow concept of ethical practice, this is an example of institutions creating and reinforcing essentially unethical practice within an apparently ethical framework. Given that accountants are not alone in operating within such professional ethics, either in the public sector or elsewhere, this effect has profound implications for ethics in the public service.

Implications and conclusions

This chapter has developed the argument that despite repeated attempts to clarify the ambiguities of ethical practice, public service ethics remain inherently unethical. The diversity of organizations which now proliferate public administration result in ethical principles providing only the lowest common denominator in ethical practice, and place even greater emphasis upon the importance of context. Given the ambiguities of ethical principles and the role of competing values in giving them meaning within particular contexts, ethical practice comes down to a personal responsibility for weighing and balancing conflicting imperatives. The ability to reach decisions based upon a careful consideration of the various values prevalent in any context is the prime characteristic of the ethical public servant. Political institutions undermine this fundamental characteristic by emphasizing norms and customs in place of context in ethical decision-making. As a result, while public service may have the appearance of high ethical standards, its practice is inherently unethical: public servants are rarely afforded the opportunity to reflect carefully upon the competing value imperatives which inform a given situation, freed from the constraints and structures of the institutions which impose order and structure on daily life.

This is not to argue that ethics are, or indeed should be, about homogeneity. Ethics are about conflicting values. If individuals have to weigh competing beliefs and loyalties in order to resolve ethical dilemmas, then it is inevitable that different individuals will resolve such conflicts in different ways. Without strong and clear frameworks ethical behaviour could lead to contradictory outcomes, not only within organizations, but also across the public sector. The implications of this for ethical practices in public service are profound. On the one hand, institutions provide a frame of reference and give some structure to otherwise chaotic and impossibly complex features of the political environment. They are both a necessary and desirable feature of political life in that they enable individuals to make sense of their environments. On the other hand, by their very nature, political institutions undermine and replace individual notions of ethical responsibility with institutional standards and norms which shape and constrain individual behaviour. In this respect they are inherently bad for ethical practice.

So what? Just because institutions abrogate personal responsibility for ethical behaviour does not necessarily mean that either the processes or the outcomes of public service will be worse than if the decisions had been based upon a careful weighing of competing values. Indeed, the way in which institutions evolve suggests that an iterative process of learning and adjustment between individual values and broader institutional norms is an inevitable feature of institutional life. Institutional norms and customs may well deliver ethical practices by default. Problems arise, however, during periods of rapid and extensive change, when managerial and organizational practices become out of step with the broader institutional framework in which they exist. In these circumstances it is conceivable that as well as introducing additional tensions into the process of change in these organizations, institutions may well militate against the development of more appropriate ethical practices to correspond with the new ethical dilemmas which emerge from new organizational or managerial structures and practices.

It is in the context of change that institutions pose the greatest threat to ethical practice in public service. At the best of times public services are inherently unethical because of the way in which institutions absolve individuals from their ethical duties and obligations, although the outcomes of public administration may be none the worse for this absence of ethics. During periods of extensive administrative change, however, the danger of absolving public servants from their ethical obligations may become only too apparent. The inherently unethical basis of public service ethics may lead to major conflicts of interest as administrative reforms really start to bite in western democracies.

References

Blake, J., Amat, O. and Dowds, J. (1998), 'The ethics of creative accounting', in C. Gowthorpe and J. Blake (eds), *Ethical issues in accounting*, London: Routledge.

Blom-Hansen, J. (1997), 'A new institutionalist perspective on policy networks', *Public Administration* Vol. 75, pp.669-93.

Chapman, Richard A. (1993), 'Ethics in Public Service', in Richard A. Chapman (ed.), *Ethics in Public Service*, Edinburgh: Edinburgh University Press.

Cooper, Terry L. (1982), *The responsible administrator: an approach to ethics for the administrative role*, New York: Kennikat.

Cooper, Terry L. (1994), 'The emergence of administrative ethics as a field of study in the United States', in Terry L. Cooper (ed.), *Handbook of Administrative Ethics*, New York: Marcel Dekker.

Fortin, Yvonne and Van Hassel, Hugo (1998), 'L'évolution de la contractualisation dans le secteur public depuis 1980', in Annie Hondeghem (ed.), *Ethics and accountability in a context of governance and new public management*, Amsterdam: IOS Press.

Gowthorpe, Catherine and Blake, John (eds.) (1998), *Ethical issues in accounting*, London: Routledge.

Greenaway, J. (1995), 'Having the bun and the halfpenny: can old public service ethics survive in the new Whitehall?', *Public Administration* Vol. 73, pp.357-74.

Jordan, Grant (1990), 'Policy community realism versus new institutionalist ambiguity', *Political Studies* Vol. 38, pp.470-84.

Lawton, Alan (1998), *Ethical management for the public services*, Buckingham: Open University Press.

Lowndes, Vivien (1996), 'Varieties of new institutionalism: a critical appraisal', *Public Administration* Vol. 74, pp.181-97.

March, J. and Olsen, J. (1984), 'The new institutionalism: organizational factors in political life', *The American Political Science Review* Vol. 78, pp.734-49.

March, J. and Olsen, J. (1989), *Rediscovering institutions: the organizational basis of politics*, New York: Free Press.

Montanheiro, Luiz (1998), 'Searching for a set of values in the ethical behaviour of the public sector', in Annie Hondeghem (ed.), *Ethics and accountability in a context of governance and new public management*, Amsterdam: IOS Press.

Nolan, Lord (1995), *First report of the Committee on Standards in Public Life*, Cm.2850-I, London: HMSO.

OECD (1996), *Ethics in the public service – current issues and practice,* Public management occasional paper 14, Paris:OECD.
Pratchett, Lawrence and Wingfield, Melvin (1996), 'Petty bureaucracy and wool-minded liberalism? The changing ethos of local government officers', *Public administration* Vol. 74, pp.639-56.
Rhodes, R.A.W. (1996), 'The New Governance: Governing without Government', *Political Studies* Vol.44, pp.652-67.
Rohr, John A. (1989), *Ethics for bureaucrats: an essay on law and values,* 2nd edition, New York: Marcel Dekker.
Sjoblom G. (1993), 'Some critical notes on March and Olsen's rediscovering institutions', *Journal of theoretical politics* Vol.5, pp.397-407.
Stoker, G. (1997), 'Governance as Theory: Five Propositions', *International Social Science Journal* Vol. 15(5), pp.47-61.
Van Wart, Montgomery (1998), *Changing public sector values,* New York: Garland.
Wright, N. and McConkie, Stanford S. (1988), 'Introduction', in N. Dale Wright (ed), *Papers on the ethics of administration,* Utah: Brigham Young University.

9 Is Democracy a Substitute for Ethics? Administrative Reform and Accountability

B. Guy Peters

Administrative ethics is important for a number of reasons (Chapman, 1993; Hondeghem, 1998), but most issues of public service ethics are derived from the basic question of bureaucratic discretion. Even in the most clearly defined and legalistic administrative systems the individual administrator is granted a great deal of latitude for making decisions on his or her own (Lewis and Birkinshaw, 1993; Hoff, 1993). In most instances this discretion creates no real problem for the public. The administrator merely follows the law and/or has a reasonable ethical sense so the citizen is treated fairly. Indeed, there is some evidence (Lipsky, 1980; Nilsson and Westerstahl, 1997) that citizens – in their role as programme clients – may be treated more than fairly, and it is citizens in their role as taxpayers who may not fare so well when bureaucratic discretion is being applied. Of course, there are other cases in which actions by the police, tax authorities, immigration officials and even teachers, demonstrate very clearly the possibilities for the abuse of administrative discretion.

There are several ways for political systems to cope with the problem of administrative discretion (see Hood, 1998a). Some systems have attempted to develop a highly professionalized administrative corps which functions as a closed career system, with the assumption that the professional values will ensure appropriate behaviour. Another strategy is to employ primarily lawyers, and to utilize legal training as a means of inculcating the desired norms into the public servants. Still other administrative traditions make use of a number of internal control devices that enforce accountability and attempt to prevent the exercise of much autonomy by public servants, even those at the very top of the administrative pyramids. Patricia Day and Rudolph Klein (1986) point to a number of alternative ways to conceptualize accountability, as well as to the increasing complexity of the accountability relationships within modern government.

These methods for coping with the problem of discretion rapidly resolve themselves into the familiar Friedrich vs. Finer debate. Does any amount of formalized, external control defend the public against the public servant who wants to abuse his or her discretion (the Friedrich position)? Or does it really hurt to supplement the positive values of most bureaucrats with a goodly amount of oversight and external control (Finer)? The obvious resolution of this debate is that it is premised on a false dichotomy and that administrative systems need both types of control, internal and external, if they are to function as most citizens would like. Even if the external controls are not really necessary, their existence helps to legitimate the system, assure the more sceptical citizen, and encourage the few public servants who have not internalized a code of conduct.

Christopher Hood (1998b) provides another approach to understanding the problem of control in bureaucracy. Building on cultural theory, he argues that a hierarchicalist conception of public administration tends to focus attention on failures of administration that result from inadequate control from above, and excessive free-lance decision-making on the part of individual public servants. On the other hand, egalitarian conceptions of public administration are more concerned with the inherent *dysfunctions* of hierarchy, and the perceived need for greater individual initiative to prevent and correct dysfunctions (see Peters, 1996, Chapter 3). While not mentioning ethical requirements *per se,* the egalitarian conception certainly does make the individual administrator the focus of error correction and responsibility.

These positions concerning controlling discretion are well known, but are none the less important because of their familiarity. Indeed, it helps to be reminded of these on-going debates as governments are proceeding down roads of reform that appear to ignore these familiar arguments about discretion and its control. The issues to be raised in this chapter revolve around the effects of numerous recent reforms of the public sector that have tended to reduce both the hierarchical and the internalized controls over the bureaucracy. While these reforms may be motivated by desires to make administration both more efficient and more user friendly, the outcomes may be less positive. In the process of producing change, some important questions of administrative control may have been ignored, or at least have been assigned a subsidiary position.

The need for imposing some form of control over the bureaucracy has not been forgotten entirely in the process of reform. Although some market-oriented reforms do appear to ignore accountability,[1] substituting the value of efficiency for equity and fairness (Self, 1993), other strands of administrative reform have been concerned explicitly with creating forms of accountability. One manifestation of that concern has been the explicit introduction of mechanisms of popular, democratic control over bureaucracy, these controls being conceptualized as substitutes for the internalized values of a professionalized civil service or for the internal controls of hierarchy. The alternative reaction has been to substitute partisan political controls for the ethical and hierarchical controls, assuming that those instruments also have some democratic legitimacy.

Therefore, to a great extent *responsiveness* as an ideal is replacing ideas of *responsibility* and *accountability* in the control of the public bureaucracy. These terms are often used interchangeably, but should be seen as implying rather different things about the control over bureaucracy. Accountability means simply having to render an account for one's actions, usually to parliament. Thus, in Westminster systems accountability is conceptualized in parliamentary terms, with the minister being (at least in principle) accountable for all the actions of his or her department (Aucoin, 2000). While emphasizing the importance of democratic controls over the bureaucracy, this form of accountability also tends to emphasize exposing failure and exceptions (often for political reasons rather than administrative reasons) rather than assessing the performance of the bureaucracy on a more regular basis.

Responsibility, on the other hand, implies commitment on the part of officials to a set of ethical and legal standards. Responsible civil servants are expected to make the most of their own decisions without close supervision, but to do so within clearly defined legal or ethical principles. Both responsibility and accountability imply that the locus of control over public administration resides largely at the elite level. In one instance the source of control is largely externalized, while in the other it is internalized, but in both citizens are left with their agents (elected or permanent) performing the tasks of control over the public bureaucracy.

Responsiveness is a more manifestly democratic term, implying that the bureaucracy will respond to the demands of the public, perhaps as mediated through political elites of some sort. Responsiveness of administration here is conceptualized as being both to political leaders and more directly to the public at large. That is, the response of the administrator in a responsive mode may be to a member of parliament functioning as an advocate of a constituent's interest. When the response to parliament is in an accountability mode it tends to be to the institution as a whole, or perhaps to a committee, rather than to an individual member. One should note here that a responsive bureaucracy may not be responsible, and may encounter difficulties when held to account for its actions, given that those actions may serve more particular than general interests.

After describing the nature of the reforms that have engendered the greater use of democratic and political means of control, this discussion next considers the likely effects of these forms of control versus others, especially those which are most familiar. The first part of the argument to be presented is that although the utilization of these more political and democratic means of control is useful in some ways, they also tend to operate *ex post facto* to detect wrong-doing, rather than to prevent it – except by the normal deterrence value of any system of punishment. In Christopher Hood's (1986) terms for describing policy instruments these democratic forms of control are useful detectors but tend to be less well suited as effectors, and further they themselves contain little in the way of mechanisms for producing appropriate actions. These mechanisms almost always depend upon the involvement of some other actors in order to produce the required types of changes in behaviour by public employees.

The second part of the argument is that these more overtly democratic forms of control may, to the extent that they are effective, actually generate somewhat perverse incentives for organizations in the public sector. Further, these forms of accountability may mis-specify the values that should be being implemented by public sector organizations, and often may do so in a manner that is potentially destructive of important public sector values. This concern with the effects of reform certainly should not be taken as an argument against democracy, nor one against more open government. It should, however, be taken as an argument in favour of the use of internalized means of control where possible, or at least the use of both populist and professional forms of accountability in tandem. It should also be taken as reflecting scepticism about the apparent efficacy of substituting seemingly democratic means for well-established professional means for policing and controlling administration.

Forms of democratic control

So far, this discussion has been focused on mechanisms of democratic control over bureaucracies without specifying what empirical referents were intended by that statement. Another word that has been applied to some of the democratization of control over the bureaucracy is the consumerization of policies. As has been argued elsewhere (Hood, Peters and Wollmann, 1996), this phrase is itself extremely ambiguous. In both conceptualizations, however, there is an attempt to enable the public affected by government action to have greater influence over the policies that impact them. The obvious difference is that in one version the emphasis is on shaping general policy, while in the other the focus is on detecting and redresing maladministration.

Part of the democratization of bureaucratic control is that there are relatively direct ways for the public to monitor poorly performing organizations and individuals within the public sector. One of the more pervasive of these ideas has been that of the citizens' charter, or perhaps more appropriately the consumers' charter. That initial populist element in the accountability regimen has been followed by the Complaints Task Force, and perhaps an even more populist conception of accountability. The assumption guiding these programmes is that citizens (largely functioning in their role as consumers of public services) are capable of assessing the performance of many public organizations, and also then transforming those assessments into enforceable decisions about what government should do, and how it should do it.

An associated version of the democratization of control over the public bureaucracy is the creation of various user groups that function as virtual boards of directors for public sector organizations (see Jensen, 1998; Adler, Petch and Tweedie, 1990). This form of control over service provision has been most apparent for policies such as education, social housing, and health care where there are numerous clients who want, and indeed often now demand, to exert some greater control over the activities of service providers. The groups that function as the mechanisms of accountability may be elected from the clients, therefore having some direct democratic mandate for enforcing accountability over the providers.

There is another way in which democracy comes into play in the control of administration, and this is through the use of political appointments to an increasing number of positions in government. A number of components of contemporary administrative reforms have tended to deinstitutionalize bureaucracy. For example, the internal deregulation of bureaucracies has shifted the focus from formalized rules for the system as a whole to more particularistic rules and procedures (see Peters, 1996, Chapter 5). One major aspect of this deinstitutionalization has been to move a good deal of implementation activity out of formal government organizations and into either deconcentrated organizations or quasi-private or private organizations. The former locus refers to organizations such as the agencies now a dominant (in personnel terms) and familiar part of British government. The latter refers to any number of options such as quangos, or increasingly entirely private organizations operating with contracts from government (Kettl, 1988; Hogwood, 1993).

In the utilization of these types of organizations government loses a good deal of its direct control over policy, and over the implementors of its policies. This loss of control is obviously evident when there is an increasing use of non-governmental, or quasi-governmental, organizations as major implementors of policy. Indeed, much of the purpose of these reorganizations of the public sector has been to reduce the level of governmental control over organizations delivering public services to enable them to be more efficient and effective, following the dictates of the New Public Management. The consequence of this may be a loss of conventional accountability, or at least the need to rethink how accountability can be enforced.

Another format for deinstitutionalizing the public bureaucracy has been deregulation, or the loosening regulation of personnel systems and the elimination of many formal civil service requirements. This strategy is also in part a mechanism for enabling government to emphasize managerialism, and presumably to enhance its efficiency. The argument implicit, or explicit, in these reforms is that traditional civil service procedures have been straight jackets for managers, limiting whom they can hire and how they can motivate, and if necessary punish, their employees (DiIulio, 1994). Likewise, an exclusive career civil service system closes government to the best possible talent, while the ability to move in and out makes government a more attractive employer for some of the best talent.

The final means for deinstitutionalizing the bureaucracy is by the use of what the Canadians refer to as citizen engagement, perhaps the most overtly democratic component of the changes mentioned here. The point of engagement is much like the consumerization of policy – to permit the public to have a direct impact over policy and administration. In terms of controlling the bureaucracy these mechanisms depend upon the public identifying malfeasance and nonfeasance and then perhaps also having at its disposal the mechanisms for at least beginning a process of rectification of problems.

The deinstitutionalization of public bureaucracies opens these reformed systems to greater patronage and to more tampering with the administration of personnel. Positions that at one time might have been covered by merit appointments are now subject to direct political appointment. The assumption is that managerial values will be used to make these personnel decisions, and indeed in many cases that may be the case. There is, however, little to prevent other less desirable criteria from being applied in the selection of personnel. For example, Paul Light (1996) has described the thickening of the federal government in the United States, with more and more political appointees being placed in control positions in the bureaucracy. These appointments have tended not to be at random, but rather have gone differentially to more politically sensitive departments and agencies (Ingraham, Thompson and Eisenberg, 1995), indicating the clear interest to use these appointments as instruments of control.

The United States has a long history of political appointments in the federal bureaucracy but there also appear to be increasing levels of political selection of personnel in other countries. For example, in European countries with a reputation for institutionalized public services and meritocratic values there are increasing uses of political appointees as means of exercising control over the public sector. L. Rouban (1998; 1997), for example, points to the increasing use of political appointments in France, and the desire to ensure that some form of accountability and control is thereby assured. In Scandinavia there is also an apparent increase in the number and influence of political appointments (Pierre, 1998; Virtanen, 1998). The list of cases could be easily extended, but the basic point remains that merit is being replaced, or at least supplemented, by political appointment with the purpose of exercising control and creating a form of accountability.[2]

The impacts of politicized accountability

For individuals raised and trained in the merit system tradition, there is an almost visceral reaction against the increased use of patronage appointments. In addition to this reaction, there may be more rational reasons for concern about the changes described above. The use of political mechanisms, whether direct or through partisan institutions, may introduce rather perverse incentives for participants in government, and produce a form of accountability that was not thought of when these changes in the public service were introduced.

Direct democracy

Although almost certainly more benign from a normative view, the use of direct democracy as a form of accountability may also create several problems for public programmes. Again, it is at least as difficult to argue against democracy as it is to argue against the merit system, but as with direct democracy for rule-making (see Budge, 1997), there may be some significant problems with the use of direct democracy for evaluating programmes and enforcing accountability on public administration.

When considering that very loose form of direct democracy in which citizens and/or customers are empowered to complain and perhaps to receive some redress, several things happen to the accountability regimen. The most obvious is that a very particular segment of the population may become the reference group for enforcing accountability under a democratic conception of accountability. That is, those citizens who feel that they have been wronged, and who have the requisite skills to complain effectively become the measure of good and bad administration, rather than a professional or legal standard of some sort.

There is good evidence that political participation, especially beyond simple voting, is not evenly distributed by social class or by education levels, so the reference group then increasingly tends to become middle-class expectations about public service. This appears to have been true in some of the experiments with education, perhaps a service with which the middle class is particularly concerned. There is less evidence concerning other policy sectors, but the same general outcome should be expected. As Schattschneider famously argued, the choir of democracy does sing with a middle class accent.

This problem of differential capabilities of exerting control over the bureaucracy is perhaps especially relevant in social policy where programme clients are often in a perceived, and generally also very real, dependency relationship with the provider. Although the stated rules of a provider organization would be that clients do have rights to equitable and courteous treatment, it is only the most self-assured of clients who might have the temerity to challenge their treatment. To do so is to threaten even worse treatment in the future. Thus, it is not only skills but also power relationships that are important in understanding how more democratic controls over bureaucracies may, or may not, be effective.

Even if clients of social programmes were sufficiently brave, and sufficiently capable of coping with the bureaucracy, they may find that they confront a moving target. That is, members of the public bureaucracy generally do not want to lose their own power over implementation, and may feel that they can do a better job than the non-professionals (see Jensen, 1998). Thus, just as clients and interest groups may evolve to counteract the powers of the bureaucracy, so too the bureaucracy will evolve to reassert its own control over its clients. This continuing game of cat and mouse over power then continues to change the patterns of interaction between the two sets of actors.

To follow on from that point, it is doubtful whether many important questions of accountability are amenable to determination by a voting process, or by the aggregation of preferences of a number of different participants. Many accountability problems involve the treatment of an individual, rather than the treatment of the aggregate. Indeed, important professional issues of accountability may arise when an individual or a small group are disadvantaged while the majority are advantaged. These problems are particularly important when defined in terms of minority ethnic groups or by gender (see Susan Corby, Chapter 4), but are important even if defined by policy preferences. The point is that accountability is not simply a question of serving the majority interest, it has ethical, legal and political interests that go beyond the majority (See Barry O'Toole, Chapter 6).

It can be argued here than an ethic of the public interest becomes replaced by the acceptance, and even celebration of private interest as a means of deciding when there has been a failure of administration. That is, while more traditional approaches to accountability tended to focus on failures to meet goals of equality or fairness, standards built more on participation, especially when participation is effectively by only a rather small segment of the society, may push in the direction of accepting inequalities providing that the inequalities favour that more participative segment.

All the above points do raise important questions about how democratic methods can be employed to promote accountability of public programmes. It should be accepted, however, that these methods do have a number of real virtues, not least that they force public organizations to be more open and to act in more transparent ways as they administer the law. That openness may not be utilized equally effectively by all segments of society, but the opportunity has been created, and the very openness itself may cause any administrator considering an abuse of discretion to consider the costs and benefits of such a decision differently than in a more closed administrative system.

Politicized controls

In most institutionalized democratic regimes, the status of political controls – other than through parliament or ministers – over the bureaucracy is suspect. Most governments have invested a good deal of time and energy in ridding themselves of patronage and other forms of political involvement in administrative life, only to see them reemerge as a mechanism for control over public organizations when the traditional mechanisms have been weakened. Although implications of such a change in accountability systems may be well understood, they may still be worth a brief discussion.

The use of these political controls is often seen by political leaders as a necessary step once some of the other mechanisms for enforcing accountability and control have been weakened or terminated. This political need arises because although a public service may be delivered by a private organization, or perhaps by a quasi-public organization, to the public it remains a public service. Therefore, the minister who heads the ministry in question may be seen as the ultimate locus of responsibility. Thus, the minister may be perceived as being responsible for programmes over which he or she has little real influence, an untenable political position.

Can we escape law and ethics?

So far, this discussion has engaged in something of a polemic concerning the populist, democratic elements of contemporary administrative reforms, and the effects of those reforms on accountability regimes. There do appear to be some genuine problems if these populist ideas are taken to the extreme and assumed to be the panacea for problems of accountability. It is also appropriate to point out the resilience of ethical, and especially legal, forms of accountability in administration. While the populism is based on democratic and deinstitutionalizing premises,[3] it also appears that the democratic elements often become translated into rights, and therefore can become justiciable. This is true despite some political attempts to enhance the discretionary character of many policies, especially social policies.

This transformation can be seen in the experience of the Citizens' Charter in the United Kingdom, and to some extent in analogous charters in other political systems. While charters may have begun simply by establishing appropriate standards of service for various public organizations, and by assuming a populist method of implementation, those standards are transformed from appropriate in a normative sense to right in a legal sense (Page, 1999), and become in some instances justiciable. Further, in general controls over bureaucracies are becoming increasingly legal and judicialized. This is true even in the United Kingdom (see Sainsbury, 1994) which has had a relatively low level of judicial involvement in policy and administrative issues.[4]

Depending upon one's perspectives, this resilience on the part of more formalized modes of control over the bureaucracy is either the good news or the bad news. If one is a believer in the efficacy of populist forms of control, and the need to consumerize the public sector, then this is indeed bad news; well-intentioned populist methods are seemingly being captured and then converted to their own use by the more traditional political institutions. On the other hand, if one is more sceptical about the utility of the populist mechanisms for accountability then these instruments for legal intervention are an important way of addressing the problems perceived in those nominally democratic mechanisms. Like so much else of importance in politics, the important issues here become those of perceptions.

Summary

This chapter has attempted to demonstrate that despite the many virtues arising from administrative reforms, and especially from those reforms that have a participatory character, there are also some important negative consequences. The principal problem identified here is that of the potential loss of accountability, or the shift of the central focus of accountability from a broadly defined public interest to a more narrowly defined set of personal or group interests. Somewhat paradoxically reforms that have as at least one goal to open public administration to the public may in the end actually reduce the level of democratic accountability.

Of course, a large part of the reason why these very reforms have been undertaken is the perceived failings of the career bureaucracy to always supply the type of accountability that many citizens would like to see. Professional ethics and norms may be lauded in the abstract, but they may not be so laudable in practice. What may be required, therefore, is some mixing of norms of professional conduct with political mechanisms that place some pressure on the enforcement of those norms. Finding the golden mean is usually a means of solving problems, especially problems arising from dichotomous choices.

Notes

1. In fairness, some of the market-based concerns with performance and quality do have elements of accountability, but not the procedural accountability with which the political system typically has been accustomed.
2. Elsewhere the distinction is made between traditional clientelism and managerial clientelism (Dudek and Peters, 1999) to make the point

that although this may appear simply to be old fashioned 'jobs for the boys and girls', the root causes may be importantly different.
3. Deakin (1994) refers to this as the state and the citizen agenda that had been fostered by the New Right.
4. The increased use of legalistic controls in the UK is in part a function of Europeanization, with the ECJ and the ECHR beginning to have real impacts (see George Szablowski, Chapter 5).

References

Adler, Michael, Petch, A., and Tweedie, J. (1990), *Parental Choice and Educational Policy,* Edinburgh: University of Edinburgh Press.
Aucoin, P. (2000), 'Accountability and Performance', in B.G. Peters and D.J. Savoie (eds.) *Revitalizing Governance,* Montreal: McGill/Queens University Press.
Budge, I. (1997), *The New Challenge of Direct Democracy,* Oxford: Polity.
Chapman, Richard A. (ed.) (1993), *Ethics in Public Service,* Edinburgh: University of Edinburgh Press.
Day, Patricia and Klein, Rudolph (1986), *Accountabilities,* London: Tavistock Press.
Deakin, N. (1994), 'Accentuating the Apostrophe: The Citizen's Charter', *Policy Studies* Vol. 15, pp.46-58.
DiIulio, J.J. (1994), *Deregulating Government,* Washington, DC: The Brookings Institution.
Dudek, C.M. and Peters, B.G. (1999), 'Clientelism in Cold Climates: The Changing Forms of Political Involvement in the Bureaucracy', Unpublished paper, Department of Political Science, University of Pittsburgh.
Hoff, J. (1993), 'Medborgskap. brugerrolle og makt', in J. Andersen et al., *Medborgskap, demokrati og politisk deltagelse,* Herning: Systime.
Hogwood, B.W. (1993), 'Restructuring Central Government: The "Next Steps" Initiative', in K.A. Eliassen and J. Kooiman (eds.) *Managing Public Organizations,* (2nd ed.), London: Sage.
Hondeghem, A. (ed.) (1998), *Ethics and Accountability in a Context of Governance and New Public Management,* Amsterdam: IOS Press.
Hood, C. (1986), *The Tools of Government,* Chatham, NJ: Chatham House.
Hood, C. (1998a), 'Remedies for Misgovernment: Changing the remedies but Not the Ingredients', in A. Hondeghem (ed.) *Ethics and Accountability in a Context of Governance and New Public Management,* Amsterdam: IOS Press.

Hood, C. (1998b), *The Art of the State: Culture, Rhetoric and Public Management*, Oxford: Oxford University Press.
Hood, C., Peters, B.G., and Wollmann, H. (1996), 'Sixteen Ways to Consumerize the Public Sector', *Public Money and Management* Vol. 16(4), pp.43-50.
Ingraham, P.W., Thompson, J.R., and Eisenberg, E.F. (1995), 'Political Management Strategies and Political/Career Relationships', *Public Administration Review* Vol. 55, pp.263-72.
Jensen, L. (1998), 'Cultural Theory and Democratizing Functional Domains: The Case of Danish Housing', *Public Administration* Vol. 76, pp.117-39.
Kettl, D.F. (1988), *Government by Proxy: (Mis)managing Federal Programs*, Washington, DC: CQ Press.
Lewis, N. and Birkinshaw, P. (1993), *When Citizens Complain*, Buckingham: Open University Press.
Light, Paul C. (1996), *Thickening Government: The Federal Government and the Diffusion of Responsibility*, Washington, DC: The Brookings Institution.
Lipsky, M. (1979), *Street-Level Bureaucracy*, New York: Russell Sage.
Nilsson, L. and Westerstahl, J. (1997), 'Representiv demorati', in S. Jonsson et al. (eds.) *Decentraliserad valfardsstad*, Stockholm: SNS.
Page, A. (1999), 'The New Administrative Law, the Citizen's Charter and Administrative Justice', in M. Harris and M. Partington (eds.) *Administrative Justice in the 21st Century*, London: Hart.
Peters, B. G. (1996), *The Future of Governing*, Lawrence: University Press of Kansas.
Pierre, J. (1998), 'Depolitisee, repolitisee ou simplement politique?: La bureaucratie suedoise', *Revue francaise d'administration publique* Vol. 86 (avril-juin), pp.301-10.
Rouban, L. (1997), *Le fin de techocratie*, Paris: PFNSP.
Rouban, L. (1998), 'La politisation des fonctionnaires en France: obstacle ou necessite?', *Revue francaise d'administration publique* Vol. 86 (avril-juin), pp.167-82.
Sainsbury, R. (1994), 'Internal Reviews and the Weakening of Social Security Claimants' Rights of Appeal', in G. Richardson and H. Genn (eds.) *Administrative Law and Government Action*, Oxford: Clarendon Press.
Self, P. (1993), *Government by the Market?*, Boulder, CO: Westview.
Virtanen, T. (1998), 'Administration et politique en Finlande – D'une elite aristocratique a un reseau issu des classes moyennes', *Revue francaise d'administration publique* Vol. 86 (avril-juin), pp.311-21.

10 Democratic Accountability and Models of Governance: Purchaser/Provider, Owner/Trustee

Colin Campbell

This chapter focuses more on executive-bureaucratic culture than public service ethics *per se*. It maintains that officials often find themselves subject to competing views of accountability. Most immediately, the resulting conflicts can greatly exacerbate efforts on the part of officials to respond appropriately to the various circumstances that they face. However, the resulting ambiguity might also cloud ethical issues. This danger arises most frequently in two extreme circumstances. The first of these pertains if accountability becomes too focused on responsiveness to the dictates of hierarchical superiors. Here the culture chooses to deal with ambiguity by so tightening hierarchy that officials effectively lose their moral agency owing to the domination of norms which reward loyalty to the virtual exclusion of other values. The second extreme occurs where the official enjoys an excess of discretion. The meaning of excess varies according to the training of public servants, especially the degree of their exposure to the vagaries of executive-bureaucratic gamesmanship. A culture which does not bring officials along gradually in the exercise of discretion can expect a high incidence of opportunistic entrepreneurship from public servants who encounter greater discretionary power than that for which their training prepared them.

Notwithstanding its acknowledgment of the danger of the above extremes, this chapter takes the view that a culture which provides officials with some significant degree of discretion serves the long-range interests of democratic accountability more than one which stresses narrow adherence to hierarchical direction. In discretionary systems, public servants prove more adaptive than those under strict hierarchical accountability when presented with unforeseen and/or unconventional circumstances.

Officials who have learned to engage their moral agency in ambiguous situations will be more likely to summon the internal and institutional resources required for them to behave responsibly when confronted with issues of ethical import. For the political leadership, the situation would appear to constitute a win-win as they receive more imaginative advice and can delegate specific decisions with a relatively high assurance that officials will take actions on their behalf which will withstand external scrutiny should problems arise subsequently.

In pursuing its argument in favour of discretionary accountability, this chapter first examines why, theoretically, the approach more fully comports with democracy. This assertion contrasts with a secular shift among Anglo-American systems (namely, the United States, the United Kingdom, Canada, Australia and New Zealand) over the past thirty years. This has introduced a bias away from discretionary authority toward hierarchical accountability. Each of these advanced democracies had moved significantly in the period from the end of the Second World War to the early 1970s, albeit in different ways and to varying degrees, from hierarchical to pluralistic views of officials' accountability. Pluralistic, in this context, means that increasingly the systems allowed officials significant latitude to proffer advice and make decisions outside the strict contours of direct responsibility toward immediate superiors. This trend reversed abruptly with the emergence of the politics of constraint during the 1980s.

This chapter focuses upon the swing of the pendulum away from pluralism back to hierarchy, a swing associated with the rise of public choice theory until its apogee in the early 1990s. The advocates of this paradigm shift construed tighter hierarchical control as a means for enhancing the democratic accountability of officials to elected politicians. However, they failed to see that fulfilment of this ideal requires more than a principal-agent relationship between officials and individual ministers. It demands, as well, vital interaction within the wider matrix of the executive-bureaucratic arena so that advice and decisions take into consideration the cost-cutting nature of governmental objectives. The chapter gives special attention to the New Zealand case. Just as New Zealand led the charge to hierarchical accountability in the mid-1980s it has, since the mid-1990s, wrestled more reflectively than the other countries with striking a balance between hierarchical and pluralistic accountability. This chapter probes in particular the transition of the New Zealand reforms in recent years from a focus on relatively narrowly construed outputs to more widely framed outcomes. Outputs are goods and services provided by departments and agencies; outcomes are the actual public and social effects achieved by outputs.

It is notable that reformers in New Zealand now stress the need for officials, and not just ministers, to view themselves as owners responsible for providing outcomes for the public. However, the term trustee is proposed here as more accurately portraying the relationship of both politicians and senior officials to the means of production of goods and services in the state. In the end, citizens own the productive apparatus of the state.

Democracy and the preference for pluralistic accountability

The principal theorists who argued for the integrity of the bureaucratic culture in the nineteenth century did not anticipate pluralism as it has developed in modern advanced democracies. Indeed, they remained strongly enamoured with the concept of the public service as a type of priesthood. Certainly, this fits with the role that the priestly class has played in civilizations as diverse as Chinese empires, pre-colonial American civilizations and, as recently as the eighteenth century, European monarchies.

This is why, in the oligarchic democracies or authoritarian regimes of the nineteenth century, theorists tended to read across from the folkways of the priestly class to the type of culture that might prevail in a bureaucracy. Although significantly secularized, these societies still saw the priesthood as one salient model for elite cadres. Thus, Benjamin Jowett, the Oxford don who advised Sir Stafford Northcote and Sir Charles Trevelyan on reform of the British civil service, envisioned a Whitehall that would function as an outlet for high-minded young men at Oxford who did not intend to become priests. He believed that a career in a reformed higher civil service would appeal to those with an altruistic bent (Chapman and Greenaway, 1980, pp.40-1). Max Weber drew even stronger parallels. He considered a firmly established bureaucracy as a status group whose positions and actions basked in the glory of institutional cogency based on discipline. Weber maintained that strong affective attachments on the part of members to a bureaucracy served as its glue just as the spiritual commitment of the priest does for the religious order (Weber, 1948, 253-4). Weber also revealed considerable scepticism about the ability of either politicians or the public generally to sway a determined bureaucracy. He styled the former as dilettantes pitted against the expert and considered the latter relatively powerless owing to the difficulty of penetrating a culture bent on maximizing the leverage gained through secrecy (Weber, 1948, pp.232-3).

The Whitehall reforms first pressed by Northcote and Trevelyan attempted to make a virtue of this situation by accepting that officials would divide between those who would influence policy and those who would simply administer. The former would work very closely with ministers. They would trade on expertise but of a different type from that stressed by Weber. The British mandarin would grasp *par excellence* how to manipulate the state apparatus, ostensibly to accomplish ministers' ends. Of course, as often as not, such officials' command of the machine reached the point where they could, if so disposed, just as easily confound ministers as help them through the maze. The point remained, however, that the British and other adherents to the so-called Whitehall model (Canadians, Australians and New Zealanders) saw no particular difficulty with officials influencing policy.

The Americans took a somewhat different approach. The division of executive and legislative authority between the President and Congress provided for in the Constitution meant that officials had to serve two masters. If the executive branch attempted to assert itself through specific guidance to officials, the Congress could counter by making legislation still more administratively prescriptive. As Bert Rockman has noted, this state of affairs stunted the development of internal coherence in the bureaucracy (1984, p.48). Indeed, the myths that emerged around the public service avowedly denied the connection between politics and administration. Thus developed the largely American conception that politicians make policy and permanent officials manage (Aberbach, Putnam and Rockman, 1981).

With the emergence of empirical research on the role of the public service in the 1950s and 1960s, US scholars increasingly acknowledged that in fact senior permanent officials did exert considerable influence on policy. Hugh Heclo's seminal work, *A Government of Strangers*, proposed a format for channelling this reality positively, his most important recommendation being that the bulk of executive-political appointees and top career civil servants merge in a single cadre called the Senior Executive Service (1977). President Jimmy Carter adopted this proposal but his successor Ronald Reagan turned the 1978 Civil Service Reform Act on its head and used it to drive still deeper the wedge between the appointive and career groups (Hansen and Levine, 1988). The approach amounted to a self-denying ordinance. Even with the extraordinarily high proportion of political appointees in US departments, an administration which refuses to tap career officials' advice will ultimately succumb to partisan excess – as was the case with Reagan's supply-side tax cuts, profligate defence budgets and, in the second term, the Iran-Contra affair. The latter debacle involved the Reagan administration in siphoning the proceeds from illegal arms sales to Iran for the equally illegal subvention of guerilla forces opposed to the Sandinista government in Nicaragua.

The argument here is that a mutual respect between politicians and bureaucrats for each other's contributions in the policy arena better serves the interests of the public. Although career officials might bring to the table greater expertise and a stronger acquaintance with the concerns of client groups, a consensus has developed around the view that they still must engage in political calculation and manipulation in order to do their work (Aberbach, Putnam and Rockman, 1981). It will serve the public interest in the long-run that the ground rules for these officials' executive-bureaucratic gamesmanship receive greater amplification.

The British government responses to two separate instances of public servants' participation in this contact sport in the mid-1980s exemplify the point. The first case involved a Ministry of Defence assistant secretary, Clive Ponting. Ponting decided to release via a plain brown envelope information revealing that Margaret Thatcher had lied to Parliament about the course of the Argentinian cruiser *General Belgrano* when the Royal Navy sunk it during the 1982 Falklands War. The government prosecuted Ponting for his action. In the trial, the judge instructed the jury that Ponting lacked the defence that he acted in the public interest because the interests of the government and the state are identical. The jury would have none of this. They voted for acquittal. Evidently, as members of the public, they believed that it served their interests to know that the prime minister had lied to them.

Two years later the same government failed to dismiss officials involved in tactical leaking in the Department of Trade and Industry against the Ministry of Defence. The message came through resoundingly that officials must collude with ministers in misleading the public even to the point of leaking information in an improper way (Chapman, 1988, pp.295-7; Hennessy, 1989, pp.167, 664-7, 728; Campbell, 1993, pp.128-9). Such circumstances seem to highlight the need for further specification of officials' discretionary accountability within the wider context of pluralism. Indeed, the Scott Inquiry established that before the Gulf War ministers had relaxed restrictions on arms exports to Iraq while continuing to tell Parliament that the government was complying with an embargo. The inquiry found that officials conspired with their political masters not just in this deception but also with attempts to suppress evidence revealing that British businessmen prosecuted for trying to evade the embargo had in fact received a nod and a wink from Whitehall (Campbell and Wilson, 1995, 258-9). Perhaps as the exception that proves the rule, Sir Tim Lankester, then permanent secretary of the Overseas Development Administration, blotted his copybook with the Conservative government in 1991. He refused to sign a government grant to Malaysia in support of an uneconomic hydroelectric project on the grounds that it constituted a bribe for defence and trade orders (Campbell, 1998, p.132). The trend in the past 30 years has seen politicians successfully narrow rather than widen the discretionary parameters for public servants.

The rise of public choice and the constriction of public service parameters

It is not necessary to assess what has taken place over the past 30 years by way of shifts in paradigms for public management without considering dramatic changes in the prevalent view of accountability in advanced democracies. This opens a huge topic that has been studied in much greater depth than allowed for in this chapter (Campbell and Halligan, 1992, pp.193-218; Campbell and Wilson, 1995, pp.249-88). The nub of the issue rests with how accountability runs through the political process.

In the classic Whitehall paradigm, the public elects a parliament in which one party gains sufficient control to form a government (whether majority, minority or in coalition). The government, under the leadership of the prime minister, assumes collective responsibility – most immediately to parliament, but, ultimately, back to the public who might not renew its mandate in the next general election. In addition, each minister is individually responsible to parliament; the theory being that parliamentary displeasure with certain policies or actions might force him or her to resign. Most ministers' portfolios involve oversight of all or part of a government department. In the Whitehall tradition, career civil servants overwhelmingly staffed these organizations in which hierarchical accountability functioned as glue. In exchange for their loyalty and, in instances of policy or managerial failure, silence, ministers imparted to career civil servants a high degree of control over management of their cadre and security of tenure.

Of course, practice has never correlated perfectly with theory. The rise of strong party discipline in the latter part of the nineteenth century meant that in the twentieth century backbenchers have exerted only limited control over cabinets. The process by which parties garner electoral support through the appeal of their leaders has often given prime ministers sufficient leverage to run command-oriented rather than consultative cabinet government. Career officials, a cadre that traces its ancestry to the royal household, frequently have pursued their own agendas. In Whitehall, this takes the form of a long-term, think-of-Britain caste of mind that often clashes with the immediacy of political exigency. Certainly failures have been seen even of the contractual core of the Whitehall system: namely, ministers who have refused to take blame and officials who have not remained silent. In any case, Whitehall accountability becomes multifaceted with officials having to mediate responsibility to such diverse objects as their minister, their departmental superiors, the prime minister, Parliament, clients, professional standards and the national interest. Thus, the iterative chain of accountability postulated by the Whitehall model rarely pertains in reality. In fact, laments of its passing might well amount to nostalgia for something that never actually existed.

Running alongside the Whitehall system, there is the presidential-congressional system of the United States. The founding fathers largely construed the arrogance of Britain to the thirteen colonies as resulting from the autocracy of the executive as embodied in the monarch. They embraced thus the concept of separation of powers as a protection against autocratic rule. Herein, both the executive and legislative branches found themselves on independent mandates. This places the career bureaucracy in the position of serving two masters, the president and Congress. It also makes cabinet government extremely difficult as career bureaucrats, ever mindful of likely responses of their patrons in Congress, often divert cabinet secretaries from an administration's agenda to one emanating from so called iron-triangles (Aberbach, Putnam and Rockman, 1981, pp.90-100). These are policy alliances between officials, legislators and their staffs, and interest groups that cluster around most major issues.

If the Whitehall tradition has erred on the side of career officials who develop and ply their own views of the national interest, the US tradition has displayed a weakness for short-term, politics-driven policymaking capable at best of only incremental change. Reformers in the US have struggled with what exactly the charisma of public service might be (see O'Toole, Chapter 6, for a discussion of the British experience).

Early in the century, the dominant model became that of competent management of complex organizations. This view enshrined the dichotomy between policy (the domain of politicians) and administration (the province of bureaucrats) discussed above. The immense national mobilization associated with the New Deal, however, put paid to this simple view. Thus, the notion emerged that officials did involve themselves in policy: they contributed neutral competence. That is, they brought their subject-matter expertise and practical experience to bear on the resolution of the challenges of the time. Whatever its accuracy, the theory made career public servants potential scapegoats. Liberals, who increasingly became frustrated with the difficulty of pushing back the frontiers of the welfare state, began to see neutral competence as the cult of Can't Do rather than Can Do. Conservatives saw bureaucrats as empire builders who parlayed their expertise and experience in ventures designed to maximize their personal utility.

The two energy shocks of the 1970s along with increased vulnerability to Asian economic competition thrust Anglo-American countries into a decline neurosis which swung the popular pendulum against further expansion of the role of the state. Indeed, the public became highly susceptible to arguments in favour of shrinking government (Rose and Peters, 1978). Public choice theory, which first emerged in the 1960s, increasingly provided the theoretical opportunity for those wanting to contract government. However, its principal advocates betrayed a decidedly American view of the political process (Buchanan and Tullock, 1962; Niskanen, 1971). Public choice stressed the immense leverage of the career public service in exploiting their expertise and positional advantage to play the political leadership, legislators and interest groups one off the other in order to maximize their budgets. Within the public choice framework, other values such as professionalism, service to the public, equity, and, to be sure, ethics, would take a back seat to controlling officials so as to minimize budgetary bottom lines.

Public choice theorists reserved special contempt for those who believed that analysis and comprehensive approaches to budgeting would bring government spending in line. This simply took politicians off the scent and led them further into the clutches of budget maximizers (Niskanen, 1973a, pp.6-8). Instead, politicians could best assert control through the automatization of budgeting. This would include much tighter coordination between Congress and the executive branch on target outlays, dollar-for-dollar personal income tax increases in order to cover spending beyond the agreed levels, and more centralized White House control of the Office of Management and Budget in reference to the political priorities of the president (Niskanen, 1973a, pp.17-19, 55-7). In practice, the separation of powers made such automatization of budgeting in the US as elusive as achieving comprehensive rationality within and between social welfare programmes proved to be in the 1960s.

This has not prevented reformers in other Anglo-American countries from attempting to adapt public choice theory to their own circumstances. The consequences have gone well beyond automatization of budgeting to mighty impingements of every sort of discretionary authority including individual discretion beyond the narrow confines of specific outputs. One of the earliest and most significant of these efforts occurred when a disenchanted group of Conservatives invited William Niskanen to the UK to offer a series of lectures on public choice (1973b). Once again, Niskanen advocated automatization of budgeting, but his recipe reflected a very limited understanding of cabinet government. For instance, he urged prime ministers to appoint ministers without consideration of representational issues such as their personal or regional backgrounds (1973b, p.60). He also recommended that ministers be shuffled randomly through the course of a government to ensure that they not align themselves too strongly with their departments. Nonetheless, Niskanen had a very large influence on Thatcher. One could certainly detect strong elements of the automatization prescription in such early Thatcher moves as imposing budget discipline with a Star Chamber of senior ministers and abolishing the Policy Analysis and Review system of interdepartmental studies of programmes.

A difficulty presents itself here, however. Public choice prescriptions still spoke very much from the background of the American experience: this contrasts sharply with that in the Whitehall systems for two main reasons. First, permanent officials in the US tend to focus their careers much more narrowly than their opposite numbers in the parliamentary systems (Heclo, 1977, pp. 116-20). This makes them more prone to defending relatively narrow bureaucratic interests. Second, and more fundamental, the parliamentary systems do not have truly transformative legislatures. That is, rank and file legislators in these systems lack the capacity to mold and reshape laws and budgets independently of the guidance provided by the political executive as embodied in the leadership of the governing party or coalition (Polsby, 1975, p.277). This means that American prescriptions about limiting budget-maximizing tendencies in Whitehall systems might amount to over-treatment. The absence of long and reasonably secure tenure in specialized fields for bureaucrats and transformative legislatures inhibits the development of strong client-patron relationships in parliamentary systems.

Misdiagnosis and over treatment

The experience of New Zealand with public choice bears special attention in this chapter because it presents in bold relief the poor diagnostics and over treatment associated with the application of public choice to Whitehall systems. In the late 1970s, New Zealand was buffeted especially severely by the energy shocks and the dissolution of preferential trade agreements with the United Kingdom. The latter had previously ensured markets for the agricultural products that still serve as the nation's core source of foreign exchange. Structurally, the state in New Zealand bore many of the marks of post-colonialism. A lack of both internal capital and foreign investment drove a strong tendency to construe the provision of essential goods and services as the domain of the public sector. The state indulged itself with the luxury of some forty departments that tended to function as fiefdoms narrowly focused on specialized policy domains. The unicameral parliament was easily the weakest of any of the Anglo-American legislatures. Prime ministers typically guided cabinet monocratically rather than consultatively. Often key senior officials exerted as much influence on the overall direction of the government as did ministers. Prime ministers frequently regarded the Treasury as if it were their own department. All of this hampered considerably the capacity of the system to empower and extend ownership within cabinet and through ministers to senior departmental officials.

The New Zealand management reforms emerged from an intense review of the role of the state conducted within the Treasury before the Labour government, which had come to power in 1984, renewed its mandate in 1987. The documents which provided an intellectual justification for the reforms cited copiously American agency literature, especially that centring on the firm (e.g. Alchain and Woodward, 1987). They asserted that the proposed reforms would establish the iterative process inferred in classic views of democratic accountability (Scott and Gorringe, 1989). Bureaucrats would become the agents of politicians who in turn would serve as the agents of the populace. They distinguished here between strategies for improving performance and those attempting to enhance accountability. The former centres on whether officials actually produce the outputs required by the politicians; the latter focuses on whether the goods and services which politicians purchase from bureaucrats align with social goals like wealth, justice and the relief of suffering.

As noted above, the classic iterative views of accountability, especially ones that assign administration to bureaucrats and policy to politicians, often defy operationalization and, indeed, prove naive in most circumstances. The New Zealand formulation revealed naivete in the following ways:

1. It alleged that special interests, due to transaction costs of gathering information and influencing policy makers, can twist public policies in their favour (Scott, Ball and Dale, 1997, p.360). This is certainly true in the US. However, the New Zealand which the reformers worked so assiduously at changing was hardly consistent with Robert Dahl's definition of a

polyarchy (1971, pp.8, 76-80). The system bore nowhere near the socio-economic diversity of the US. It remained relatively closed, as opposed to open, with respect to access to decision-makers. Also, political contestation followed the set-piece format of parliamentary adversarial politics rather than public contestation of all participants found in the US. Under the circumstances, it might be assumed that the transaction calculus for influencing policy in New Zealand would lack both complexity and intensity, but it should not be assumed that gathering information and influencing policy makers would be prohibitively expensive for all but the representatives of special interests. Some groups would never gain access because they lacked cache within the framework of post-colonial elitism. Others would not have to deploy elaborate machinations to obtain access simply because they used informal contacts and consequently incurred relatively minor costs.

2. The New Zealand reformers also imported from American institutional economics the notion of agency problems in the alignment of the incentives which prevail in public sector delivery systems with the policy objectives of legislatures and authorized governing bodies (Scott, Ball and Dale, 1997, p.360). Agency problems undoubtedly existed. However, whether they did so in anywhere near the degree that they do in the US is highly dubious. In the US, the calculus associated with the separation of powers and the transformative nature of Congress compounds exponentially the difficulty of aligning implementation with the intentions of policy-makers. In fact, during the in mid-1980s New Zealand even fell short of the complexity of alignment in other Whitehall systems, especially Canada and Australia. New Zealand cabinets had a history of relatively monocratic guidance meaning that their deliberations often fell short of exerting a transformative impact on policies proposed by the prime minister and/or the treasurer. Indeed, the Labour government achieved its reforms through prior agreements between the treasury, finance minister, and a few allies. Indeed, notwithstanding their sweeping implications, the reforms often received assent without vetting by the cabinet Policy Committee which was supposed to be the formal ministerial group for reviewing policies to assess their implications for other departments (Goldfinch, 1998, pp.196-7).

3. The New Zealand reformers committed the fallacy of the 99-year lease. Those acquainted with British real estate practice will know that many individuals who own property actually do so only to a portion thereof, by holding, say a long-term lease of 99 years. In politics, governments can succumb to the comparable illusion of a long-term lease. For instance, Thatcher, after her 1987 election proclaimed that the Conservative Party

would control the government well into the twenty-first century. The New Zealanders succumbed to the 99-year lease fallacy in styling ministers as owners of their departments (Scott, Ball and Dale, 1997). This serves as a highly error-prone stance for several reasons. First, New Zealand follows a constricting, three-year electoral cycle that allows the ultimate owners, the public, to assert their will relatively frequently. Second, ministers might focus more on their career progress through cabinet hierarchy than upon the task of running their departments so that they become absentee landlords. Third, the public, as actual owners, might resort to other surrogates to act upon their behalf. These include rank and file legislators and the bureaucracy. Shaun Goldfinch captures how the operation of the 99-year fallacy might have triggered public resentments that led ultimately to the institution of mixed member proportional representation:

> In a country that strongly values political participation, changes imposed in the face of public opposition, often in secret and in the face of explicit election promises to the contrary, may have caused resentment and undermined the legitimacy of the political system to some extent (Goldfinch, 1998, p.179).

Of course, the first election conducted under mixed member proportional representation led to a coalition government and an exponential complication of the calculus for transactions among and between politicians and bureaucrats.

Other assessments of the New Zealand reforms have isolated in great detail dysfunctions stemming from the naive construction of democratic accountability as bilateral principal/agent relationships between the public and politicians and then between politicians and bureaucrats. Among these, two articles by Robert Gregory have made perhaps the most direct assault on the resultant reemphasis of the policy/administration dichotomy (1998a; 1998b). Both articles concern the accountability issues surrounding the 1995 Cave Creek disaster in which 14 people lost their lives in the collapse of a faultily constructed viewing platform. In the aftermath of the incident, the purchaser/provider framework clouded rather than clarified responsibility (1998b, pp.522-3).

From the perspective of the purchaser, the Minister of Conservation, the chief executive of the Department of Conservation (DOC) bore responsibility for the effective construction of a safe platform. From the standpoint of the chief executive, the government's failure to adequately fund the department had made the production of such outputs very difficult. That is, the fiscal straightjacket of a more-with-less syndrome had severely impinged upon the capacity of the public service to produce outputs that effectively serviced desired outcomes. The government had also eliminated potential monitors of the alignment of outputs with outcomes. Specifically, DOC's predecessor agency, the Forest Service, included design and construction personnel who did not move to DOC at the time of its creation. In addition, the government had abolished the former oversight agency for construction, the Ministry of Works and Development (Gregory, 1998b, p.521). Echoing Allen Schick's (1996, p.62) assessment of the government's reforms, Gregory concluded that the purchaser/provider decoupling seemed:

> ...disconnected from the vital and fluid world of experience, and is not well suited to fostering the moral and ethical competence necessary to serve higher, less measurable values...it is not a guarantor of good political and social judgement on the part of individual governmental officials (Gregory, 1998b, p.536).

Similar defects as those detected by Gregory reared their heads again on 20 February 1998, when the major power supplier to the city of Auckland cut off electricity to the central business district for several days due to underwater cable failures. The report of a ministerial inquiry into the crisis urged the government to take greater care to ensure that the power company's plans, asset management and customer contracts respond to the public interest (Ministry of Energy, 1998).

Generalizing the New Zealand lessons

It should be noted that these experiences have not fundamentally challenged the monocratic nature of the New Zealand tradition of executive-bureaucratic guidance. Thus, they do little to show either how the New Zealand reforms might pertain to more consensual traditions or how New Zealand itself might cope with coalition government.

Jonathan Boston and June Pallot provide an excellent assessment of why the National Party government developed during 1993-1994 a new policy-making framework whereby it distilled strategic result areas (SRAs) which transcended departmental outputs and identified outcomes that it sought within a three-year period. The government had come to the conclusion that the format which disaggregated governance into purchaser/provider relations between ministers and officials obscured long-term strategic goals and the integration of these with on-going policy decisions, especially those concerning the budget (Boston and Pallot, 1997, p.382). Meanwhile, the agency responsible for reviewing departmental chief executives' performance agreements with their ministers had come to the conclusion that the quality of these varied too widely. It sought especially to broaden their frame so as to incorporate ownership issues which would help align outputs with outcomes (Boston and Pallot, 1997, p.389).

Notwithstanding their compelling rendering of the developments surrounding these changes in the government's thinking, Boston and Pallot fail to provide a comprehensive diagnosis, largely because they appear to construe bureaucratic organizations rather than the cabinet itself as responsible for a higher degree of integration. This applies especially to their characterization of the Department of the Prime Minister and Cabinet as providing overall monitoring and coordination of policies. Most students of Whitehall systems would view such an agency as simply providing support for cabinet and its committees in fulfilling these functions (Boston and Pallot, 1997, p.395).

Scott, Ball and Dale quote at length from Allen Schick's assessment of the New Zealand reforms passage which makes it appear as if his report contains not a discouraging word (1997, p.369 citing Schick 1996, p.4). To be sure, Schick's analysis gives due credit to reformers for breaking down some of the command-and-control orientation of departments by introducing greater incentives for managerial initiative. However, Schick also identified numerous shortcomings in the reconstituted system. These included considerable unevenness in departments' sense of mission and performance, the straightjacket effect of the sinking lid on operating budgets, the failure to incorporate cost and performance data in budget decision making, and, generally, the tendency for narrow concerns to crowd out collective ones and for the short-term to obscure the long-term (pp.3-7). Schick makes his clearest contribution by underscoring the need for shifting the focus of ministers' relations with their departments from purchaser/provider towards that of owner. This would enshrine their responsibility for achieving overarching social and economic objectives which go beyond the parameters of departmental outputs (p.44).

In a very pointed passage, Schick infers that the public choice format has not given sufficient focus to the fact that ministers must serve as *trustees* [my term] of the long-range viability of departments in addition to obtaining value for money as the purchasers of agency outputs.

> But Ministers must also be mindful of the organizational strength of their department; they should be institution builders, and they should forbear from demanding so much by way of outputs and from

pushing the purchase price down so far as to jeopardize the department's long-term capacity to perform (p.43).

The use of trustees, above, is deliberate for the obvious reason that ultimately the public owns the department. The nomenclature assists us in avoiding the fallacy of the 99-year lease. It also allows for others besides ministers to share in the trustee role, especially bureaucrats, whether career or contractually engaged, who bear a day-to-day responsibility for the departments' organizational integrity.

Notwithstanding the deftness with which Schick's critique expands the parameters for reform, it fails, much like that of Boston and Pallot, adequately to point toward mechanisms which might draw ministers and their departments from parochialism. Schick's prescriptions also betray a lack of understanding of how collective decision making might work in Whitehall systems. Indeed, Schick seems to view central guidance through the prism of the type of monocratic direction frequently attempted (but rarely achieved) by US presidents through the White House and the Executive Office of the President:

> I take the view that there is a continuing need for strong policy and managerial leadership from the centre. The central departments must prescribe and enforce accountability requirements, and they must deal with matters that cross departmental lines... (p.33).

The simple fact remains that central departments can simply support the prime minister and cabinet in achieving such coordination. No manner of central departments or cluster thereof can compensate for a failure of ministers to identify and commit themselves to coherent strategic goals. This point is not lost in Campos and Pradhan's comparisons of the Australian and New Zealand reform efforts (1997, pp.443-4). It is the central theme coming from an earlier study which chronicles how the Australians achieved a high degree of integration between strategic planning and budgeting while greatly improving the performance of departments (Campbell and Halligan, 1992).

Why trustees?

Resurrection of the term trustee in your author's lexicon takes him back more than thirty years when he was a budding legislative studies scholar (a pursuit he abandoned some twenty years ago). At the time, the most thoroughgoing analysis of legislators' representational roles was *The Legislative System: Explorations in Legislative Behavior* (Wahlke et al., 1962). The authors of this work struggled with the salience, in modern democracy, of Edmund Burke's apologia to the electors of Bristol. Burke had exhorted his constituents to understand that a parliament served not as a congress of agents for disparate interests but as a deliberative assembly seeking to discern the general good, resulting from the general reason of the whole (Wahlke et al., 1962, p.269).

Wahlke and his colleagues took an agnostic stance toward this lofty expectation. In fact, they indulged what would strike rational choice theorists as heresy. They argued that different actors in the policy arena can adopt different rational principles (pp.9-10). Democratic reformers (including the social or Christian variants) will operate with a clear conception of the public good. The rationality of those who perceive themselves as agents of their constituents and/or vested interests will plough much narrower furrows. However, threatening either type of rationality when it becomes monotonic we find the politico:

> ... who rationally perceives the actions demanded of him by various 'forces' outside the legislature ... and who rationally weighs the strength of these pressures against his own rational preferences for the various courses of action urged upon him, then strikes a balance and acts accordingly (p.10).

Significantly, the authors found in their study of four state legislatures that majorities ranging between 55 and 81 per cent of respondents adopted the Burkean 'trustee' representational role (p.281). In each case, the politicos proved the next largest group (ranging between 13 and 29 per cent). Thus, agents (or delegates) formed clear minorities ranging in size between 6 and 20 per cent. The findings provide a snapshot of the challenge facing public choice, which itself emerged in the 1960s. Wahlke and his colleagues, who in fact seemed slightly partial to politicos, conceded that Burke's pious formula might best suit the realities of complex democratic systems:

> People themselves may pay lip service to the notion that a representative should not use his independent judgment, but in fact they are unlikely to be able, or may not care, to give him instructions as was possibly the case at an earlier time when the tasks of government were comparatively simple ... Rather than being a 'pious formula,' the role orientation of trustee may be a functional necessity (p.281).

Regarding senior officials, the bulk of research during the 1970s equally suggested that top bureaucrats found themselves operating with a degree of independence within the executive-bureaucratic arena. This empirical work perhaps did not go so far as to sustain Norton C. Long's assertion in the 1950s that legislators had become less representative, responsive and responsible than bureaucrats (Long, 1952, p.810). However, the evidence from several studies suggested that officials see themselves as playing significant integrative roles within the policy arena (Suleiman, 1974, p.13 and ch. 8; Putnam, 1973, pp.268-9; Aberbach and Rockman, 1977; Presthus, 1973, pp.60-3; Campbell and Szablowski, 1979). By the early 1980s, it became conventional wisdom that many senior bureaucrats deploy the full range of behind-the-scenes political skills and passionately commit themselves to attaining specific policy goals (Aberbach, Putnam and Rockman, 1981). Subsequent research has suggested that command-oriented governance, which emerged during the 1980s under neo-liberal administrations, has tempered if not reversed this reflex (Aberbach, 1991; Campbell and Halligan, 1992, pp.217-8; Campbell and Wilson, 1995, pp.306-8).

Such reeling in of public servants has produced ambiguous results. Wholesale efforts to blinker the strategic perspectives of officials inevitably diminished policy integration. Further, when difficulties arose, it became increasingly difficult to apportion responsibility between and among political leaders and senior officials. Now, with the emphasis on the politics of budgetary surplus, the compelling need for budget stringency will evaporate as a justification for command leadership. Surpluses will necessitate relearning how to manage choice. This, in turn, will call for a more interactive dialogue between politicians and bureaucrats about strategic objectives. The trusteeship of both cadres concerns the future. Under the politics of constraint, the imperative of addressing the building fiscal crises sharply proscribed deliberations about future programmatic options. The encouragement of wide strategic perspectives among officials struck neo-liberals, perhaps with some justification, as a luxury. Under the politics of surplus, strategic choice becomes a necessity and requires a strong analytic base both with regard to options and implementation. This is the core competency of the senior civil service.

Ownership and trusteeship

If there is a shift back to ownership and trusteeship and from a purchaser/provider format, there may be fairly dramatic consequences for the foci of participants in the political process regarding inputs, outputs

Stakeholders	Bias in Emphasis	
Public	**Purchaser/Provider**	**Owner/Trustee**
'General'	Inputs → Outputs	Outputs ← Outcomes
'Special Interests'	Inputs ← Outputs	Outputs → Outcomes
Politicians	**Purchaser/Provider**	**Owner/Trustee**
Rank-and-File	Inputs ← Outputs	Inputs → Outputs
Committee	Inputs ← Outputs	Inputs → Outputs
Party (Ruling)	Inputs → Outputs	Outputs ← Outcomes
Minister	Inputs → Outputs	Outputs ← Outcomes
Cabinet	Outputs ← Outcomes	Outputs → Outcomes
President/PM	Outputs ← Outcomes	Outputs → Outcomes
Bureaucrats	**Purchaser/Provider**	**Owner/Trustee**
Central Agencies		
Coordinative	Outputs ← Outcomes	Outputs → Outcomes
Macro-economic	Inputs → Outputs	Outputs ← Outcomes
Budgeting	Inputs ← Outputs	Inputs → Outputs
Line Departments		
Permanent Heads	Inputs ← Outputs	Outputs → Outcomes
Chief Executive	Inputs → Outputs	Outputs ← Outcomes

Figure 1 Stakeholders' Perspectives Work Effects on Their Emphasis on Inputs, Outputs, and Outcomes

and outcomes. Figure 1 portrays the various elements of political systems in regard to the likely tendencies of their foci. The purchaser/provider column assumes a focus on goods and services while the owner/trustee one infers an emphasis on longer-term issues associated with stewardship. The format asserts that the general public tends toward a focus on outputs regardless of whether the prevailing rhetoric assumes a purchaser/provider or owner/trustee format. Arcane discussion of resource allocation often escapes the general public as would discussion of long-range implications of goods and services. This would seem to apply to support for state-funded education. Members of the general public will focus on their children's experiences or, more generally, the performance of pupils in their local school in standardized tests. These indicators will play more heavily in their assessment of state school performance than concern for inputs (such as whether their system requires more teachers), or outcomes (such as whether the prevailing approach to pedagogy will adequately prepare young people for successful careers in the fluid world of high-tech society).

The two separate sets of assumptions displayed in Figure 1 reveal that special interests can be pulled in opposite directions depending upon an emphasis of purchaser/provider or owner/trustee rhetoric. If society views teachers simply as providers of educational services then they will tend to focus on input issues such as salaries and staff numbers associated with their ability to proffer their product. If, on the other hand, society entrusts teachers with stewardship of the educational system, they might focus less on inputs and, indeed, become force maximizers. If so, they would become akin to John J. DiIulio's principled agents. That is, they would ... go above and beyond the call of duty, and make virtual gifts of their labour even when the rewards for behaving that way are highly uncertain at best (DiIulio, 1994, p.277 as cited by Schick, 1996, p.24). Such a stance would heighten an emphasis on outcomes as a strong sense of stewardship would presumably not be adopted without wanting as well actually to achieve durable results.

Turning to politicians, Figure 1 distinguishes between rank-and-file legislators, committee members, members of the ruling party caucus, ministers individually, cabinet and the president or prime minister. It proves less than sanguine about rank-and-file legislators and committee members. Under the purchaser/provider format both groups would tend to focus on inputs as, presumably, pressures from intense constituents and special interests would stress resourcing levels. A shift to the owner/trustee format would perhaps focus both groups more on outputs. However, the particularist nature of most claims that the public and special interests lodge at this level would still find the two groups locked in the realm of trade-offs between inputs and outputs.

The ruling party caucus and ministers individually under the purchaser/provider format will reveal a bias toward outputs. In the former case, this is owing to the requirement that the government appear efficient in the provision of goods and services as part of its resume for renewing its mandate; in the latter, ministers earn their spurs within cabinet hierarchies in part through their management skills. A switch to an owner/trustee format widens the compass of both groups toward the interplay between specific outputs and more generalized outcome matters. Although they will still tend to focus on outputs, government politicians assuming this emphasis will become increasingly informed by issues surrounding the legacy that an administration wants to leave. It is within this matrix that cabinet collectively and the president or prime minister focus most of their attention. If there is an absence of teamwork within cabinet, ministers will not imbibe this dimension of governance as intensely as otherwise. In any case, an owner/trustee format will put strategic questions associated with an administration's legacy in bolder relief.

The prevailing format bears implications for officials as well. First, looking at the central coordinating agencies, it has to be recognized that these can differ considerably with reference to their cultures and time frames. Thus, agencies assisting the president or prime minister and/or cabinet toward coherent policy commitments take more strategic views. However, where an administration finds itself in the electoral cycle will determine whether its perspective leans toward its legacy (typically at the outset of a term), or political survival (more likely as election deadlines become imminent). Thus, there will be a swing in the course of a term from a stress on outcomes to one focusing on outputs, and even, especially with the onset of campaigns, inputs.

As for agencies responsible for macro-economic policy, these usually lack sufficient interest in the vagaries of inputs to focus their attention at that level. In addition, their sensitivity to episodic neuralgia in investment markets obscures their view of the long-term. Thus, the language that they best understand would pertain to the medium term realm of outputs. Budget agencies would reveal a bias toward inputs as a focus. The gravitation of rhetoric from a purchaser/provider to owner/trustee format would concentrate strategy-oriented agencies' focus on outcomes, macro-economic agencies on the relation of outputs to outcomes and, most dramatically, budget agencies' on the forest (outcomes) rather than the trees (inputs).

Similarly, changes in format can work effects on the heads of line departments, whether they hold their positions with an assumption of tenure until retirement or under contractual terms requiring that they deliver efficiently specific goods and services. If a purchaser/provider format is assumed, this obviously dovetails with the exigencies of contract-based employment and would orient chief executives toward a focus on outputs. If applied to traditional permanent department heads, however, it might have them riveted on inputs. Especially with ever smaller resources, permanent heads would become determined to protect their departments' resources from encroachments by an approach imported from the private sector. It has already been noted that in New Zealand an adjustment of rhetoric toward ownership has signalled an attempt to broaden the focus of chief executives so that the outputs they proffer relate to the government's core goals. It has also been seen that permanent heads, through coordination with their colleagues and exposure to cabinet consultations, can lift their game to a focus on outcomes. Group dynamics, such as the weekly meeting of permanent secretaries in the UK, and the Canadian practice of giving key guidance roles to committees of deputy ministers in times of crisis, prove important to wrenching top officials from the daily issues faced by their departments.

Adoption of the trustee format as discussed here resonates with more recent thinking on both the differences between public and private sector management and the introduction of public choice paradigms and the need for more consultative decision making in developing and transitional societies. For instance, Laurence E. Lynn, Jr. has taken public choice theory to task for missing the point that the logic of competitive markets differs from that of governance so dramatically because the latter involves a host of collective goals which would not attract profit-seeking investors, and is held together with the glue of decision makers functioning with authority derived from constitutions and legislation (Lynn, 1997, p.10). In this respect, Mark Moore has highlighted the multi-dimensionality of the responsibilities assumed under the rubric of public management (1995). Here officials must devise strategies which look outward (toward external constituencies), upward (toward superior hierarchical authority), and downward (toward primary work and production workers).

Conclusion

This chapter has argued that democratic accountability in the executive-bureaucratic arena requires a delicate balance of contributions among and between the political leadership and career bureaucrats. This is fostered by consultative frameworks that empower cabinet colleagues through collective deliberations and animate the potential of public servants through positive engagement of their aptitudes and capacities. Granting officials high degrees of discretion over the types of policy advice they submit, the use of their resources and the administration of programmes best serves the norms of inclusion embedded in pluralistic democracy. However, this proposition is an anathema to those distrustful of the motives of public servants. Under the banner of public choice, the sceptics have achieved considerable success in Anglo-American democracies in constraining the discretion of officials in the provision of public goods and services.

New Zealand, which pressed the public choice framework the hardest, has relented somewhat in the past few years on the grounds that its system focused excessively on outputs and insufficiently on outcomes. It has shifted its strong focus on purchaser/provider dynamics between politicians and officials in order to incorporate the notion that both cadres bear considerable commonality of interest through shared ownership of public organizations.

While endorsing this course correction, this chapter has advocated conceptualizing ownership as trusteeship. The latter emphasis takes root in the proposition that mutuality in the discernment of the public good serves as much better glue for executive-bureaucratic relations than ownership that can prove illusory if not out and out ephemeral. Although the term trusteeship, notwithstanding its long lineage in legislative studies, might strike the reader as eccentrically this author's nomenclature, it does invite stronger assessments of the degree to which political executives and bureaucrats take into consideration issues associated with the strategic integration of policies. Especially now that Anglo-American systems seem to be moving from fiscal stringency to surplus they will increasingly find themselves managing choice again. This will require a more vibrant dialogue between political leaders and officials than pertained through the past twenty years.

References

Aberbach, Joel D. (1991), 'The President and the Executive Branch', in Colin Campbell and Bert A. Rockman (eds.) *The Bush Administration: First Appraisals,* Chatham, NJ: Chatham House.

Aberbach, Joel D. and Rockman, Bert A. (1977), 'The Overlapping Worlds of American Federal Executives and Congressmen', *British Journal of Political Science* Vol.7, pp.23-47.

Aberbach, Joel D., Putnam, Robert D. and Rockman, Bert A. (1981), *Bureaucrats and Politicians in Western Democracies,* Cambridge, MA: Harvard University Press.

Alchain, A. A. and Woodward, S. (1987), 'Reflections on the Theory of the Firm', *Journal of Institutional and Theoretical Economics* Vol.143, pp.110-36.

Boston, Jonathan and Pallot, June (1997), 'Linking Strategy and Performance: Developments in the New Zealand Public Sector', *Journal of Policy Analysis and Management* Vol.16, pp.382-404.

Buchanan, James M. and Tullock, Gordon (1962), *The Calculus of Consent: Logical Foundations of Constitutional Democracy,* Ann Arbor: University of Michigan.

Campbell, Colin (1993), 'Public Service and Democratic Accountability', in Richard A. Chapman (ed.) *Ethics in Public Service,* Edinburgh: University of Edinburgh Press.

Campbell, Colin (1998), *The US Presidency in Crisis: A Comparative Perspective,* New York: Oxford University Press.

Campbell, Colin and Szablowski, George J. (1979), *The Superbureaucrats: Structure and Behaviour in Central Agencies,* Toronto: Macmillan.

Campbell, Colin and Halligan, John (1992), *Leadership in an Age of Constraint: The Australian Experience*, Sydney: Allen & Unwin.

Campbell, Colin and Wilson, Graham (1995), *The End of Whitehall: Death of a Paradigm*, Oxford: Blackwell.

Campos, Ed and Pradhan, Sanjay (1997), 'Evaluating Public Expenditure Management Systems: An Experimental Methology with an Application to Australia and New Zealand', *Journal of Policy Analysis and Management* Vol.16, pp.423-45.

Chapman, Richard A. (1988), *Ethics in the British Civil Service*, London: Routledge.

Chapman, Richard A. and Greenaway, John R. (1980), *The Dynamics of Administrative Reform*, London: Croom Helm.

Dahl, Robert A. (1971), *Polyarchy: Participation and Opposition*, New Haven, CT: Yale University Press.

DiIulio, John J., Jr. (1994), 'Principled Agents: The Cultural Basis of Behavior in a Federal Government Bureaucracy', *Journal of Public Administration Research and Theory* Vol.4, pp.277-320.

Goldfinch, Shaun (1998), 'Institutional Elites and Radical Economic Policy Making in New Zealand, 1984-93', *Governance* Vol.11, pp.177-208.

Gregory, Robert, (1998a), 'A New Zealand Tragedy: Problems of Political Responsibility', *Governance* Vol.11, pp.231-40.

Gregory, Robert (1998b), 'Political Responsibility for Bureaucratic Incompetence: Tragedy at Cave Creek', *Public Administration* Vol.76, pp.519-38.

Hansen, Michael and Levine, Charles H. (1988), 'The Centralization-Decentralization Tug-of-War in the New Executive Branch', in Colin Campbell and B. Guy Peters (eds.) *Organizing Governance: Governing Organizations*, Pittsburgh: University of Pittsburgh Press.

Heclo, Hugh (1977), *A Government of Strangers*, Washington, DC: Brookings.

Hennessy, Peter (1989), *Whitehall*, London: Secker& Warburg.

Long, Norton C. (1952), 'Bureaucracy and Constitutionalism', *American Political Science Review* Vol.46, pp.808-18.

Lynn, Lawrence E., Jr. (1997), 'Public Management and Government Performance: A Consideration of Theory and Evidence', a paper prepared for a working group of the International Public Management Network, Potsdam, Germany. June 26-27.

Ministry of Energy (1998), *Report of the Ministerial Inquiry into the Auckland Power Supply Failure*, Wellington, New Zealand.

Moore, Mark (1995), *Creating Public Values: Strategic Management in Government*, Cambridge, MA: Harvard University Press.

Niskanen, William A. (1971), *Bureaucracy and Representative Government*, New York: Aldine, Atherton.

Niskanen, William A. (1973a), *Structural Reform of the Federal Budget Process*, Washington, DC: American Enterprise Institute.

Niskanen, William A. (1973b), *Bureaucracy: Servant or Master? Lessons from America*, London: Institute of Economic Affairs.

Polsby, Nelson W. (1975), 'Legislatures', in Fred I. Greenstein and Nelson W. Polsby (eds.) *Government Institutions and Processes*, Vol.5 of *Handbook of Political Science*, Reading, MA: Addison-Wesley.

Presthus, Robert (1973), *Elite Accommodation in Canadian Politics*, Toronto: Macmillan.

Putnam, Robert (1973), 'The Political Attitudes of Senior Civil Servants in Western Europe', *British Journal of Political Science* Vol.3, pp.267-90.

Rockman, Bert A. (1984), *The Leadership Question: The Presidency and the American System*, New York: Praeger.

Rose, Richard and Peters, B. Guy (1978), *Can Government Go Bankrupt?* New York: Basic Books.

Schick, Allen, (1996), *The Spirit of Reform: Managing the New Zealand State Sector in a Time of Change*, a report prepared for the State Services Commission and the Treasury, Wellington: State Services Commission.

Scott, Graham and Gorringe, Peter (1989), 'Reform of the Core Public Sector: The New Zealand Experience', *Australian Journal of Public Administration* Vol.48, pp.81-92.

Scott, Graham, Ball, Ian and Dale, Tony (1997), 'New Zealand's Public Sector Management Reforms: Implications for the United States', *Journal of Policy Analysis and Management* Vol.16, pp.357-81.

Suleiman, Ezra (1974), *Politics, Power, and Bureaucracy in France: The Administrative Elite*, Princeton, NJ: Princeton University Press.

Wahlke, John C. (1962), *The Legislative System: Explorations in Legislative Behavior*, New York: Wiley.

Weber, Max (1948), in H.H. Gerth and C. Wright Mills (eds.) *From Max Weber: Essays in Sociology*, London: Routledge & Kegan Paul.

11 Contracting, the Enterprise Culture and Public Sector Ethics

Martin Painter

The adoption of contracting in the public sector has grown apace in recent years, in conjunction with the ideological dominance in many countries of 'more market' political arguments, and the growth of an 'enterprise culture'. Modern public sectors deploy the language and techniques of the contract in a number of ways. For example, agencies that deliver services to the public sometimes make 'contracts' with their customers. Secondly, performance contracts are a common feature of both individual and organizational work within agencies. A third example is the use of competitive tendering to contract out various forms of work to private providers. Sometimes this can result in a public agency winning the tender. The use of this third form of contracting as a method of monitoring and control of public policy outputs and outcomes is an instrument with peculiar dimensions and characteristics. It is not just a tool for efficiency improvements, but a set of practices that can transform the normative and regulative character of public institutions, and hence the constraints, incentives and opportunities that shape the actions of agents of the state. As a method of control and regulation of these actions, contracting is the antithesis of the constraints and duties embodied in office-holding. The question is whether, in this context, ethical conduct can be expected to wither or flourish (Moss, 1997; Shergold, 1997). The prognosis is not good.

Office-holding and public ethics

Ethical conduct in the public sector of liberal democracies is built on the foundation of office-holding. Public offices embody duties and obligations that reflect the complex web of constitutional, legal, and political responsibilities inherent in the conduct of public administration. Office-holders experience day in, day out the conflicts and dilemmas that these multiple accountabilities and responsibilities bring. Conscientious office-holders cannot be mere ciphers because the exercise of judgment is routinely called for. They are constantly called upon to look to their own resources of moral reasoning to make hard choices. Neither can they be free moral agents and step outside their office to act as if they were private citizens in the performance of their official duties (Minson, 1998, pp. 49-52; Jackson, 1987). The location of the foundations of ethical conduct in the responsibilities associated with office-holding does not exclude a role for individual ethical reflection and choice, but in exercising that choice officials are required, as argued by Barry O'Toole in Chapter 6, to put their public duties first.

The barometer of public sector ethics is the health and robustness of the public institutions within which officials hold their offices. When such institutions are routinely corrupted, and sanction unethical conduct, or punish responsible acts of conscience, moral agents within them are frequently rendered powerless, short of acts of near futile heroism. Individuals acquire the power to do good routinely when the institutions return to health. The first requirement for institutional health is for some measure of independence and permanence; the second, a plurality of forms and structures of offices within an inclusive tradition. For example, in a Westminster system, the government of the day expects loyalty and faithful service from its officials, but this expectation competes with others. The expectation of blind loyalty has on many occasions been accompanied by the punishment of principled behaviour. The dangers of unitary regulation and control of public offices are considerable, and the safeguards lie in a plurality of relatively autonomous offices of guardians, watchdogs and monitors. The existence of tensions between unitary and other principles of control are common in systems of public offices. In such a context, many different kinds of institutional, legal and political safeguards protect and advance often competing public values throughout the system. Some such values, like merit, encourage self-reflective autonomy, and are designed specifically to provide the institutional context within which ethical conduct can thrive (Painter, 1990; Uhr, 1996).

Office-holding versus contracting

In supplanting the obligations of office-holding with the market-mimicking, legalistic, arm's-length monitoring systems of the contract, some of the bedrock on which ethical conduct in the public sector has been built is being disturbed. What are the fundamental characteristics first, of office-holding and second, of contracting, as systems of regulation of administrative activity? In creating an office and employing an office holder, the state specifies at the same time a set of role obligations and tasks, and a relationship of subordination that allows for direction and intervention. The office holder learns the obligations and tasks, and over time acquires skill in the exercise of discretion so that intervention is the exception. Training, induction, and possibly the promise of security reinforce a set of mutual obligations between the institution and the office-holder. Experienced superiors promoted through the ranks can intervene selectively to correct errors via a generalized power of command in a master-servant relationship. Tasks can be added, duties changed, new skills imparted and acquired. Regularity, predictability and great flexibility are possible in such a system. Offices can be re-assembled in new ways, and new tasks can be matched with known talents and skills. Loyalty and dedication can be rewarded by offering new challenges to the most proficient. Generalized competencies in public office-holding can be developed over time and put to good use. Over-arching control and accountability systems can institutionalize key values and principles across the whole of government through a variety of mechanisms, such as inspection, audit and review by legal tribunals.

What has just been described might sound like the classic Weberian bureaucracy, but it only emphasizes some aspects of that form, in particular the location of an autonomous, impersonal entity – the office – in a hierarchy or, more accurately, in a plurality of co-existing hierarchies in a multi-centred and multi-layered public sector. What holds these offices together, or at least distinguishes them as a system, is not only the existence of some unitary authority structure representing the public power, but also the exigencies imposed by sharing authority. Exchange and interdependency characterize the networks and communities of cooperation that straddle this system and enable it to work (Hindmoor, 1998). In sharing the obligations of office-holding, participants have at least that much in common. Both in requiring compliance with an order, and in seeking agreement in a negotiation or a discussion with more or less equals, the public office holder draws on common sources of legitimacy and familiar role expectations. Responsibility and accountability have common roots and meanings. Trust in such a system builds on common norms as well as frequency and regularity of exchange, rather than on external enforcement mechanisms.

In transaction costs language, governance structures come in two types: the hierarchy and the market. The former relies on authority, the latter on contracts in order to regularize and make possible exchanges. Contracting stands in stark contrast to the hierarchical relationships that normally regulate a system of public offices. It is deliberately temporary and task specific and eschews the generalized master-servant relationship as a form of control and regulation (Hood, 1986). The contract specifies the obligations of two independent and freely transacting parties and identifies the manner in which they will be enforced. In a commercial context, the contract is a legal agreement that contains, among other things, specifications of the task to be achieved, the price to be charged, the method of payment, and the manner in which compliance and successful performance are to be monitored and enforced. The contractor is a temporary mercenary, albeit one for whom reputation and reliability may be important economic assets. While in such a circumstance, self-interest dictates that the contractor meets obligations, the purchaser must routinely anticipate and guard against defalcation and opportunism. The contractor in turn expects the purchaser to 'turn the screws'. The relationship is arm's length and, while compliance is monitored by the purchaser, it is externally enforced. Transparency, formality, legality and high levels of specificity are essential to the conduct of the relationship.

Coupled with competitive tendering, contracting by the public sector seeks out from the marketplace of productive units a service provider who strikes a commercial agreement specific to the undertaking of a particular task. Competitive tendering attempts to bring to bear the disciplines of the market on reducing costs and making efficient, high quality provision. It also brings other parts of the world of the market-place into the service provision system. The market is not a norm-free environment, and the operations and structure of particular markets are constructed by law and regulation. Trust and other less than spontaneous forms of exchange are routine and essential. In its basic form, however, the contract as a model for regulating exchange, coupled with the device of periodic competitive tendering to select the contractor, presumes the possibility of their absence. The relationship is deliberately impersonal, relies on external enforcement and assumes the worst of both parties.

The differences between contracting and office-holding can be illustrated by the phenomenon of 'in-house' tendering and contracting, common in many local government bodies. In its purest form, this requires the complete organizational separation of the provider from the purchaser so as to remove conflicts of interest. The provider agency may even be cast loose to compete with private providers, with all that this entails for business survival or failure. More commonly, the in-house agency is forced to compete for a segment of the service field with private providers, and this 'market-testing' then provides the benchmark for the purchaser's pricing of the remainder. Either way, the aim is to focus the minds of agencies on the bottom line of price and efficiency, and the minds of government service purchasers on the objectives of policy and the specification of performance criteria to measure their achievement. Agency managers must be risk managers, and develop an enterprise culture. In their turn, government policy makers and purchasers must become accustomed to regulating and monitoring at arm's length, where the contract and its enforcement becomes the principal instrument of control and accountability.

As a method of service performance or delivery, contracting would seem to be particularly appropriate where the task is routine and predictable so that performance is relatively easily monitored, and where there is also a market of multiple providers so that there is effective competition (for example, tasks such as office-cleaning and refuse collection). Like many techniques of administration and control, it finds its indiscriminate advocates and imitators across all types of public sector activity, from legal and policy advice to the delivery of personal health and welfare services. Another area of growth has been the use of employment contracts in Senior Executive Services, coupled with performance agreements, seeking to make transparent the expectations and requirements that governments have of their senior advisers, and providing for summary termination if performance is unsatisfactory. Most of the discussion here is focused on contracting for service provision, however. Attention has been focused elsewhere on both the benefits and the potential hazards of contract employment in the senior ranks (Boston, 1997; Mulgan, 1998; Weller and Wanna, 1997).

Some dilemmas of public sector contracting

The purported failures of in-house systems of provision based on hierarchies of public offices were captured in public choice and principal-agent theories and their critiques of bureaucracy, which form the foundation of many justifications for contracting (Boston, 1996; Althaus, 1997; Boyne, 1998). In assuming that office-holders would be self-interested and opportunistic, economic theories of bureaucracy turned the virtues of systems of public offices into vices: permanency was an invitation to complacency; the system of generalized hierarchical supervision was a recipe for mutual collusion and shirking; and the only enterprise and enthusiasm to be expected were in the pursuit of personal and organizational aggrandizement, and the concealment of error. There was an inherent conflict of interest between the role of 'purchaser' and 'provider' in this view, hence the need to separate the roles and make use of contracts. One remedy, again given the assumption of self-interest and opportunism, was to harness them through competitive tendering and contracting out, or the development of internal markets accompanied by contracts. Not only would contracting reduce costs, due to the downward pressure on prices resulting from competitive tendering, it would result in continuous quality improvement as providers sought to outdo each other in meeting service specifications. In order to achieve this, the purchaser would be required to put in place clear service objectives with accompanying measurable performance indicators, each being essential pre-requisites for business-like efficiency improvements.

The pros and cons of contracting and competitive tendering have been thoroughly and repeatedly canvassed in an extensive literature (for example, Boyne, 1998; Hodge, 1998). One set of costs or limits flows from the consequences of the impersonality and the adversarial nature of the contract relationship. Principal-agent theory warns us that high levels of information asymmetry always characterize such relationships – the agent always knows more about what is going on than the principal, and uses that power to his or her advantage. The principal in response puts in place intensive and possibly intrusive forms of monitoring and external scrutiny, which reduces levels of trust, and which in turn increases the likelihood of shirking by the agent. A vicious circle is set up. The kinds of social relationships that build trust and mutuality and assist in achieving common goals (in this case, those set out in the contract specifications) are undermined. Other kinds of problems arise because of the creation of a 'market for contracts'. The letting of a contract is the award of a temporary monopoly, and the aspirant monopolist engages in exactly the kind of rent-seeking behaviour that supposedly characterized the bureaucratic monopoly, which the brave new world of contracting is intended to combat (Boyne, 1998, pp. 700-1). Indeed, because of the commercial stakes involved and the once-off nature of the decision to award a contract, the incentives and opportunities for bribery and other irregularities are particularly high, perhaps more so than in the public monopoly, which is likely to be extracting more benign forms of rent.

In some respects the differences between office-holding and a contractual relationship are only ones of degree. Mutual self-interest among otherwise antagonistic parties is the way the master-servant relationship is often best depicted, and the same might be said of contracting. If the two shade together, however, the outer boundaries are worlds apart. This is seen in some inherent tensions in the practicalities of contracting. The gap between theory and practice is often wide. The structural logic of contracting demands a high level of impersonality and the erection and maintenance of legal fences and procedural buffers of the kind that are not required in a hierarchy of public offices. Contract managers, however, learn that 'cooperative' and 'continuing' relationships with contractors facilitate smooth implementation, and that mutual learning and obligations develop which make their supervisory jobs easier. They then find themselves chastised for engaging in 'collusion' and for losing sight of the need for arm's length objectivity.

The Australian Government's Industry Commission (1996, pp.82-3) described the ideal principal-agent relationship as follows:

- for each principal-agent relationship, it is clearly established who is *responsible* for different aspects of the service;
- sufficient *information* is readily available so that ... performance ... is transparent; and
- there is opportunity for *redress* where substandard performance is identified and a capacity for that to be corrected or sanctions to be imposed.

Revealingly, a commentary on this formulation elaborated that although 'open consultation' between purchaser and provider was necessary, 'reliance on unspoken assumptions by either party will potentially undermine the contractual relationship' (Senate, 1998, p. 1/2). Note that it is precisely such 'unspoken assumptions' as trust, respect and commitment to a common enterprise that the assemblage of public offices seeks to achieve within its ranks in order to facilitate cooperation and obedience alike. In the networks and policy communities of the public sector's complex structures of governance, such modes of exchange and building of commitment are essential in oiling the wheels of policy management and administration (Hindmoor, 1998).

Recent discussions of best practice in Australian Government contracting have brought these issues out. The same contradictions are found wherever one looks. The *Commonwealth Procurement Guidelines* (Department of Finance and Administration, 1997, p.165) recommends that contract management should be based on:

- commitment to open communication, trust and mutual support;
- flexibility; and
- working with the supplier to identify possible improvements.

- A partnering arrangement can establish the basis for a mutually beneficial relationship.

Another manual promotes a 'non-adversarial' contract model and advocates the development of 'extra-contractual' relationships as a means of fostering a cooperative working arrangement (MAB/MIAC, 1997). The jargon refers to 'partnering', 'strategic alliances' and 'teaming' (Department of Finance and Administration, 1998, pp.29-30). A recent Senate Committee report, drawing more closely on the Industry Commission's ideal of the principal-agent role splits, threw cold water on these instruments for achieving effective contract management. To them, the problem was to ensure the strict legal enforceability of the contract, and the danger of 'partnering' lay in the temptation to prop up a non-performing contractor: '[t]he committee's concern is that if too much emphasis is given to the informal "partnering" approach agencies may not give sufficient emphasis to ensuring that the formal contractual relationship which must underpin it is sound' (Senate, 1998, p.9/4).

Conceptual confusion and sleight of hand serve political ends. The rhetoric of contracting has become a common feature of political discourse in public sector and welfare reform, and the use of terms such as 'partnering' and 'team building' to allay political opposition from groups whose material interests are adversely affected by contracting (such as unionized employees) is sometimes closer to reality than the language of competition. The Labour Government in the UK, for example, having rejected 'compulsory competitive tendering' in local government, talks of creating a 'more positive climate in which local authorities and their potential partners in the private and voluntary sectors can approach competition...' (DETR, 1998).

But the advocacy of closer ties of mutuality and cooperation in the contract relationship also reflects some very real dilemmas of contracting government services in a commercial environment, in which cost and profit are the principal motivating logics in the relationship. Other kinds of contractual model advocating less adversarial relationships are theoretically feasible. Christopher Hood (1997) has drawn attention to the use of contracts in a model of an 'empowering' contract state, where co-production by citizens with an urge to participate in public life provides the normative setting, rather than the norms of the market place. The citizen 'carer' working as a case manager in a voluntary organization helping the unemployed is poles apart from the opportunistic entrepreneur who sees a business opportunity in placing the unemployed in work. The purpose of the contract between state and provider in the model of the 'empowering' contract state is to forge a mutual partnership between like-minded public spirited actors in state and society respectively.

In practice, mutually empowering and commercial contracts co-exist uneasily in contemporary welfare service provision. Contracts in this context represent one of a variety of funding and service provision relationships forging cooperative agreements between government and non-government agencies over service delivery. Where elements of competitive tendering are in place in setting up the contract relationship, the commercial setting becomes paramount – even in the case where a contract is won by a community sector welfare provider. Other, competing providers may be purely commercial enterprises, while the community sector providers significantly 'privatize' in their form and culture as they adapt to the realities of such contracting. The bottom line, imposed by the terms of the contract, is that the service must be provided at the cost and quality specified in the contract. Similar standards and practices that identify the nature of the provider as an accountable business entity are imposed on all.

Public sector ethics, the enterprise culture and contracting

When office-holding is replaced by contracting and competitive tendering, a number of profound consequences flow for the structural and institutional foundations of ethical public service conduct. These reflect a broader set of dilemmas arising from the introduction of an enterprise culture more generally into the public sector. Some take an optimistic view of the nature of these developments. This is that the new public management generally has enabled a new spirit of freedom and autonomy to pervade public sector management. In 'letting the managers manage', by demolishing rigid bureaucratic formalisms, and in encouraging risk and enterprise, public servants have been freed from restraints and allowed room to define and act out their own meanings of professional and personal ethical conduct. Paul du Gay, in a critique of enterprise culture, describes how the modern public servant is set free as 'an entrepreneur of oneself, because enterprise offers the means of obtaining self-realization and self-perfection' (du Gay, 1994, p.662). Public employees achieve self-fulfilment by using their initiative and by seeing projects through to the end in more autonomous, decentralized settings. They prefer to put themselves on the line than to have a supervisor look over their shoulder, and submit willingly to the risks of ex post performance review in exchange for greater managerial freedom.

It is no accident that the advent of this new form of management has been accompanied by a spate of officially produced, elaborate and detailed codes of ethical conduct. At the same time as freeing managers to work at arm's length, enjoining them to take risks, and handing them new levels of personal autonomy, more must be done to ensure that the manager is aware of and internalizes the ethical standards that used to be regulated and learned by example under supervision. In the new, devolved world of agencies, government norms and values that could be taken for granted are deliberately relaxed. Corporate mission statements and codes of conduct provide the substitute.

The romantic vision of the self-actualizing moral being, harnessed in ethical tandem with the dismal image of the opportunistic egoist in defence of the enterprise culture in the public sector, is a fundamental contradiction. Examples abound. The Australian Government Attorney-General's Department has commercialized its legal services, such that government agencies pay commercial rates for its legal advice, and may seek such advice elsewhere if it can be provided more cheaply and effectively. Tendering and contracting regulate much of the Legal Practice's relations with the rest of the public sector. In 1995 the Department published an ethical code for the Legal Practice, *Guidelines on Our Values, Ethics and Conduct*. The Solicitor-General, Dale Boucher, explained the underlying philosophy:

> it is largely through identification of values, whether they are inner or explicit, that an ethical code can be meaningfully formulated.... [E]thical guidelines [are] a vital component of ... devolution, that is, giving people in the organization power to make decisions and also changing forms of service delivery through, for instance, commercialization. Identifying values and ethical principles are part and parcel of operating effectively and efficiently, making the best use of public resources and tapping the creative and innovative abilities of staff. And this can best be done by giving them freedom to act in an ethical framework, cast against a sense of corporate identity (Boucher, 1996, p.4).

This model of the 'ethical manager' fails to acknowledge the power of the commercial bottom line. Boucher was at pains to deny the view that 'ethics cannot or do not exist in a commercial environment.' He went on to point to the value of commercial benchmarks in 'invigorating' the legal service, and the stimulus to 'continuous improvement' due to competition. The four 'core values' identified in the code were integrity, responsiveness, excellence and competitiveness. The 'corporate identity' that these reflect is suited to the promotion of the Legal Practice as a successful tenderer for contracts, one that has the necessary professional reputation, the required customer focus and the ability to deliver a product more efficiently and effectively than others. Such would seem appropriate for any corporation, and John Uhr found himself wondering where was the 'larger legitimacy of these core values, which ... should derive from the core business of the department.' (Uhr, 1996a, p.7). Simply stating that this is to advise government on appropriate legal policy is not enough – such is the obligation of any lawyer to a client. The public duty of the department has a special character:

> the duty of care of the private legal expert is to the best interests of the client, whereas that of the Attorney-General's officers includes an important element of 'constitutional care', that is, care for the constitutional systems and its nutrient values of representative democracy and the rule of law.... [T]he whole-of-government responsibility of departmental officers to take care of the best interests of duly-constituted government, [is] a more fundamental responsibility than taking care of the interests of a commercial client (Uhr, 1996a, p.7).

The vital point is that the interests of a client – in this case, a government or one of its executive agencies – and the public interest need not coincide.

Boucher also recognized what he called 'additional obligations' arising from public sector activity, which to him meant complying with the 'codes and standards which apply in the APS such as the Public Service Act, the Privacy Act, the Freedom of Information Act... and so on' (Boucher, 1996, p.4). How can this be reconciled with the entrepreneurial cast of the contracting agency's corporate identity? If these 'codes and standards' are applied as guides and frames of reference for the exercise of managerial discretion, they will sometimes contradict the requirements for 'responsiveness, excellence and competitiveness'. The monitoring and enforcement of these codes and standards also conflict with the requirements for corporate and personal managerial autonomy in the pursuit of efficiency and effectiveness, and for the single-minded focus on the client's, or purchaser's, specifications in framing advice or exercising discretion. The purchaser of the service, not the contractor, is responsible for ensuring that conformity with codes and standards is part of the contracted 'product'. A private sector legal practice will see no reason to internalize codes and standards other than those intrinsic to legal practice, and the commercialized public agency may suffer a competitive

176 *Martin Painter*

disadvantage from so doing. Commercialization, in other words, is likely to weaken the reach of these codes and standards. Attempts to reconcile contracting with traditional forms of public sector accountability, the subject of the next section, highlight this problem.

Contracting and accountability

Public Service Commissioner Peter Shergold, speaking at the same ceremony that launched the Attorney-General Department's *Guidelines*, put his colleagues on the spot:

> so what is it that the public sector has that the private sector does not? In the delivery of government services, why are we apparently the preferred supplier? Part of the answer lies in the high levels of accountability to which we are subject and the strong set of values and codes of conduct to which we are committed... [O]ur bottom line is a matter of ethics, not of profits. Throughout the service we continue to share a common set of values; an ethical framework...; a strong accountability to the Government, Parliament and the Australian public; responsiveness both to governments and the Australian public; and merit as the basis for staffing (Shergold, 1996, p.1).

Advocates of contracting claim for it an enhancement of accountability because it requires a much sharper specification of distinct principal and agent responsibilities, and a system of monitoring and reporting to achieve contract compliance. Outcomes-focused accountability, it is argued, is the best kind. The ultimate responsibility for ensuring that the values embedded in accountability procedures are maintained and enhanced remains with the purchaser. The values or ends considered important, including such things as procedural fairness and respect for the public, should be specified as clear performance standards and then monitored and enforced as part of the contract. In that case, the contractor can be fenced off from the kinds of monitoring and oversight characteristic of the multiple accountabilities of public sector work, even if the purchaser is still subject to them. The Australian Government Department of Administrative Services recently advocated this point of view: '[i]ncluding more detailed specifications of objectives and responsibilities in the contracts makes accountability more readily identifiable, which means the intervention of an independent arbiter should not be necessary' (Senate, 1998, p.8/4).

A significant flaw in this view of arm's-length accountability is that the contracting out of so much service delivery (invariably accompanied by shedding of staff) strips away the level of detailed knowledge and expertise required to write detailed specifications and monitor substantive outcomes. Where the artificial, adversarial divide between purchaser and provider does not exist, but hierarchies, networks or communities better characterize the form of the relationship between the overseer and the operative, knowledge is more likely to be shared, in a climate of trust and mutuality. Contrast this with the following comment from one non-government provider in the welfare sector in Melbourne:

> the level of expertise which seems to be available in the various bureaucracies has diminished to such an extent that they no longer actually know what they are tendering for. Consultation does not take place. Documentations turn up, you go through them and you want to ask questions; but you are not allowed to ask questions because this is a breach of the tender process, even questions of clarification (House of Representatives, 1998, p.25).

Therefore placing the onus of accountability purely on the purchaser may be futile. The purchaser will feel victim to the powerlessness of information asymmetry, and will almost certainly, as a matter of survival, shift the blame on the agent. Prisons administration in the UK provides numerous recent examples (Barker, 1998). The problem goes deeper, however. The purchaser's outcomes responsibility is defined one-dimensionally, and side-steps the multiple and often conflicting accountability requirements of the public sector. Indeed, escape from these seems not so much a by-product as an intention of contracting. The Department of Finance in Australia has argued that the multiple sources of oversight and redress characteristic of much of the public sector proper should not need to be imposed on the service provider: '[a]lthough contracted service providers must be accountable for outcomes and service quality, care should be taken to ensure that the value of contracting out is not reduced by duplicating public service reporting and monitoring in the private sector' (Senate, 1998, p.2/4). As Richard Mulgan (1997) has pointed out, one of the principal aims of contracting out is to achieve savings by shifting a service to the private sector, and a primary source of such savings is freedom from government 'red tape'. To this point, most commentators and law-makers in Australia have agreed with the view that the sharp line between public and private sectors that has been drawn around the jurisdiction of the Ombudsman (for example) should in principle be maintained with respect to contracted out services. In exceptional cases, such as contracting of employment services, special provision might be made so that the Ombudsman could look directly at the contractor's treatment of a client upon receiving a complaint (Senate, 1998, p.8/4). Otherwise, the Ombudsman should normally address only the proficiency of the purchasing or monitoring agency in ensuring the quality of the service provision through its management of the contract.

The focus on an outcome as the 'deliverable' in the contract, for which the contractor is held to account by precise performance standards and external enforcement, only captures a small part of the picture. What distinguishes public services is the importance of a diversity of procedural values (Painter, 1990). The one-dimensional principal-agent split does not encompass the multiplicity of role obligations entailed in performing a public office and delivering a public service. Marcia Neave, President of the Administrative Review Council, in her evidence to the Senate Finance and Public Administration Committee stressed such aspects: 'ensuring that public administration is lawful; that people behave fairly, rationally, openly and efficiently in their dealings with the community ... we are concerned to ensure those values will be maintained as government services are increasingly delivered in new ways' (Senate, 1998, p.14/7).

The case of the damaged letter box, quoted by the Committee, well illustrates this point (Mullins, 1996). The mail deliverer contracted by Australia Post damaged a pensioner's letterbox. He asked Australia Post for compensation, but was dissatisfied with the offer. The contractor would not claim on his insurance because the cost was less than the excess. Australia Post could not compel the contractor to meet the cost or to reach a settlement. The Ombudsman, acting on the pensioner's complaint, negotiated a settlement. In sum:

> the mail delivery contract in question was apparently deficient in at least two respects: it did not specify what might be regarded as implicit in a contract, namely that *contracted mail deliverers should exercise due care and attention in the conduct of their work;* and it did not provide a clear means of redress (emphasis added) (Senate, 1998, p.6/4).

Australia Post now writes into its contracts a procedure for compensating customers and recovering the cost from the contractor.

The need to specify the obvious in the contract, especially when it is in general terms such as 'exercise due care and attention', goes against the grain of writing precise, easily enforceable contracts that focus primarily on measurable, substantive outcomes. Clearly from the above, the contract is not the most appropriate instrument to facilitate the transfer of procedural values such as fairness, respect for cultural diversity, probity and so on. The more multi-faceted the task, and the more uncertain the outcomes, the more unsuited is the activity to the contract as an instrument of control. Contracts are not well fitted to the task of specifying and demanding many public sector 'taken for granted' duties, rights and obligations from the contractor, particularly if they entail the exercise of discretion, and in some cases the intervention of a superior or an arbiter, when faced with judgments about competing or ambiguous values. Nor do the accountability processes that come with the arm's length contractual relationship sit easily with the constituent's expectation of personal attention to legitimate grievances. As Mulgan points out, contracting must mean some reduction in accountability 'through the removal of direct departmental and ministerial control over the day-to-day actions of the contractors and their staff' (Mulgan, 1997, p.26). If external monitors of values such as anti-discrimination and privacy also enjoy inhibited access to inspect and remedy, then the prospects for maintaining and policing fundamental tenets of routine, everyday ethical conduct in the delivery of public services are not good.

Advocates of market mechanisms claim to have answers to such accountability and 'quality assurance' problems. In some cases, where the government-funded service provider is not the sole provider, customers can vote with their feet, as they do when choosing between restaurants or between supermarkets. However, most contracts for government services are let to monopoly providers who periodically compete for the field, so the customer or client has no such leverage. In the absence of an 'exit' option, the customer is left to rely on complaints mechanisms backed up by external arbiters, or on internalized norms and standards. Recently, under the spell of the enterprise culture, government agencies have been enjoined to mimic the private sector in the development of such norms and standards, and to develop a 'customer focus'. Commonwealth agencies that contract out services must develop 'service charters':

> the charters are plain language documents detailing the services provided, the standards of service which can be expected, clear statements as to who is responsible if the service is not provided at the level promised, and guidance on how to complain if something goes wrong. Charters can be expected to address, where relevant, such service quality issues as reliability, tangibles such as appearance of physical facilities and equipment, responsiveness, assurance and empathy. The Committee believes that service charters, where

appropriate, should contain a code of ethics, or at least address ethical issues (Senate, 1998, p.8/4).

As already discussed, in the search for mechanisms to ensure the maintenance of public service standards by private contractors, the Committee placed the primary responsibility not on the contractor but on the purchaser, who retains the onus of ensuring public accountability. Such is consistent with the theory and practice of contracting – it is the role of the principal to define and assure the standards. It is deeply ironic, then, that one mechanism for such assurance is for the government agency to publish a service charter to guarantee the customer focus of a commercially-focused private provider.

Such charters in any case are only partial answers to the range of assurances and accountability mechanisms that the public requires from public service providers. It is stretching the meaning of the word 'customer' to apply it to prisoners, the unemployed, or the disabled. None but a very small and relatively unimportant range of values, rights and expectations that are entailed in the manner in which such groups and individuals should be related to, are encompassed in the exchange relationship that underlies the imagery of 'customer service'. Even the idea of 'client' service misses some strands of the complex web of obligations, checks, and accountability mechanisms that are entailed in many of the relationships between the state and citizens (Weller, 1997; Vardon, 1997). Ultimately, we must turn to the core of public offices and office holders, and the values and standards they institutionalize and transmit, to locate public responsibility and to anchor the guarantees of ethical conduct.

Conclusion

Modern public sector management reforms in Australia and elsewhere have taken contracting into more and more areas of public service management and delivery. In the name of efficiency, state employees and agencies in many fields of activity have been replaced by contracted private individuals or businesses. The risks of such practices are well known. When it does business, the state has always been vulnerable to venality and abuse of power, and elaborate systems of rules and audit are nothing new in preventing and remedying unethical conduct in the implementation of contracts.

More fundamentally, in supplanting integrated or networked hierarchies of public offices by fragmented public agencies and private firms regulated by contract, one of the basic building blocks of public ethics – office-holding in a system of public service – may be dismantled. Some of the consequences of this are alluded to by Richard Chapman in Chapter 7. Attempts by agency chiefs to write codes of ethics that at the same time defend traditions of public ethical values and celebrate the enterprise culture, fight an uphill battle against the logic of risk and enterprise in the marketplace, and in market-mimicking relationships. Attempts by contract managers to adapt the contract to some of the more complex dimensions of public service delivery, such as the generic values of fairness and decency, highlight the inappropriateness of such instruments to the task. Arm's length adversarialism, mutual suspicion and contract enforcement legalism thwart many of the normal, negotiated or taken-for-granted practices and habits of public sector administration. Every agent in a principal-agent chain which is held together by contracts has the incentive to ignore or evade wider public interest requirements. Tensions and contradictions are made evident in the manner in which traditional, multiple forms of accountability are mostly by-passed or supplanted by narrow, one-dimensional mechanisms of contract enforcement and service delivery. In sum, the replacement of the generic, comprehensive forms of supervision, regulation, networking and teambuilding inherent in a system of public offices, by the particularistic, task-specific forms inherent in the contract, is a threat to the basis of ethical conduct in the management and delivery of public services.

References

Althaus, Catherine (1997), 'The application of agency theory to public sector management', in Glyn Davis *et al.* (eds), *The New Contractualism?*, Melbourne: Macmillan, pp.137-54.
Barker, Anthony (1998), 'Political responsibility for UK prison security – ministers escape again', *Public Administration* Vol. 76, pp.1-24.
Boston, Jonathan (1996), 'The ideas and theories underpinning the New Zealand model', in Jonathan Boston *et al.* (eds), *Public Management: the New Zealand Model*, Auckland: Oxford University Press, pp.16-41.
Boston, Jonathan (1997), 'The new contractualism in New Zealand: Chief Executive performance agreements', in Glyn Davis *et al.* (eds), *The New Contractualism?*, Melbourne: Macmillan, pp.180-98.
Boucher, Dale (1996), 'An ethical code ... not a code of conduct', *Canberra Bulletin of Public Administration* Vol. 79 February, pp.3-5.
Boyne, George A. (1998), 'Competitive tendering in local government: a review of theory and evidence', *Public Administration* Vol. 76, pp.695-712.

Davis, Glyn, Sullivan, Barbara and Yeatman, Anna (eds) (1997), *The New Contractualism?*, Melbourne: Macmillan.

Department of Environment, Transport and the Regions (DETR) (1998), *Modern Local Government: In Touch with the People*, London: DETR.

Department of Finance and Administration (1997), *Commonwealth Procurement Guidelines*, Canberra: Department of Finance and Adminstration.

Department of Finance and Administration (1998), *Competitive Tendering and Contracting: Guidance for Managers*, Canberra.

du Gay, Paul (1994), 'Making up managers: bureaucracy, enterprise and the liberal art of separation', *British Journal of Sociology* Vol. 45, pp.655-74.

Hindmoor, Andrew (1998), 'The importance of being trusted: transaction costs and policy network theory', *Public Administration* Vol. 76, pp.25-44.

Hodge, Graeme (1998), 'Contracting public sector services: a meta-analytic perspective of the international evidence', *Australian Journal of Public Administration* Vol. 57, pp.85-97.

Hood, Christopher (1986), *Administrative Analysis*, Brighton: Wheatsheaf

Hood, Christopher (1997), 'Which contract state? four perspectives on over-outsourcing for public services', *Australian Journal of Public Administration* Vol. 56, pp.120-31.

House of Representatives Standing Committee on Family and Community Affairs (1998), *What Price Competition? A Report on the Competitive Tendering of Welfare Service Delivery*, Canberra: Parliament of the Commonwealth of Australia.

Industry Commission (1996), *Competitive tendering and contracting by public sector agencies*, Melbourne: Australian Government Publishing Service.

Jackson, Michael (1987), 'Office conduct or moral conduct?' *Canberra Bulletin of Public Administration* October, pp.83-5.

Management Advisory Board/Management Advisory Improvement Advisory Committee (MAB/MIAC) (1997), *Before you sign on the dotted line... ensuring contracts can be managed*, Canberra: MAB/MIAC Report No 23.

Minson, Jeffrey (1998), 'Ethics in the service of the state', in Mitchell Dean and Barry Hindess (eds), *Governing Australia: studies in contemporary rationalities of government*, Cambridge: Cambridge University Press, pp.47-69.

Moss, Irene (1997), 'Does entrepreneurial government reduce the scope for scrutiny of the public service?', *Australian Journal of Public Administration* Vol. 56, pp.3-10.

Mulgan, Richard (1997), 'Contracting out and accountability', *Australian Journal of Public Administration* Vol. 56, pp.106-16.

Mulgan, Richard (1998), 'Politicization of senior appointments in the Australian Public Service', *Australian Journal of Public Administration* Vol. 57, pp.3-14.
Mullins, Joanna (1996), 'Handling complaints related to government services delivered by contract', *Canberra Bulletin of Public Administration* Vol. 79, February, pp.109-17.
Painter, Martin (1990), 'Values in the history of public administration', in John Power (ed.), *Public administration in Australia: a watershed*, Sydney: Hale & Iremonger.
Senate Finance and Public Administration References Committee (1998), *Contracting out of Government Services Second Report*, Canberra: Parliament of the Commonwealth of Australia.
Shergold, Peter (1996), 'Integrating traditional values with newer management approaches', *Canberra Bulletin of Public Administration* Vol.79 February, p.1.
Shergold, Peter (1997), 'Ethics and the changing nature of public service', *Australian Journal of Public Administration* Vol. 56, pp.119-24.
Uhr, John (1996), 'From merit to multiculturalism' in John Uhr (ed.), *Ethical Practice in Government*, Canberra: Federalism Research Centre, pp.7-22.
Uhr, John (1996a), 'Core value or core business?', *Canberra Bulletin of Public Administration* Vol. 79 February, pp.5-7.
Vardon, Sue (1997), 'Are prisoners clients?', *Australian Journal of Public Administration* Vol. 56, pp.127-9.
Weller, Patrick (1997), 'Are prisoners clients?', *Australian Journal of Public Administration* Vol. 56, pp.125-7.
Weller, Patrick and Wanna, John (1997), 'Departmental secretaries: appointment, termination and their impact', *Australian Journal of Public Administration* Vol. 56, pp.13-25.

12 Between Autonomy and Accountability: Hong Kong's Senior Civil Servants in Search of an Identity

Anthony B.L. Cheung

Accountability and autonomy: Concepts and uncertainties

In his discussion of *accountability* in public service, Colin Campbell (1993) delineated between *hierarchical* accountability and *democratic* accountability. Civil servants as officials operating in large and complex government departments have to be accountable, not only to their immediate superiors in the Weberian hierarchical sense, but also to the political leadership that derives its legitimacy through its claim to embody the will of the people as defined in democratic elections. According to Campbell, democratically-oriented civil servants take the notion of political legitimacy a step further by anticipating changes in the popular mandate in times of elections and by assessing their impact on government priorities and agenda-setting (Campbell, 1993, p.112). As far as public service ethics are concerned, few will dispute with, for example, Luiz Montanheiro's (1998) notions of the impartial and accountable bureaucrat and the open and honest politician.

In the case of Hong Kong, it is not so simple and straight-forward for civil servants to be politically impartial and accountable. Not only is there not yet in existence a democratic system of governance in which the political executive takes its right to govern on the basis of the popular mandate as expressed during democratic elections, but throughout the 155 years of British colonial rule until 30 June 1997, senior civil servants, mainly those of the Administrative Class and hereinafter referred to as 'administrative civil servants', had in effect formed the permanent government, embodying both the roles of policymakers and administrators in what S.K. Lau (1982, pp.26-9) described as 'a bureaucratic polity'. Quite contrary to the path as depicted by J.D. Aberbach, R.D. Putnam and B.A.

Rockman (1981) in the evolution of the bureaucrats-politicians interface, the Hong Kong administrative civil servants had all along been the kind of 'pure hybrid' (Image IV of Aberbach et al's description) combining the functions of policy formulation, interests brokering and ideals articulation, functions which were conventionally within the sphere of politicians. Not until the 1990s were other emerging political players (such as popularly-elected politicians and parties) seen to be beginning to demand a share of those functions and powers. However, the principle of political accountability has remained blurred and indeterminate, constituting the main outstanding ethical issue for the civil service as an institution.

Civil servants are traditionally expected to be autonomous within their own administrative role. Such administrative autonomy has more recently been reinforced by the New Public Management paradigm (see Hood, 1991) which advocates greater freedom and autonomy to managers subject to performance accountability. Civil servants also get more involved in the process of policy formulation, as indeed recognized by Aberbach et al. (1981), but there is never any doubt as to the subordination of the civil service to the elected political leadership. Politically they are not supposed to be their own master, but, again this is not the case in Hong Kong.

In exercising their near-autocratic powers, administrative civil servants in the past enjoyed a high degree of 'political' autonomy. They were the only dominant players in a politically monolithic environment where they had full control over political and fiscal resources, policy decisions and the allocation of privileges, patronage and appointments, as well as the capacity to arbitrate and resolve societal conflicts. They were used to pretending to be the custodian of the public interest and considering themselves above politics and sectoral interests, although in practice they were allied with the established elite interests (see Barry O'Toole, Chapter 6).

Amidst post-1997 demands for increased accountability and reduced autonomy, the civil service faces a political crossroads. In their search for a clearer constitutional identity, the muddled nature of the political system has not helped to steer a way forward. It is, however, not true to say that the autonomy and accountability of the Hong Kong civil service had remained unchanged throughout the years. On the contrary, the bureaucracy undertook significant trajectories in the past few decades on both fronts, due to external pressures and internal innovations. Before discussing the challenges imposed by the new Special Administrative Region (SAR)[1] political order, it is useful to review those past developments (see Figure 1).

	Before 1960s	**1970s – mid-1980s**	**Mid-1980s – 1997**
Autonomy	*Administrative domination:* • Administerization of society • Bureaucratic polity • Preservation of public order and stability and self-sufficiency	*Bureaucratic rejuvenation:* • CDO scheme • Quasi-ministerization of policy officials • McKinsey reforms • ICAC	*Institutional reforms:* • Public sector reform • Customer-orientation • Managerialization strategies to re-manage internal and external constituencies • Further politicization of policy officials
Accountability	*Government by discussion and co-optation:* • Administrative absorption of elite interest • An exclusionary corporatist system	*Government for the community:* • Organizing the community • State interventions and services • Inclusionary state	*Accountability reforms:* • District administration scheme • Representative government • Integrity enhancement initiatives (Ombudsman, open government, access to information, privacy protection) • Facing the legislature and the media

[CDO= City District Office; ICAC= Independent Commission Against Corruption]

Figure 1
Major changes in the autonomy and accountability of the Hong Kong civil service under British colonial rule

Authoritarian autonomy (until the 1960s)

Up to the late 1960s the conventional form of colonial administration had been followed whereby senior civil servants, mainly administrative class officers who were recruited from Britain, acted as 'political officers' as in other typical British colonies (Lugard, 1970), to keep an effective control over the indigenous population with the assistance of co-opted local Chinese leaders, under a regime of indirect rule where social problems and politics were 'administerized'. Under the doctrine of self-sufficiency the colonial government performed the minimum state functions of keeping law and order and of providing some essential public works. The indigenous Chinese population was basically left alone, living under their own Chinese law and customs and looked after by their own community leaders. How to cope with societal demands had always been a key preoccupation of the bureaucrats: their concern was how to contain and suppress 'societal politics' and to maintain administrative domination.

A process of 'administrative absorption of politics' was pursued whereby 'the government co-opts the political forces, often represented by elite groups, into an administrative decision-making body, thus achieving some level of elite integration' (King, 1981, p.130). G.B. Endacott (1964, p.229) rationalized such a system as 'government by discussion', serving a community 'in which the ends of government are accepted without cleavage' and providing 'an efficient administration within an accepted social and economic framework, bound up with a laissez-faire economy' (p.244).

Using A. Stepan's concept (1978), the early colonial state could also be depicted as an 'exclusionary corporatist state' which only incorporated local Chinese social and business elites but provided for minimal interaction and integration between 'state' and 'society' (i.e. the local predominantly Chinese society). The stability of the regime was built on a low level of popular mobilization and participation. This absence of political activity and the transient and refugee mentality of the early population, reinforced a sense of political apathy and impotence (Miners, 1975; Rear, 1971). Preservation of the social order and stability, being the primary value of the colonial civil service, was founded on an acquiescent local elite and a non-demanding population inculcated with a culture of 'utilitarianistic familism' (Lau, 1982). The relationship between government and people was not that of accountability to the people, but subordination of the people.

Autonomy with some legitimacy: Strengthening the administrative regime (from the 1970s to the mid-1980s)

The period from the early 1970s to the mid-1980s (prior to the conclusion of the Sino-British talks on the future of Hong Kong) can be broadly described as one of bureaucratic rejuvenation by the civil service, mainly under the leadership of the reform-minded Governor Sir Murray MacLehose (until 1981). Such rejuvenation aimed at establishing a basis of legitimacy for a strengthened administrative regime to govern in the absence of a popular mandate, through various means of institutional and community building efforts.

The 1967 Communist-inspired riots revealed deep-seated problems of government legitimacy and elite-mass integration (King, 1981). Departing from the previous hands-off approach of indirect rule, the colonial bureaucracy now aimed at adopting a style of governance which was more proactive and people-oriented. A new City District Office (CDO) scheme was introduced in 1968, with young locally-recruited administrative officers posted to various districts to better coordinate government activities at the local level and to bring government closer to the people. Their role was to explain government policies and report back community opinions and sentiments to central agencies. Short of a participative democracy, some kind of two-way political communication was put in place. CDOs set up mutual aid committees and owners' corporations in residential blocks and area committees at the district level, which together with permanent territory-wide campaigns like the Clean Hong Kong Campaign and the Fight Crime Campaign, helped to instill a sense of community belonging and identity.

At the same time, the civil service was modernized through management reorganization. The 1973 review by management consultants McKinsey and Company, was likened by some (Harris, 1988, pp.135-41) to the 1968 Fulton Report on the reform of the British civil service. It proposed reorganizing the Government Secretariat into a number of 'policy' and 'resource' branches headed by super-secretaries; strengthening policy and programme coordination among government departments; and streamlining resource allocation processes in line with the rationalist approach to public administration then popular in North America and Western Europe. Top administrative officers who occupied the new 'branch' portfolios were expected to behave increasingly as quasi-ministers. In 1974 MacLehose established the Independent Commission Against Corruption (ICAC) which was highly successful in breaking up corruption syndicates within government departments and in educating the public not to accept bribes or to bribe public officials. The ICAC represented not just a major institutional innovation, but was also a 'charismatic institution' to help regain legitimacy for the unelected government.

By the mid-1980s the Hong Kong government was clearly no longer the *laissez faire* regime it used to be. Public housing, education, healthcare and welfare services were vastly expanded and labour reforms were pursued. Large-scale transport and new town infrastructural projects were also started. With economic growth and affluence becoming almost the sole criterion to legitimize colonial rule, the government's interventionist strategies were geared towards capitalist accumulation as its *raison d'etre*.[2] In order to subdue and contain societal politics, the colonial bureaucracy had opted for institutional rejuvenation and proactive policy interventions, moving towards a more 'inclusionary' form of state corporatism (Stepan, 1978), so as to strengthen both the institutional capacity and legitimacy of the administrative regime.

Autonomy with some accountability: Nurturing a political regime during the post-1984 transition

Continuing the 1970s efforts of institutional and community building, the political transition period following the 1984 Sino-British Joint Declaration saw significant changes in the political and institutional aspects. These included promoting accountability reforms in line with the British Government's decolonization agenda for Hong Kong; building a representative government rooted in the local population; and initiating public sector reforms, partly in response to global public management reform trends and partly to achieve some kind of depoliticization of the civil service in the light of political changes.

Introducing accountability

In 1980 a district administration scheme was launched, introducing 'district boards' which were partially elected on a universal franchise (Hong Kong Government, 1980),[3] to advise the government on any matters affecting the well-being of those residing or working in the district. The district administration scheme was subsequently subsumed within what the government claimed to be the basic layer of Hong Kong's three-tier system of representative government comprising district boards, municipal councils and the Legislative Council (Hong Kong Government, 1987, Ch. II). The introduction of 'representative government' was part of the British

Government's decolonization agenda to transfer the powers of administration to a locally-rooted system (Hong Kong Government, 1984a, 1984b). Political reforms during the post-1984 transition were pursued amidst China's suspicion and objection, by a civil service elite still keen to retain executive control.

Attempts at establishing some degree of political accountability were aligned with further initiatives to enhance integrity. These included the establishment of a Commissioner for Administrative Complaints in 1989 (renamed the Ombudsman in 1996), a Commissioner for Privacy in 1996, and the promotion of open government and access to information. Under Governor Chris Patten, who set an example for public accountability by introducing his own Governor's Question Time in the Legislative Council, senior civil servants had to actively explain government policies and behave in an increasingly ministerial fashion by addressing matters of public concern before the media and in Legislative Council panels. Patten also introduced performance pledges for all government departments and public agencies, and annual policy progress reports and policy commitments for all Policy Secretaries.

Following direct elections in 1991 which saw the rise of the first generation of elected 'politicians' claiming to have the popular mandate, the Legislative Council had become more assertive and demanding of the administration. Chief Secretary Anson Chan brought out the sentiments of her senior civil service colleagues when she slammed legislators in 1994 for 'using every available public opportunity to criticize and belittle' civil servants (*Eastern Express,* 27 October 1994). The attitudes of senior civil servants towards the move to representative government remained ambivalent. According to a 1994 survey, only 59.9 per cent of directorate officials felt they should be accountable to the Legislative Council while 24.0 per cent felt otherwise and 16.1 per cent were not sure (Lee, 1994, pp.42-7). Tensions continued between the senior civil servants' desire to retain their political autonomy and their official rhetoric about respecting the need to be accountable to the legislature and to promote democracy.

Institutional reforms to promote managerial power

With the launch of the 'Public Sector Reform' programme in 1989, the administration began to focus on management reforms which promoted efficiency and served to strengthen managerial autonomy. New reforms included: the setting up of self-accounting trading funds and rationalization of public corporations and non-departmental public bodies; devolution of resource management responsibilities and budgetary reforms; greater emphasis on the 'policy' management functions of the policy branches (now renamed bureaux); procedural and structural changes within the civil service to promote awareness of costs and results; and the transformation of civil servants from administrators into better managers (Finance Branch, 1989; Cheung, 1992).

What makes Hong Kong an odd case in the current global trend of public sector reform is the fact that reforms were neither driven by social or economic problems, nor the result of a perceived decline in administrative efficiency (Cheung, 1996b). The official reason was that 'stimulated by Hong Kong's economic success, the community is quite rightly demanding more and better public services' and hence the civil service had to become more efficient, not only to improve financial and performance management, but also to address the more qualitative aspect of its work, in particular customer and staff issues (Efficiency Unit, 1995, p.3). As has been argued elsewhere, what 'efficiency' has contributed to public sector reform is very often in terms of providing a rhetoric of *realpolitik* to enable complex patterns of political and intra-bureaucratic interests to be articulated within the shifting practice of public administration (Cheung, 1996b). In the case of Hong Kong, public sector reform measures can be viewed as a set of strategic responses to reshape the public sector institutional configuration, so as to 're-manage' the changing realities of both internal and external constituencies within the new political order, thus strengthening the institutional capacity of the civil service to face new challenges to its autonomy.

Crises of autonomy and accountability: Dilemmas after 1997

The logic of democratization and decolonization, if followed through in Hong Kong in her transition to become a highly autonomous SAR, would have required the civil service to be politically *less autonomous* and *more accountable*. However, the reality points to a blurred scenario where senior civil servants do not all necessarily accept less autonomy and greater accountability, and where the new political order does not allow them to be so even if some may prefer to play a more back-seat role as politically neutral bureaucrats.

Not used to subjugating itself to local political forces, the senior civil service was seen to have tried hard during the process of political transition to assert its authority by politically downsizing the legislature and restructuring institutional arrangements through public sector reform so as to maintain a degree of effective control over the changing external environment. Nevertheless, with the notions of citizen rights, democracy and accountability now commonly accepted as the foundations of a modern society such as Hong Kong, whether it likes it or not, the civil service has to cope with more challenges to its hitherto unquestioned supremacy. Both the political and administrative worlds of the civil service have definitely become more complex and multifaceted, giving rise to a crisis of political identity for senior civil servants.

The resistance to role change of senior civil servants

W. Seibel (1996, p.74) has described the key feature of the German administration as follows: 'What characterizes German public administration since the eighteenth century is its early modernization relative to the political'. A well-developed administrative system in advance of its political institutions was considered instrumental in allowing Germany to function even when the political regime collapsed, as it did in 1918 and again in 1945. There is a high degree of similarity between Seibel's depiction of German public administration and the administrative state of Hong Kong in both colonial times and the present SAR era. The fact is the *political* regime was virtually non-existent during the years of colonial rule, thus enabling the civil service *administrative* regime to expand in powers and functions, taking upon itself roles which otherwise would have been played by properly constituted democratic institutions. The civil service's self-reforming capacities were amply demonstrated during the 1970s and 1980s when it survived a series of social and economic turmoils. Such capacities were partly imposed by sheer circumstances under which there were just no other effective institutions in society to share with it the responsibilities of governance. They were also partly created by senior administrators who saw themselves as the real rulers and who were willing to take the necessary adjustment and renewal initiatives, whether political, administrative or managerial, when times and situations so demanded. In the process a strong administrative regime had been established.

Having gone through years of bureaucratic reforms and localization, and been cast in the role of providing the major basis of stability and continuity to SAR governance, the senior civil service, in particular the administrative civil servants, emerged as a powerful governing force. Any expectation that this senior civil service would now quietly settle into an instrumental, politically-neutral administrative arm of the government was probably unrealistic. The process of 'ministerialization' of the top administrative civil servants since the McKinsey reforms gave rise to a new hybrid of *political-bureaucrats*, even more tightly organized and more united both in ethos and in the will to govern, than elected politicians. In practice they now form the 'government party'. As far as they are concerned they are the 'Executive'. They still try to preserve their political and administrative autonomy as in the past. Their vision is more guided by the 'getting things done' kind of administrative pragmatism than by values such as democratic accountability.

The administration-biased nature of the SAR political system

The advent of 'representative government' and its concomitant process of political representation of societal interests has not resulted in any loosening of administrative power in the real sense. On the one hand, senior civil servants are unwilling to give up their powers of governance. On the other hand, the political representatives elected by geographical popular interests and industrial and professional functional interests[4] were prevented by the Basic Law to take up the powers of governance from the civil service. In the minds of the Chinese Government and her appointed Basic Law drafters when finalizing the mini-constitution, the imperative to continue with Hong Kong's 'executive-led' tradition dictated that the government should be placed in the safer hands of senior civil servants rather than politicians.

Such a paradox has created uncertainties in the role and values of senior civil servants. While political change and constitutional rhetoric imply that they should move towards becoming a politically neutral and accountable institution of public administration serving the interests of the community as articulated through political elections, in practice senior civil servants, particularly those holding policy-making powers at the Secretary level, are still responsible for both policy and administration. Instead of having the politicians taking up the functions of articulating, brokering and integrating diverse interests in society, such functions continue to fall squarely on top civil servants who are expected to lead rather than to follow. The introduction of the political representation of interests has not, therefore, created a strong 'political' regime.

After the establishment of the SAR, the 'political regime' is still not much in sight. The new Chief Executive has yet to create an executive institution of his own. The Legislative Council's functions and powers have been severely curbed by the constitutional provisions of the Basic Law.[5] Political parties and groups which emerged during the pre-1997 transition are still in their formative stage and have yet to develop an effective role in the new SAR system of governance.

Challenges from within the 'executive authority'

Tung Chee-hwa seemed to be seeing eye to eye with the bureaucrats when he campaigned on a platform of depoliticization.[6] However, Tung also claimed he would exercise 'strong leadership' and expected the non-civil service members of his Executive Council to play a more prominent political role in formulating policy blueprints and promoting government policies. A vocal and assertive Executive Council team would certainly provide an important bulwark to counter-balance the power and influence of the top civil service team headed by Chief Secretary Anson Chan, seen by some pro-Beijing elements as a protégé of Governor Patten.[7] While previous members of the Governor's Executive Council owed their position and status to the senior civil servants who nominated them, and worked as the latter's loyal partners rather than political competitors, Tung's Executive Councillors are his own choice and owe their political allegiance to him, rather than to the bureaucracy.

Despite Tung's denial of any intention to move towards a ministerial system of political appointees, the nightmare of top mandarins is that Tung might one day reduce or take away their policy-making powers, rendering them as simply 'civil servants'. Two competing 'executive-led' models are interfacing: the mandarins favouring a civil service-dominated system, and Tung and his advisers probably preferring a more presidential kind of executive government. In the short run, Tung has to depend much on the senior civil service for implementing policies effectively and for maintaining a smooth-running administration. He could not afford to alienate the mandarins. However, in the long run, as he accumulates more experience of governance and greater political capital, particularly if he plans to run for a second term in 2002 as most expect him to do, Tung may be tempted to cause a wider reshuffling of his team of principal officials.[8]

Impact of the change in public trust of the civil service

The extent to which the senior civil service can hold the balance of power in the new government depends largely on both its competence in governance and its meritocratic integrity as perceived by the public at large. The hitherto good image of the civil service has been seriously questioned and subsequently damaged by a series of incidents and crises occuring after the transfer of sovereignty, causing many to doubt its institutional competence and ability to provide leadership.

In December 1997 the messy way in which government departments executed a quickly conceived plan to slaughter over 1.2 million chickens in the territory in a bid to stop the spread of the 'bird flu' sounded the first major alarm. This was then followed by several health and food scare incidents, the red tide incident, the failure to cope with unemployment and other problems created by economic recession, and most seriously the chaos surrounding the opening of Hong Kong's new expensive international airport at Chek Lap Kok in July 1998, which finally began to convince some that the days of the myth of civil service invincibility are gone.

The civil service is also subject to an integrity crisis of a different kind. From late 1998 the Director of Audit has published several damaging value-for-money reports which accused outdoor staff of several departments (Water Supplies, Housing, and Urban Services) of over-reporting their working hours and being poorly supervised. These generated public outcries against the sleaze of civil servants whose better pay and conditions *vis-à-vis* private sector employees facing lay-offs and salary cutbacks have not helped to find sympathy. An incident involving the Director of Social Welfare travelling on a government-paid first-class air flight to attend an international conference in Israel, with a stopover in Britain for private matters, was severely criticized by the media and the public as being extravagant and out of tune with the present economic recession, not to mention that he was spearheading a government campaign to review the Comprehensive Social Security Assistance scheme with an aim to reducing benefits to some so-called 'unworthy' and 'lazy' welfare recipients. The refusal by top civil servants to take responsibility for the new airport saga, even after the release of critical reports by a special committee of inquiry, the Legislative Council and the Ombudsman, further reinforced the public dismay with the institutional competence and integrity of the hitherto sacrosanct bureaucracy.[9] In August 1999 the Commissioner of Inland Revenue had his contract terminated for failing to report his wife's business as a tax consultant, and for having infringed departmental guidelines by directly ruling on 7 tax cases in which his wife acted as tax representative. Both the upper echelons and the rank-and-file of the civil service are subject to waves of bureaucrat-bashing.

Without public support and the basis of legitimacy it provides, it will be difficult for the administrative civil servants to steer a strong path in face of challenges from various political players. Partly to face up to the public uproar and to pacify angry legislators, but more importantly to take the opportunity to shape up the civil service, Tung Chee-hwa announced major plans on 15 January 1999 to review existing systems for the discipline and performance appraisal of civil servants and to link pay and conditions to performance. A consultation document on *Civil Service Reform* was published in March 1999 (Civil Service Bureau) which called for a revamp of civil service performance management, with the aims to introduce more flexible appointments and eventually turn all basic rank staff into contract staff. The document also argues in favour of bringing 'outsiders' into senior ranks of the civil service through lateral entry instead of relying solely on internal promotion. In the name of improving civil service personnel management, the opportunity has been created to allow the Chief Executive to appoint non-civil servants to senior and top posts in the future. Rank-and-file civil servants are bewildered by the impact of reform on their job security, while some senior civil servants begin to sense a potential threat to their hitherto monopoly over governmental power. The time right now seems politically bad for senior civil servants to try to assert their autonomy and power.

Conclusion

In the absence of competitive and democratic politics, senior civil servants historically exercised almost unchallenged 'rulership' over Hong Kong. This historical legacy which has continued very much until today despite the change of sovereignty, is beginning to encounter institutional tensions. To the senior civil servants, two major problems have arisen. *First*, the domination by administrative power and administrative values and discretions of the decision-making system has suppressed the development of other important values such as political responsibility and democratic checks and balances. Civil servants have to learn to be politically accountable and are reluctant to do so quickly. *Second*, public expectations of the performance of the civil service are now two-fold: the institution is being appraised in terms of both its political and administrative competence. In other words, administrative domination now carries both political power and political risk.

At present, senior civil servants in Hong Kong as elsewhere have to be accountable for their performance in terms of policy delivery and outcome, as well as the use of public resources. In such accountability, they are being monitored and checked by several institutions – the Legislative Council, the Director of Audit and the Ombudsman, apart from their superior the Chief Executive. In terms of political accountability, even if senior civil servants became resigned to accepting a role subordinate to the 'political masters', the question remains as to whom their political masters are. Constitutionally speaking, the Chief Executive appoints all top civil servants and the whole civil service should be at his disposal in the exercise of his governmental authority. Yet, in the present circumstances of Hong

Kong, where the Chief Executive is not popularly elected but widely seen as someone hand-picked by Beijing and only nominally elected by an election committee without popular mandate, there is much pressure for civil servants also to be accountable to the elected Legislative Council, and through it to the electorate.

The notion of democratic accountability of the senior civil service, even if the matter is put on the reform agenda, is still indeterminate. The issue will involve not only a shift of attitudes, core values and expectations, but also the clarification of institutional relationships and constitutional doctrine. Senior civil servants have to settle for the role of an influential administrative power in partnership with a political regime in some form of 'shared leadership'. To achieve that, not only has the political regime to be further nurtured and strengthened, but it has also to be sorted out how that political regime is to be constituted in terms of the interface between the Chief Executive and the Legislative Council. The search for the political identity of the senior civil service cannot be divorced from the democratic evolution of Hong Kong's system of governance which right now is in a kind of quagmire.

Notes

1. Hong Kong reverted to China on 1 July 1997 to become a special administrative region with a high degree of autonomy under its Basic Law promulgated in April 1990.
2. By the early 1980s, then Financial Secretary Philip Haddon-Cave (1984) preferred to describe the government philosophy as one of 'positive non-interventionism' implying the state's readiness to intervene when industries with social obligations ran into trouble and when an institution needed regulation to prevent inequitable practice.
3. District Boards became fully elected on universal franchise in 1994 under the Patten political reform.
4. In the first 10 years of the SAR, the Basic Law provides that the Legislative Council should mainly consist of two types of legislators, those directly elected by geographical constituencies (from 20 seats in 1997 to 30 by 2003, with the increased seats to be drawn from a transient electoral college) and those elected by functional constituencies of industrial, business and professional interests.
5. Under Article 74 of the Basic Law, legislators may not introduce bills relating to public expenditure or political structure or the operation of the government. The written consent of the Chief Executive is required

before bills relating to government policies are introduced. Furthermore, the adoption of bicameral voting (between directly-elected members and functionally-elected members: Annex II Section II of Basic Law) ensures that as long as the two categories of legislators do not see eye to eye in political stances and policy orientations, there is little opportunity for the Legislative Council to pass any motion or resolution of its own.
6. Tung asked, for example, 'Is our civil service too bogged down in the politics of our legislative process? Should they be devoting more time and energy to the formulation and efficient implementation of policies?' (Tung, 1996).
7. The first battle over who should be in charge of government policy formulation was fought in late March 1997 (before Tung assumed office) when top civil servants expressed great displeasure over Tung's appointment of three of his Executive Councillors to lead policy teams comprising policy Secretaries to formulate policy proposals on housing, education and elderly welfare, for inclusion in his forthcoming inauguration speech. In face of the bureaucratic opposition and a media uproar over the potential role conflict, Tung was forced to back down by emphasizing that those three Executive Councillors would simply perform a research role and not convene any formal policy teams. The relationship between the Executive Councillors and top civil servants continued to be tense after the transfer of sovereignty. One example is the delay by the administration to nominate Antony Leung as the new chairman of the Education Commission, despite it being well known that Leung was Tung's choice and his assigned Executive Councillor to look after education.
8. Tung has already appointed a non-civil servant Elsie Leung as Secretary of Justice. It was widely rumoured in early 1999 that a pro-Beijing politician Wan Ka-shuen was being considered for appointment as Solicitor General. He subsequently withdrew his application for the job because of strong opposition from the legal community and the Democratic Party to his appointment. Rumours also abound that consideration is being given to appoint all Secretary-rank officials in future on fixed-term contracts so that suitable civil servants would first retire from the civil service in order to take up the posts as political appointees, thus paving the way for more non-civil service appointments to be made. When Tung announced in March 1999 the postponement of Anson Chan's retirement as Chief Secretary until 2002, he indirectly created the practice of his top officials staying in office in line with his own term, hence paving the way for future 'ministerial' appointments to be made

to tie in with the Chief Executive's term of office. In July Tung announced the appointment of Dr. E.K. Yeoh, chief of the Hospital Authority and a non-civil servant, to be Secretary for Health and Welfare upon the retirement of the incumbent civil servant Katherine Fok.
9. Some newspapers called for those responsible top officials of the government and the Airport Authority to resign. The Legislative Council inquiry even pointed its fingers to Chief Secretary Anson Chan who was subsequently forced by circumstances to extend her apology without reservation at the Legislative Council's debate on 3 February 1999.

References

Aberbach, J.D., Putnam, R.D. and Rockman, B.A. (1981), *Bureaucrats and Politics in Western Democracies*, Cambridge, Mass: Harvard University Press.
Campbell, Colin (1993), 'Public Service and Democratic Accountability', in Richard A. Chapman (ed.), *Ethics in Public Service*, Edinburgh: Edinburgh University Press, pp.117-34.
Cheung, A.B.L. (1992), 'Public Sector Reform in Hong Kong: Perspectives and Problems', *Asian Journal of Public Administration* Vol. 14, pp.115-48.
Cheung, A.B.L. (1996a), 'Performance Pledges – Power to the Consumer or a Quagmire in Public Service Legitimation?', *International Journal of Public Administration* Vol. 19, pp.233-60.
Cheung, A.B.L. (1996b), 'Efficiency as the Rhetoric? Public-Sector Reform in Hong Kong Explained', *International Review of Administrative Sciences* Vol. 62, pp.31-47.
Cheung, A.B.L. (1997), 'Rebureaucratization of Politics in Hong Kong: Prospects after 1997', *Asian Survey* Vol. XXXVII, pp.720-37.
Civil Service Bureau (1999), *Civil Service into the 21st Century*, Civil Service Reform consultation document, March, Hong Kong.
Eastern Express, 27 October 1994, Hong Kong.
Efficiency Unit (Hong Kong Government) (1995), *Serving the Community*, Hong Kong: Government Printer.
Endacott, G.B. (1964), *Government and People in Hong Kong, 1841-1962: A Constitutional History*, Hong Kong: Hong Kong University Press.
Finance Branch (Hong Kong Government) (1989), *Public Sector Reform*, February, Hong Kong.
Haddon-Cave, P. (1984), [1980] 'The Making of Some Aspects of Public Policy in Hong Kong' (Introduction to the First Edition) in D.G. Lethbridge (ed.), *The Business Environment in Hong Kong*, Hong Kong: Oxford University Press.

Harris, P. (1978), *Hong Kong: A Study in Bureaucratic Politics*, Hong Kong: Heinemann Asia.

Harris, P. (1988), *Hong Kong: A Study in Bureaucracy and Politics*, Hong Kong: Macmillan.

Hong Kong Government (1980), *Green Paper: A Pattern of District Administration in Hong Kong*, June, Hong Kong: Government Printer.

Hong Kong Government (1984a), *Green Paper: The Further Development of Representative Government in Hong Kong*, July, Hong Kong: Government Printer.

Hong Kong Government (1984b), *White Paper: The Further Development of Representative Government in Hong Kong*, November, Hong Kong: Government Printer.

Hong Kong Government (1987), *Green Paper: The 1987 Review of Developments in Representative Government*, May, Hong Kong: Government Printer.

Hood, C. (1991), 'A Public Management for All Seasons?', *Public Administration* Vol. 69, pp.3-19.

Huque, Ahmed Shafiqul, Lee, Grace O.M. and Cheung, A.B.L. (1998), *The Civil Service in Hong Kong: Continuity and Change*, Hong Kong: Hong Kong University Press.

King, Ambrose Y.C. (1980), 'An Institutional Response to Corruption: the ICAC of Hong Kong', in C.K. Leung, J.W. Cushman and G. Wang (eds), *Hong Kong: Dilemmas of Growth*, Canberra: Research School of Pacific Studies, Australian National University, and Hong Kong: Centre of Asian Studies, The University of Hong Kong.

King, Ambrose Y.C. (1981), 'Administrative Absorption of Politics in Hong Kong: Emphasis on the Grass Roots Level', in Ambrose Y.C. King and Rance P.L. Lee (eds), *Social Life and Development in Hong Kong*, Hong Kong: The Chinese University Press, pp.127-46.

Lau, S.K. (1982), *Society and Politics in Hong Kong*, Hong Kong: The Chinese University Press.

Lee, J. (1994), 'Civil Servants', in D.H. McMillen and S.W. Man (eds), *The Other Hong Kong Report 1994*, Hong Kong: The Chinese University Press, pp. 39-60.

Lugard, F.J.D. (1970), *Political Memoranda: Revision of the Instructions to Political Officers on Subjects Chiefly Political and Administrative, 1913-1918*, third edition, International Specialized Book Service.

McKinsey & Co. (1973), *The Machinery of Government: A New Framework for Expanding Services*, Hong Kong: Government Printer.

Miners, N.J. (1975), 'Hong Kong: A Case Study in Political Stability', *The Journal of Commonwealth and Comparative Politics* Vol. 13, pp.26-39.

Montanheiro, Luiz (1998), 'Searching for a set of values in the ethical behaviour of the public sector', in A. Hondeghem (ed), *Ethics and Accountability in a Context of Governance and New Public Management*, Amsterdam: IOS Press.

Rear, J. (1971), 'One Brand of Politics', in K. Hopkins (ed), *Hong Kong: The Industrial Colony*, Hong Kong: Oxford University Press, pp.55-139.

Scott, I. (1989), *Political Change and the Crisis of Legitimacy in Hong Kong*, Hong Kong: Oxford University Press.

Seibel, W. (1996), 'Administrative Science as Reform: German Public Administration', *Public Administration Review* Vol. 56, pp.74-81.

Stepan, A. (1978), *The State and Society: Peru in Comparative Perspective*, NJ: Princeton University Press.

The Basic Law of the Hong Kong Special Administrative Region of the People's Republic of China (1990), Hong Kong: The Consultative Committee for the Basic Law of the Hong Kong Special Administrative Region of the People's Republic of China.

The Sino-British Joint Declaration on the Question of Hong Kong (1984), [Joint Declaration of the Government of the United Kingdom of Great Britain and Northern Ireland and the Government of the People's Republic of China on the Question of Hong Kong], September, Hong Kong: Government Printer.

Tsang, Steve Y.S. (1988), *Democracy Shelved: Great Britain, China, and Attempts at Constitutional Reform in Hong Kong, 1945-1952*, Hong Kong: Oxford University Press.

Tung, Chee-hwa (1996), *Building a 21st Century Hong Kong Together*, 22 October, Hong Kong.

13 Ethics, Governance, and Constitutions: The Case of Baron Haussmann

John A. Rohr

This chapter is a product of a year's research (1998-1999) at the Woodrow Wilson Center in Washington, working on a comparative study that examines the relationship between constitutional principles and administrative institutions in Canada, France, the United Kingdom, and the United States. Building upon a previously published article (Rohr, 1998, pp.103-19), the research project aims at offering a gentle corrective to some of the excesses seen in the New Public Management (NPM) literature. The purpose here is to remind the public administration community that managerial innovations cannot change the fact that administration is governance. Many other things it may be as well, but it remains a form of governance. The constitutional foundations of administrative practice underscores this point because in the aforementioned countries there is nothing more inherently governmental than a constitution.

Although the writer's project encompasses a broad range of public administration questions, this chapter deals only with ethics. One of the advantages of grounding the study of public service ethics in a country's constitutional tradition is that the connection between ethics and governance is *immediate*, i.e., it need not be *mediated* by the customary philosophical doctrines of deontology, utilitarianism, or natural law and their progeny. Important as these philosophical teachings are, their writ runs far beyond public service ethics and gives the discussion an upward tilt toward timeless truths that risk losing touch with the highly contingent, fact-driven world of ethics in public administration. Witness the marked tendency to explain deontology in terms of Kant's famous condemnation of all forms of lying (Kant, 1994, pp.280-1). Kant's argument is at its best when one considers questions of purely personal rectitude. A good man does not lie. It is less convincing when the discussion turns to lying for reasons of state, e.g., to foil speculators ready to diminish the value of one's nation's currency. The outcome may well be the same – don't lie – but even the most convinced deontologist will acknowledge that the argument is more complicated than it was at the purely personal level.

There is a problem, however, with the constitutional approach to ethics: its inherent relativism. Since constitutions differ from one country to another, so will the ethical standards derived from them. It should be noted, however, that constitutionally based relativism is far more capable of yielding meaningful standards than its vulgar, curbstone counterpart that finds the ultimate wisdom in the tired, old question: 'Who are you to impose your values on me?'

To illustrate the link between relativism and meaningful standards, consider the current debate in the United States over the implementation of the Government Performance and Results Act (GPRA) a statute passed in 1993 aimed at enhancing administrative performance by requiring the legislative and executive branches to work closely together in developing and integrating 'strategic plans', 'annual performance plans', and 'annual performance results'. If implemented wisely, the statute offers American public servants an opportunity for significant ethical action in trying to correct recent excesses in the always stressful relations between Congress and the executive departments. This issue arises only because of the American constitutional principle of separation of powers. It would make no sense in a parliamentary regime. In this sense it is of *relative* ethical value, but it is capable of yielding meaningful ethics standards for American public servants who take seriously their oath to uphold the constitution of their country.

Although the GPRA provides no direct and specific guidance for administrators in parliamentary regimes, it may serve to expand their moral imagination by stimulating them to reflect on how a set of interesting American principles might be creatively adapted to efforts to improve performance in their own countries. Pursuing this goal of expanding moral imagination, the study considers several examples from earlier times, among them the story of Baron Haussmann whose administrative career is here examined. Haussmann's virtues and vices are best understood as functions of the regime of Napoleon III whom Haussmann served so well.

To provide context for the discussion of Haussmann, other topics in the study will examine the peculiar ethical problems of such administrators as pre-civil war postmasters in the United States who faced enormous pressure to refuse to deliver abolitionist pamphlets within slave-holding states (John, 1995); Quebec technocrats who chafed under the limitations of provincial government and yearned for an independent state as a worthy domain for their administrative talents (Lachapelle, 1993); and British civil servants who learned to vary their application of the constitutional principle of civil service anonymity with the vagaries of the concomitant principle of ministerial responsibility (Woodhouse, 1994).

Haussmann's Life and Times: A Brief Overview

Georges-Eugène Haussmann was born in Paris in 1809. He attended the prestigious Lycée Henri IV, then as now, a wise choice for parents with grand ambitions for their children. After studying law at the Sorbonne, he entered the prefectoral corps in 1831 and proceeded to fill a wide variety of administrative posts during the Orleanist regime of Louis Philippe, the 'citizen king'. He was serving as prefect of the Gironde when, in 1853, Emperor Napoleon III appointed him Prefect of the Seine, 'the most important administrative appointment in the administrative state' (Jordan, 1995, p.49), a position he held until a financial scandal led to his dismissal in 1870. He served briefly, but without distinction, in the Chamber of Deputies of the Third Republic. Haussmann died in 1891.

He is best known for bringing about nothing less than the transformation of Paris with the grand boulevards and elegant parks that grace that city today. No less important were his stunning improvements in sanitation, lighting, and transportation. Neither Haussmann's friends nor his foes nor Haussmann himself would dispute the judgment of Napoleon III that he was a 'great administrator' (Jordan, 1995, p.180). Haussmann's spectacular successes were due primarily to his effective and, at times, ruthless use of power which, in turn, rested on his informal status as a favourite of Emperor Napoleon III and his formal status as Prefect of the Seine, a position which made him the de facto mayor of Paris.

Since this chapter focuses on the relationship between constitutions and administration, here is a brief chronology of the constitutional changes during Haussmann's lifetime. He was born under the Empire of Napoleon I, which was replaced by the Bourbon Restoration of 1815, and which, in turn, yielded to the Orleanist regime, also known as the July Monarchy, in the revolution of 1830. In 1848, another revolution brought the Second Republic to power whose president, Louis Napoleon, a nephew of the first Napoleon, was elected by popular vote. In 1851, Louis Napoleon led a *coup d'état* against the republic he headed, an action legitimated by the overwhelming support he received in a plebiscite. The next year saw the establishment of the Second Empire with Napoleon III at its head. In 1870, France suffered a crushing defeat in the Franco-Prussian War, which ended the Second Empire. After the bloody suppression of the Paris Commune in 1871, the first steps were taken toward what would eventually emerge as the Third Republic with a series of constitutional laws voted in 1875.

Virtues and vices

Haussmann's vices are more interesting for our purposes than his virtues because they are more directly related to the constitutional standards of the regime in which he flourished. To do justice to his memory, however, the brighter side of his character should not be ignored.

Virtues

To do this, the common misapprehension that the splendid, wide boulevards he designed for Paris were really military highways intended to move troops more quickly against oppressed and unruly Parisians should be corrected. Although military considerations were not entirely irrelevant, far more important were the aesthetic values of open spaces, such practical matters as the public health benefits of clearing out dismal slums and the commercial advantages of expediting the flow of traffic. Military plans, such as they were, had been laid long before Haussmann's arrival. The rue de Rivoli, for example, had been begun by the first Napoleon as a convenient path to dispatch soldiers to the troublesome neighborhoods on the east side of Paris as well as for the aesthetic purpose of leading into an open urban space around the Hotel de Ville. To the extent that military purposes played any part in Haussmann's plans, there is the ironic fact that the most important military use of his boulevards came in 1871 when the supporters of the Paris Commune used them to descend upon the centre of Paris (Jordan, 1995, p.343).

Many of Haussmann's virtues would be welcome in civil servants of any regime, for example, his indomitable energy and his unflagging loyalty to his political master. Although sharp practices in matters of public finance would eventually lead to his downfall, there is no evidence that these practices redounded to his personal financial advantage (Jordan, 1995, p.223). For purposes of ethical analysis, however, his most interesting virtue was surely his clear-headed view of the public interest as he understood it. This virtue is mentioned last not because it is least, but because its problematic character tends to spill over into the category of vice, thereby serving as a bridge between Haussmann's virtues and vices. In his *Mémoires* written after his fall from power, he asserts that '[t]he only practical form of Democracy is the Empire' and that 'I was an imperialist by birth and conviction' (Jordan, 1995, p.5). He explains the link between imperialism and democracy as follows: 'It [imperialism] is a democracy whose authoritarian form assures stability, whose chief receives from the People an indispensable title that allows him to treat on equal footing with the most powerful sovereigns, but whose strong constitution does not permit him to compromise the imprescriptible and inalienable rights of the Nation' (Jordan, 1995, p.335).

Haussmann's commitment to the empire was rivalled only by his devotion to Paris as its centre. In the very first sentence of his *Mémoires,* he introduces himself to the reader as 'quite simply a parvenu Parisian, determined to make a name for himself, even a controversial name, in his beloved natal city'. No small part of the 'controversial name' he won for himself was due to his incessant conflicts with fellow Parisians who saw little advantage for themselves in Haussmann's spectacular public works. Haussmann's reply was characteristically direct: 'Paris belongs to France and not to Parisians by birth or by choice ... [T]he central power, which represents the nation, ought to be armed at Paris with the necessary authority to make the general interest prevail over all the others'. David Jordan summarizes nicely Haussmann's view of the public interest: 'Grandeur, rational order, purposeful and incessant movement, progress, cleanliness, an urban life lived in public are the qualities he forcefully imposed on Paris' (Jordan, 1995, pp.5, 334, 367).

There is something admirable about a man with a firm sense of who he is and what he must do, but something unsettling as well. Jordan had it right in referring to the qualities of life Haussmann '*imposed* on Paris' (emphasis added). Haussmann was a single-minded man. He describes himself as one who always 'followed a direct route, without letting myself to be diverted'. This, he believed, gave him a certain advantage over adversaries more devious than himself: 'clever men, little accustomed to the straight and narrow, did not lie in wait for me along this road'. Those who dared to cross the self-righteous Haussmann paid dearly for their transgressions: 'I strike back with usury,' said he (Jordan, 1995, p.5).

Vices

Baron Haussmann was not a pleasant man. To find flaws in his character is not difficult. Indeed, such an endeavour is soon overwhelmed with an embarrassment of riches. To keep the discussion of Haussmann's vices within manageable bounds, only three of them are mentioned here: arrogance, sharp practices and political meddling.

Arrogance

An arrogant public official is unwelcome in any regime, but the offence is less serious in an authoritarian one. Haussmann was insufferably arrogant by any standard, but the long success he enjoyed under the Second Empire suggests that the authoritarian milieu of the regime spared him the early dismissal he almost certainly would have merited had he served during a republican era.

Examples of Haussmann's arrogance abound. Consider his title of 'Baron', which he claimed through his maternal grandfather, Georges-Frédéric Dentzel, a brigadier general under Napoleon I upon whom the latter conferred the title of baron of the empire. Haussmann's critics pointed out that he had no legitimate claim to the title since such honours could not be handed on through the maternal line, but Haussmann felt no embarrassment because 'many of his contemporaries used titles just as questionable'. (Chapman and Chapman 1957, p.150; Des Cars, 1978, p.242).

His arrogance did not escape his superiors. One of the letters in his personnel file from his early days in the provinces notes that in fulfilling his assignments, 'he is inclined to substitute his own personal policy and ideas for those of his superiors, by reason of the excellent opinion he has of his personal merit' (Chapman and Chapman, 1957, p.33). In the same vein, the duc de Perigny, who served as Minister of the Interior in the early years of the Second Empire, recounts in his *Mémoires* the interview in 1853 that prompted him to select Haussmann for what he knew would be the extremely difficult post of Prefect of the Seine. Acknowledging that, paradoxically, he was more impressed by Haussmann's 'character faults' than by 'his remarkable intelligence', he went on to observe that the prospective prefect delighted in explaining the great events of his administrative career and that he 'could have gone on for six hours without stopping provided the conversation stayed on his favourite topic, himself'. Well aware of the toughness the new prefect would need to implement the ambitious urban renewal projects of Napoleon III, Persigny took considerable pleasure in knowing he had the right man. Somewhat ominously, he added, 'while this fascinating personality revealed itself to me with a certain brutal cynicism, I could barely contain my utter satisfaction' (Des Cars, 1978, p.242).

For a good example of Haussmann's high opinion of himself, consider his instructions to the painter charged with decorating the Municipal Council chamber at the Hôtel de Ville in 1865. Four murals were called for. The first three depicted Clovis choosing Paris as his capital, Philippe-Auguste embarking on a crusade to regain the Holy Land, and Francis I establishing the Hôtel de Ville. The fourth mural presented none other than Haussmann himself receiving from Napoleon III the decree annexing several communes adjacent to Paris (Jordan, 1995, p.151).

He enlisted his arrogance in advancing his own career on one of the many occasions when he found himself at odds with the Council of State and Napoleon's ministers. As Prefect of the Seine, Haussmann was technically subordinate to the Minister of the Interior. Ordinarily, this hierarchical disadvantage had little practical significance because Haussmann could usually finesse ministerial opposition by his ready access to the Emperor. In November 1860, Haussmann found several of his projects languishing in the Council of State and various ministerial bureaus. Weary of these delays, he decided to draft a decree for the Emperor's signature creating a new 'Ministry of Paris' with himself as minister. The Emperor found this too bold an innovation, but offered him instead an invitation to attend cabinet meetings as well as an appointment as an extraordinary member of the Council of State. The draft decree Haussmann prepared for the Emperor's signature was accompanied by a letter reminding His Majesty that there was to be a banquet the very next day at which Haussmann was to 'propose the Emperor's health'. To coax the Emperor to sign the decree, he bluntly assured him that 'I should be happy to have a new cause for gratitude for the generosity which your Majesty has already shown me' (Chapman and Chapman, 1957, p.149).[1]

Haussmann's arrogance assumed international implications at a banquet sponsored by the municipality of Paris to honour the King and Queen of Belgium. Having 'by now become very blasé about crowned heads,' Haussmann created quite a stir when he took the Queen by the arm and 'snapped at the King: "Come along, then, King of the Belgians, take Mme Haussmann's arm..." And he led the way to dinner' (Chapman and Chapman, 1957, p.207).

Haussmann's arrogance did not desert him as his career came to an unhappy end. At the first hint in December, 1867, of the revelations of the financial legerdemain which would eventually bring him down, Haussmann stonewalled in the grand style worthy of an imperial favourite:

> Everyone has seen that threats have no effect on an administration convinced of its duty... A great administration knows neither anger

nor resentment. It remains calm and firm in the struggles which it has increasingly to wage against ill-founded pretensions (Chapman and Chapman, 1957, p.226).

The press was not moved. The rumours of scandal continued apace with a string of political misfortunes for the Emperor, which forced him to make significant changes in his cabinet at the end of 1869. The new members of the government were of a more liberal persuasion than their predecessors. Part of the liberal agenda was to demand Haussmann's resignation, a measure in which the Emperor reluctantly acquiesced. Imagine the Emperor's astonishment when his personal letter advising Haussmann that he would have to resign received the following reply: '*I refuse to resign*. I do not wish to appear to evade the difficulties of the final hour. I wish to render my accounts, to pay off the debt of the City, and go out by the main doorway, handing over my administration to my successor in good order'. For good measure he added: 'A man like me does not resign, neither does he cling to power. Either you sack him or keep him' (Chapman and Chapman, 1957, p.239). The Emperor sacked him.

As a final example of Haussmann's arrogance, consider his way of referring to the poor of Paris as 'nomads'. There was a cruel irony in this particular appellation, for these nomads were, as Jordan aptly notes, 'a tribe of his creation, some of them displaced by the demolitions, many newly arrived to enlist in his construction and demolition armies' (Jordan, 1995, p.293). Contempt for such people was a necessary concomitant of Haussmann's administrative triumphs. His interest lay with boulevards, sewers, parks and lighting – areas of state responsibility which benefited rich and poor alike. His favourite metaphor for the city as a body with lungs, bowels and arteries 'considered neither the soul nor the repose of the body itself, neither the citizen nor their daily private lives' (Jordan, 1995, p.295). Had he cared about people as people, he would not have succeeded in his great life work. His arrogance led him to believe his own high-minded rhetoric on public spiritedness which caught so well the spirit of the regime he served so faithfully.

Financial irregularities

A recurring theme throughout Haussmann's long tenure as Prefect of the Seine was the resentment of elected officials toward him. He solved part of this problem in 1855 when he persuaded the Emperor to call for legislation changing the municipal council of Paris from an elected to an appointed body whose members were *de facto* chosen by Haussmann himself and then officially appointed by his nominal superior, the Minister of the Interior (Jordan, 1995, p.216). Parliament, however, presented a more difficult problem. When Haussmann became Prefect of the Seine in 1853, he was pleased to discover that his predecessors had left a modest surplus in the municipal treasury. Although the prevailing orthodoxy of the day, championed by elected officials, held that 'every surplus belongs to the public', Haussmann saw the surplus as the fiscal foundation for an extensive and largely clandestine plan for borrowing the capital needed for the Emperor's ambitious urban renewal projects. Thus, Haussmann embarked on a creative financial adventure that would eventually lead to his downfall, but not before he had accomplished far more than either he or the Emperor dreamed possible at the outset. As a public financier, Haussmann was far ahead of his time. He grasped intuitively the remarkable potential for growth in what would come to be known as deficit spending, but what he called 'productive spending'.

At first he relied upon shrewd schemes of shuttling funds back and forth between the city's 'ordinary' and 'extraordinary' budgets in such a way as to mask the true extent of the city's debt. The key to his system, however, was the establishment of the Public Works Fund for Paris *(Caisse des Travaux de Paris)* in 1858. Not coincidentally, this fund was established at the same time that he annexed the suburbs surrounding Paris. Informed opinion estimated that it would take ten years to provide adequate sewers, lighting, and water in the annexed zone if ordinary revenues alone were relied upon. This was far too long for the impatient prefect. Hence, he prevailed upon the Emperor to issue a decree creating the Public Works Fund. Because his fund was established by imperial decree as opposed to parliamentary statute, Haussmann escaped the burden of close legislative scrutiny. The Fund was his *caisse noire*.

The Cour des Comptes occasionally questioned some of Haussmann's uses of the Fund, but its writ ran no further than to call the alleged irregularity to the attention of a parliament whose reduced role in the imperial regime enabled it to do little more than issue feckless after-the-fact warnings that Haussmann ignored. For all practical purposes the Emperor's favourite was untouchable.

When Napoleon's health and political power began to wane in the late 1860s, Haussmann became an attractive target for those whose real aim was to topple the imperial regime itself. A constitutional change in 1867 brought ministers into a closer working relationship with parliament. This institutional change, combined with a rejuvenated and increasingly hostile press, gradually subjected Haussmann's financial practices, especially his questionable dealings with Crédit Foncier, to a closer scrutiny than they could bear.

The indomitable Jules Ferry led the attack, charging that Haussmann 'lacks all sense of legality' and that '[h]e breaks the law with abandon' (Chapman and Chapman, 1957, p.229). Haussmann conceded his methods were unorthodox, but insisted they were legal as well as effective. It is beyond the scope of this chapter to try to settle the legality of Haussmann's creative public finances. For present purposes, the interesting point is the argument he made to support the legality of his actions. Acknowledging that there was no statute to support his Public Works Fund, he argued that there was ample precedent for his reliance upon an imperial decree as the legitimating source of his revenue-raising policies. He noted that under the Second Republic, a decree, not a statute, had enabled the state to purchase the toll concessions on bridges over the Seine and the city of Paris proceeded to issue bonds to finance the purchase. There was no challenge to this arrangement at that time, despite the absence of any national law to support it. If a republic can regulate its finances by decree, surely an empire can do the same.[2]

Political meddling

Throughout his long career, Haussmann was always involved in politics. A clearer illustration of the inherently political character of administration than the brilliant career of Georges Haussmann can hardly be imagined. As a young man of 21, he played a minor role as a messenger in the Revolution of 1830 that ushered in the reign of the 'citizen king', Louis Philippe. Fortunately (and characteristically), Haussmann backed the winning side. He showed considerable bravery during the three days of fighting in the streets of Paris and received a minor wound which became 'the stroke of good fortune he exploited to launch his career' (Jordan, 1995, p.57). Having received some legal training, he decided to apply for a post in the prefectoral corps shortly after the revolution of July, 1830. He probably selected this corps because it was part of the Ministry of the Interior where his father had some influence. When he submitted his application, he mentioned the wound he had received in helping to bring the Orleans regime to power as well as his distinguished lineage as grandson of a general of Napoleon on his mother's side and of a member of the Legislative Assembly of 1791 on his father's side. He also invoked his friendship with the duc d'Orléans, a classmate from his days at Lycée Henri IV and a son of King Louis Philippe. The young duke was Haussmann's patron until his premature death in 1842, a serious blow to his ambitious client. Through the long years from 1831 to 1853 when Haussmann was working his way up the ladder of the prefects' corps, he carefully cultivated the good will of the rich and powerful, without, however, shrinking from controversy with them when professional duty required it.

The revolution of 1848 presented an acute problem for Haussmann as a loyal supporter of the fallen Orleans Monarchy. His *Mémoires* reveal his careful political calculations as he navigated the swirls and eddies of that tumultuous year, 1848. At the time, Haussmann was serving as subprefect in the Department of the Gironde. Upon the abdication of Louis Philippe at the end of February, the Second Republic was proclaimed at first in Paris and then gradually throughout all of France. When the representatives of the newly-proclaimed republic offered Haussmann the opportunity to retain his office of subprefect, he declined, stating that 'I could absolutely not, without dishonour, become the representative of the policies of the republic after having served the recently overthrown July Monarchy for seventeen years' (Jordan, 1995, p.84). He was then offered the position of president of the *Conseil de Préfecture* of the Gironde which his tender conscience permitted him to accept because he found it 'pure administration' – a rather ironic comment in view of the politically charged character of Haussmann's administrative career.

By the summer of 1848, the revolution had turned exceedingly violent and Haussmann watched in dismay as four different prefects arrived in rapid succession to represent the republic in the Gironde. Amidst this instability, Haussmann was offered a promotion which he shrewdly declined, saying he was reluctant to 'reenter the administration before the Constitution was voted and a definitive government installed' (Jordan, 1995, p.88). Writing of these events some forty years later, he candidly acknowledged that he did not want to be too closely identified with the shaky republic, especially as he sensed a growing sentiment for more firm government under Louis Napoleon. Thus Haussmann found himself well positioned when Louis Napoleon was elected President of the Second Republic from which position he led the *coup d'état* that resulted in the Second Empire and the long reign of the erstwhile republican president as Emperor Napoleon III.

Haussmann's appointment as Prefect of the Seine in 1853 was, of course, the crucial event in his career. He was selected with Napoleon's ambitious urban projects in mind. Although Haussmann was neither an architect nor an engineer, the Emperor and his able Interior Minister, the duc de Persigny, saw other attractive qualities in him. We have already observed the delight Persigny took in Haussmann's 'brutal cynicism'. No less important, however, were his demonstrated skills in the overtly political arena of electoral campaigns. Napoleon's *coup d'état* of 2 December 1851 had to be legitimated by a plebiscite. As Prefect of the Gironde, an area not known for its support of Napoleon I, Haussmann was expected to deliver a strong majority in support of the *coup d'état* and therefore of Louis Napoleon's elevation from President of the Second Republic to Emperor Napoleon III. (At that time, it was not unusual for prefects to use their influence in elections to support the government of the day in Paris whose representatives they were). He did not disappoint his political masters. The plebiscite, held on 21 December 1851, found the Gironde giving Napoleon overwhelming support – a larger majority than he had won as candidate for President of the Republic in 1848. After the empire was established, Haussmann continued to succeed in seeing to it that elections in his *departement* returned candidates favourable to the Emperor. These matters weighed heavily in his favour when it came time to select a new Prefect of the Seine.[3]

Since Paris had no mayor at that time, the Prefect of the Seine exercised many of the functions normally associated with the office of mayor. Although constitutional theory made the Prefect of the Seine the subordinate of the Minister of the Interior and prevented him from dealing directly with the Emperor, Haussmann skilfully circumvented these legal niceties and managed to interact with Napoleon on virtually a daily basis. This personal contact with the Emperor was the key to Haussmann's power and served him well until the power of the Emperor himself faltered and with it the power of his loyal servant. Thus, Haussmann, like so many of his tribe, eventually met the unhappy fate of those who put their trust in princes.

Conclusions

At the outset of this chapter, it was introduced as part of a larger work comparing the relationship between constitutional principles and administrative institutions in four countries. The inherent relativism of a comparative study was indicated as its most serious problem. This is particularly true in the domain of administrative ethics as opposed to such mundane areas as public finance, personnel management, and administrative law. Ethical relativism brings to the table the heavy baggage of centuries of debate over the ultimate meaning of good and evil – a topic far beyond the modest scope of this chapter and one that has been touched upon in a rather preliminary way elsewhere (Rohr, 1978).

The complexity of comparing ethical traditions is compounded when one leaves the friendly confines of liberal democracy and enters the less familiar world of authoritarian regimes such as the Second Empire. This must be done, however, if a constitutional approach to administration is to have any merit as a theory. The smug assertion that liberal democratic regimes alone are morally acceptable cannot be sustained. Not only would this be unrealistic, but, more importantly, it would be a form of historical imperialism that stands aloof in self-righteous judgment on how the vast majority of human beings have organized their civic lives over the centuries. No case is made here for moral equivalence. Not only is liberal democracy preferred to its authoritarian counterpart, there are convincing arguments that support this preference. It does not follow, however, that the moral excellence of liberal democracy deprives authoritarian regimes of moral legitimacy. This is why the ethical dimension of Haussmann's career under the Second Empire is so interesting, even though it exposes the soft underbelly of a constitutional approach to public administration.

One might question stopping with the relatively benign authoritarianism of the Second Empire. What about Hitler, Stalin, *et al.*? To this objection, two answers are offered.

First, it should be questioned whether Nazi Germany, the Soviet Union and similar regimes had constitutions at all. To be sure, one can always find some sort of official texts in such regimes, but a real constitution, whether written or not, requires some minimal adherence to the rule of law and some *effective* constraint on the powers of those who govern. The Constitution of 14 January 1852 guarantees that the Second Empire passes this test, but twentieth century totalitarian regimes do not.

Secondly, it is argued that, for thoughtful persons, public service ethics presupposes that one has made, or at least should have made, a prior judgment on the moral legitimacy of the regime in which one serves. Recall Aristotle's distinction between a good man and good citizen. One who faithfully serves a thoroughly unjust regime may well be a good citizen but may also be a bad human being, for example, a good Nazi is by definition a bad person. Consequently, the question of public service ethics cannot arise in a thoroughly unjust regime because an unfavourable answer to the fundamental question on the moral legitimacy of the regime itself precludes further inquiry.

Notes

1. For a detailed discussion of the working relationship between Haussmann and the Emperor, see the chapter entitled 'Le Paris d'Haussmann: à la recherché d'une rélance économique,' in Louis Girard (1986), *Napoleon III*, Paris: Fayard.

2. For further examples of sharp financial practices by Haussmann, see Chapman and Chapman, pp.27-8.
3. For further examples of Haussmann's service to Napoleon III while still Prefect of the Gironde, see Girard, pp.181-2.

References

Chapman, Joan M. and Chapman, Brian (1957), *The Life and Times of Baron Haussmann: Paris in the Second Empire*, London: Weidenfeld and Nicolson.

Des Cars, Jean (1957, 1978), *Haussmann: la Gloire du Second Empire*, Paris: Librairie Académique Perrin.

Girard, Louis (1986), *Napoléon III*, Paris: Fayard.

John, Richard R. (1995), *Spreading the News: The American Postal System from Franklin to Morse*, Cambridge: Harvard University Press.

Jordan, David P. (1995), *Transforming Paris: The Life and Labors of Baron Haussmann*, Chicago: University of Chicago Press.

Kant, Immanuel (1994), 'On a Supposed Right to Lie from Altruistic Motives', in Peter Singer (ed.), *Ethics*, New York: Oxford University Press.

Lachapelle, Guy *et al.* (1993), *The Quebec Democracy: Structures, Processes, and Policies*, Toronto: McGraw-Hill Ryerson.

Laronze, Georges (1932), *Le Baron Haussmann*, Paris: Libraire Félix Alcan.

Rohr, John A. (1978, 1889), *Ethics for Bureaucrats: An Essay on Law and Values*, 2nd ed. New York: Marcel Dekker, Inc.

Rohr, John A. (1998), 'Comparative Constitutionalism as a School for Administrative Statesmen', in Michael Hunt and Barry J. O' Toole (eds.) *Reform, Ethics and Leadership in Public Service: A Festschrift in Honour of Richard A. Chapman*, Aldershot: Ashgate.

Woodhouse, Diana (1994), *Ministers and Parliament: Accountability in Theory and Practice*, Oxford: Clarendon Press.

14 Ethics in Public Service for the New Millennium

Richard A. Chapman

The beginning of the new millennium provides an opportunity to take stock of current experience, reflect on the past, and consider the nature of future problems, challenges and opportunities. This is as true in public administration as in other spheres of human activity. In particular, given growing concern about such matters, especially those considered in this book, the advent of the twenty-first century is an opportunity to review the complexities of ethical issues now facing public administration, some facets of which are as old as civilization itself. Indeed, the practice of public administration stimulated the ancient Greeks to ask philosophical questions about morality – questions to which students can still provide no easy answers. Over the centuries, questions of ethics raised by Aristotle, Plato, and others, have been reconsidered in the light of contemporary experience, and as societies have become increasingly complex, so the challenge of producing acceptable answers has become more and more difficult.

Earlier chapters have reviewed a selection of what their authors believe to be some of the most significant problems; they have also indicated some of the difficulties in resolving them. In general the outlook does not appear optimistic. This is partly because while in the past scholars have analysed issues and, where possible, suggested ways forward, practitioners have not appeared particularly interested in what has been written. Sometimes, indeed, it seems to observers that whatever is, is thought to be good. It is the outsiders who appear more anxious than the insiders. Again, this may always have been so. Nevertheless, efforts continue to be made to re-emphasise the warnings by a variety of means, especially in lectures, books, artlicles, and evidence to official committees.

Most recently this has been reflected in a spate of conferences, books and articles on ethics in public service. While the apparent apathy of practitioners may be one reason, it is not the only one: the reasons are many. They include, for example, the expansion of world communications; the interdependence and effects on all countries of others, sometimes referred to as globalization; the increasing sophistication of the social sciences, itself reflecting the increasing sophistication of society; and the striving for more democratic and consequently more accountable structures and processes of government. In the specific field of public service ethics the focus had been accentuated by a number of lapses from the highest standards of public service. Indeed, nearly every liberal democracy has had its share of such cases, and they have attracted widespread attention in the media. This has resulted in an unprecedented re-examination of the structures and processes of government, the ways public services are designed and delivered, and the effects of those public services on the lives of individual citizens. Students of public administration are particularly interested in the roles of officials, how they should behave, and what they ought to do in given circumstances. The practice of public administration and, consequently, the methods and processes used in studying it, have been evolutionary. However, it has become increasingly complex in the last century. Nevertheless some of the questions raised in the ancient past are as relevant today as they ever were. It is in this context that the contributions to this volume have focused on a number of facets of ethics in public service. The opportunity at this particular time has been used to consider present conditions and matters attracting current attention, and to engage in informed speculation on where current trends and emphases might lead.

Ethics in public service is about the practical application of moral standards in government. All ethical behaviour is concerned with how an individual feels he or she ought to behave. It is about values, and the application of those values in any given context. Recognizing that there have to be practical limitations to any field of study, the authors of this book have chosen primarily to focus on administrative experience, to consider it largely in the context of liberal democracies, and to examine it in as much depth as practicalities permit. It seemed not unreasonable to limit such studies to the societies considered in this volume, because they generally permit more openness to both citizens and scholars, openness being thought a desirable feature of democracy. Perhaps more important, however, especially in comparative studies, it should be noted that there is relatively little open discussion of public service ethics in countries which are not democratic. Moreover, public service often does not exist in authoritarian regimes in the same way that it is found in modern democracies.

Neither, of course, is it found without additional complications in private sector organizations that are nowadays so often contracted to provide public services. The key factor in understanding public service ethics is the significance of the political environment which provides the framework for public service and which conditions its practice.

The political environment

In liberal democracies it is the political environment which determines the scope and objectives of the public services; it is the political environment which determines the values to be applied when delivering these services; and it is the political environment which affects the ways public servants work and is the most important factor in the differences between public administration and management or administration in other contexts.

Public administration, as used here, encompasses not only the provision of particular public services, many of which can be quantitatively measured, but also the quality of services, and, in some cases, especially at the highest levels, the making or contributing to decisions about what should be done. In other words, public administration is not just about the management of public services, which itself raises a whole plethora of ethical problems; it is also about contributing to the setting of the values and goals of the wider society and to the qualitative aspects of government work. Of course, in modern democracies elected governments ultimately decide programmes for action and are responsible to electorates. Nevertheless, policies for action cannot be decided by politicians alone; administrators make significant contributions. Indeed, in some contexts and in some countries more is left for administrators to decide than in other contexts or other countries. The relative balance of these activities varies according to the constraints of the political environment in different places and at different times. Much depends upon the pressures and preferences of the people and of their representatives.

Not only are there differences between public service ethics in different types of political system, and between countries which regard themselves as liberal democracies, there are also important differences between work in public services and work in other contexts. This is generally recognised in areas of high political salience. Few, even among enthusiasts for making public administration more business-like, would disagree that diplomacy is a distinctly public sector activity, and few would fail to recognise the monopoly characteristics of work in a national treasury, police force, fire service, or the drafting of legislation. However, there are many shades of grey between the clearly recognisable contrasts of work in the public services and work elsewhere. Towards the end of the twentieth century there was a shift in emphasis about what should be regarded as the province of public service and what should be contracted out to other organizations. There was also a clearly recognizable shift in many liberal democracies towards emphasizing the virtues of being business-like, to rolling back the state, to encouraging leadership and to being entrepreneurial, to setting up new structures freed of the constraints of bureaucracy, to introducing performance related pay in the public services, to giving contracts to firms to provide various types of public services following processes of competitive tendering, and to privatization. These and associated practices became regarded as features of 'new public management'. Buzz-words indicating 'goodness' became popular and indicated virtue to the point where criticism, or even the expression of reservations, could be regarded as disloyal. Good words included 'new', 'market', 'entrepreneurial', 'competition', and 'strategic'; bad words included 'bureaucratic', 'public service', 'traditional'. In particular, there was much evidence that being business-like was thought to be good and that working in the public sector was for the unambitious and inefficient. Public servants in liberal democracies, because of their responsibilities to ministers and the constraints of the political environment, could not defend themselves in public even when ministers were critical of them or were not supportive in the face of unjustified condemnation. Even when pay increased, public service morale declined.

These changes reflected the mood of the time and their implementation was led by politicians. The changes were therefore the consequences of a shift in the political environment and, in particular, of an ideological change in emphasis. In some cases this was the result of elections which returned more representatives with neo-liberal beliefs – but it should also be noted that the shift was not purely to conservatives in the partisan sense, because the changed emphasis was also apparent in politicians who were social democrats or socialists. The important point to note is that very important changes occurred in public service, the changes were the result of changes in the political environment and, moreover, the changes had consequences in terms of how officials behaved, how they felt they ought to behave in their daily work, and therefore on the practical application of moral standards. Two elements of the political environment, of particular relevance for understanding ethics in public service, relate to the role of constitutions and public accountabilities. These will be briefly considered here as they are themes which emerge as significant in the earlier chapters of this book.

The role of constitutions

The significance and practical effects of a constitution is probably the most important factor in public service within liberal democracies. In the modern world there are no democracies without constitutions. This statement covers both the written aspects of a constitution and the 'unwritten' aspects which include customs and conventions. The United Kingdom is one of the few countries that does not have a single written document that might be called the constitution, but there is, nevertheless, a constitution and a fairly clear understanding of what is acceptable and what is not acceptable according to that constitution. Most other modern democracies have written constitutions, but even they also have features of government, including unwritten rules, customs and conventions, that are not included in the basic document but that are accepted as being of constitutional significance. Whether or not a democratic country has a single document which lays down the basic structures and functions of the organs of government, it is fairly clear what is or is not constitutionally acceptable. Sometimes a constitution embodies in its preamble, if not in itself, a statement of rationale or values which should be respected. Sometimes a bill of rights is incorporated within a constitution or supplements it. Constitutions may not of themselves ensure democracy, but no modern democracy exists without one. Constitutions are a fundamental part of the political environment within which public administrators work.

It could be argued that constitutions are in some respects more important than elections in democracies. A government may be dependent for its legitimacy on elections, but questions may be asked about the timing and frequency of elections, as well as the turnout and the type of electoral system. There may be many questions about each of these, and the answers to the questions, or interpretations of them, may determine the legitimacy and acceptability of governments. The essential point to emphasize, in this present discussion, is that constitutions, as well as elections, legitimize democratic governments. Indeed, they may be seen as the guiding influence on what and how public services are provided. They provide the framework for all aspects of the structure and organization of government. The institutions of government are of fundamental importance for public service. Constitutions are therefore important for stating the general purposes or aims of government, values that are expected to be observed, and for determining who should decide, and how decisions should be made about the more specific ends or policies of government.

Technically in a secondary position, but perhaps as important in influencing ethical behaviour in public service, because of their more direct impact on day to day activity, is the mass of rules subordinate to any constitution. These rules may include, at their most significant, codes of conduct, but they may also encompass even the most routine set of office procedures. All have their part to play in determining and guiding administrative behaviour. They have contributions to make in terms of the education and training of officials. They may also be important for the education and understanding of citizens in relation to their system of government and for sensitizing them in relation to personal rights and expectations. In these respects, rules of various sorts have a vital and important part to play in affecting the behaviour of officials when discretionary decisions have to be made.

The effect on public administration of a constitution, and of the rules which are subordinate to it, might be more easily understood if contrasts are made with management in other contexts, perhaps by drawing attention to the most extreme features of the business sector. It is possible to imagine a spectrum with the public sector at one extreme. At the other extreme is the business sector. In the public sector within a liberal democracy the ends or purposes of officials are to achieve the objectives laid down by government according to stated or implied values, standards and procedures that have been constitutionally laid down. This is what is meant by public service, and the essential loyalty of an official is to public service understood in this way. The public good is ultimately determined by government. In general terms (ignore the refinements for the moment) the public servant regards public service as his or her motivating force. This may be seen to apply even when government policies may appear to be contradictory or may be reversed more than once. Personal, group, or other interests are subordinated to serving the public interest.

Two examples may be helpful here. Anthony Sampson, reporting comments about the British civil service from ministers and ex-ministers, wrote in 1962 that one of his interviewees had said: 'I remember when we took office in 1951, the same civil servant who had been looking after nationalization had already got out a plan for denationalization. He went about it with just the same enthusiasm' (Sampson, 1962, p.235).The second example comes from comments Edward Bridges made about the civil service in 'Portrait of a Profession', his 1950 Rede Lecture. In that lecture Bridges stressed that a senior civil servant should have some of the qualities

> called for in the academic world, namely the capacity and determination to study difficult subjects intensively and objectively, with the same disinterested desire to find the truth at all costs, the same

willingness to face the truth when it turns up in unexpected places, and in what may be for practical purposes an inconvenient form, the same readiness to scrap much hard work which has already been done when one finds that one has started on the wrong track.

He then went on to explain that few civil servants were ever completely responsible for the work they were doing:

On all important questions it is necessary to make sure that the Minister approves what is being done; and, apart from ministerial responsibility the complications of much Government work call for a far greater degree of consultation with colleagues and consideration for other and wider interests than is commonly found in other occupations. Through the nature of his work, therefore, he has much less consciousness than other professional men that the work he does is his own individual achievement, and is inevitably far more conscious than others that the work he does is part of something greater than himself (Bridges, 1950).

At the other extreme from public service is work in the business sector. Here, motivation is ultimately to the owners of the organization, whose intentions are to make profits. Where the purpose of an enterprise is to provide a service, then a service is provided to contribute to the economic purpose of the enterprise and for no other reason. Sometimes the result may be to work according to values that may not be acceptable in public service, though they may be perfectly acceptable in the business sector. An extreme example may be helpful here.

In the late 1960s Ford in America, at a time of considerable commercial competition, decided to produce a compact car called the Pinto. The car was developed quickly and in early safety tests only three out of eleven cars passed: the problem was that in crashes from the rear the fuel tanks exploded. The car nevertheless met the proposed minimum safety standards required by the National Highway Traffic Safety Administration. Ford then made a cost-benefit analysis which included such factors as productivity costs, property damage from accidents, victim's pain and suffering, and funeral costs. Other factors were also considered: for example, it was believed that Americans were not primarily interested in safety. The costs of correcting the fault would have made the car unacceptably expensive, so Ford went ahead and marketed the car as it had been developed, until the company was prosecuted for 'reckless homicide'. The key factor in the decision to produce the car was its saleability; that is, whether it would make a profit when all the relevant factors were taken into account (Barry, 1991, Ch. 1; Snoeyenbos, Almeder and Humber, 1983). These were essentially ethical considerations, but they were subordinated to the purpose of the enterprise. Of course, it may be argued that the continuation of the purpose of the enterprise, making a profit, also had ethical implications, since it guaranteed the continuation of the firm and of the employment of staff. In other words, there are competing ethical considerations – safety versus employment. Similarly difficult considerations may apply in other contexts such as safety provisions on railways or in aircraft; people take risks and cost-benefit calculations have to be made, however tragic may be their consequences.

The intention here is not to argue that employees in the business sector lack ethical standards and are unprincipled. This would be nonsense and easily refuted. The point is that at the extreme end of the spectrum away from public service the motivating values and conditions of work in the private sector are very different. In between these extremes, of course, there are variations with their own positions of complexity and, potentially, conflict. It is important to stress that ethical dilemmas cannot be avoided, they will always occur. Sometimes ethical principles are not compatible and the ethical task is to resolve the conflict. In the public sector these dilemmas have particular interest for citizens and for students of public administration because they are practical features of the executive work of government, and because the overarching principles guiding the work are to be found in the constitution.

Public accountabilities

In contemporary political systems, and when considering trends that are envisaged to continue into the new millennium, there are many intermediate positions between the extremes of the public sector and the business sector. Some of these have been present for most of the twentieth century. The nationalized industries, for example, were set up, as Professor William Robson put it, to 'secure freedom from parliamentary supervision over management on the one hand and Treasury control over personnel and finance on the other' (Robson, 1960, p.59). In the last two decades of the twentieth century, practical experience has evolved new arrangements along comparable lines and with comparable intentions, such as the creation of executive agencies and other developments that have been associated with 'new public management'. One consequence is that business sector organizations have been delivering public services – for example, they have been providing services under contract, services that previously may have been provided only by the public sector. Even if the detailed provisions of particular services appear to clients or customers to be much the same, irrespective of provenance, there are nevertheless differences. Any such provision by the private sector is to fulfil the conditions of the contract (which may involve a service to the people); and it should be noted that the conditions of contracts become an increasingly important responsibility of the public service. Any comparable provision by organizations wholly within the public sector is to the public interest as represented by the government (which also may involve a service to the people) and it should be noted that the associated conditions and values are influenced by the political environment. In some respects there are similarities, and at some levels it may be difficult to distinguish between the two. In other respects there is a world of difference between operating in a public service with the many implications of working in a political environment, and operating in a private company with somewhat different values, conditions of service and, ultimately, accountabilities.

One of the essential characteristics and qualities of working in the public service within a modern democracy and one of the elements of the political environment is the emphasis on public accountability. This is easy to express in general terms, and forms of accountability are easily shown to be significant in all democratic political systems, though in practice it is by no means uncomplicated.

In the United Kingdom the practical experience was put well by H.E. Dale, nearly sixty years ago, when he explained some of the differences between public administration and business management. The British civil service, he pointed out, works under the supreme control of a committee accountable to over six hundred elected 'shareholders', of whom up to about three hundred are likely at any one time to be opposed to current policies. Any fairly large section of this body is able to raise a set debate on any part of the organization's business or on any transaction they may select at almost any time. The leaders of the opposition group are at liberty to propose that the committee, or at least the 'director' responsible for a mistake, shall be publicly reprimanded; and if the proposal is carried, the 'director', and perhaps the whole committee, will have to resign at once. In addition, any of the 'shareholders' is entitled at any time to ask any question he chooses about any matter of business, from issues of broad policy down to the smallest detail, and to have a full and accurate reply within two or three days. Furthermore, the 'shareholders' with these rights and powers sit at the organization's supreme headquarters for several hours a day, on five days a week, for about eight months a year (Dale, 1943;

Chapman, 1988). An important consequence is that the work regarded as most important for the most senior management officials is not in practice concerned so much with management as with politics in the most comprehensive and non-partisan sense of the word.

Officials in the British civil service are hierarchically accountable; this is the pattern in the bureaucracies of most democratic countries. Ultimately, accountability is to ministers who, in turn, are accountable to the legislature; and, in the United Kingdom, Parliament is formally accountable to the people at elections which are held not less frequently than every five years. This affects the ways of working of most civil servants in British government departments. The accountability has a 'trickle down' effect, so that civil servants are sensitized into appreciating what is politically significant, politically sensitive, and requires particular care. The creation of agencies and the executive work of departments providing large scale services has resulted in large numbers of people at hierarchically the lowest levels being engaged in what is now referred to as 'governance', where political sensitivity may be accorded much less significance than in the past. Nevertheless the principle still applies: all public sector accountability in liberal democracies is conditioned, as already explained, by the political environment. The lowest level official whose routine actions unexpectedly attract attention in a parliamentary question never forgets the significance of such accountability. The significance of accountability in this context is not something that can be evaluated in quantitative terms by, say, the number of ministerial resignations that follow from administrative embarrassments. It is of a different order: accountability here is qualitative and value-laden, and it conditions the daily activities of large numbers of officials. Moreover, accountability of local government officers to councillors is, or has been, as observable as the accountability of civil servants to ministers.

If accountability to politicians is of special importance in public service within a democracy, requirements to be 'efficient', as indicated by good administrative practice and hierarchical responsibility, are of almost equal importance. This may be similar to accountability in other contexts but there are also differences of emphasis. Often procedures can be more 'bureaucratic' in public service because there is more documentation of details (often because decisions have to be consistent with values approved by the political environment, and the decisions may have to be justified in public, in accordance with those values). Ultimately, too, in terms of the administrative hierarchy, there is the possibility of an official being summoned to give evidence to a parliamentary committee. Whatever the context, there are pressures to ensure that public service organizations operate to the highest possible standards of management and in accordance with well established principles or criteria. Procedures are created to ensure that there is accountability up a hierarchy, ultimately to elected representatives. The organization has to be both efficient because of the need to ensure value for taxpayers' money and because efficiency encompasses the qualitative and value-laden expectations of the society: for example, a public service organization that delivered a service but denied citizens equality and fairness of treatment without good reason would attract serious public criticism. Consequently accountability in public service may be more complex in practice than accountability in the business sector, where the management challenges may be similarly demanding but less complex, more easily comprehensible, and apparently less bureaucratic. Trying to make public sector organizations more business-like without fully appreciating all the implications of proposed changes may have effects quite different from what was intended.

It might be comforting to think that a new approach to accountability in the public service could resolve all the difficulties currently experienced or foreseen. Unfortunately, however, this is not possible: accountability cannot be reduced to some sort of ready-made practical formula. Nor can the difficulties of exercising discretion be resolved by creating a new and more comprehensive code of conduct. This is not to say that more research into problems of accountability would not be valuable, nor is it to deny the values of codes of conduct. It is, however, to emphasize that these issues cannot be resolved by pretending that public sector organizations are the same as private sector organizations. It is also to emphasize that broad judgments and expectations of business-like efficiency deny the lessons of elementary observations in the social sciences.

An example using current (end of 1999) proposals for modernizing the UK civil service may be helpful here. A recently announced programme of civil service reform intends to promote stronger leadership in the civil service. Sir Richard Wilson, Head of the Civil Service, said: 'Over the next 20 years we want the service to have a stronger sense of leadership, not just from the top but all the way down the line' (*The Independent*, 16 December 1999). It is not yet completely clear what is envisaged in practice, but sometimes the sort of leadership appropriate in business organizations is not acceptable in the public sector. Derek Lewis found this when he became Director General of Her Majesty's Prison Service (Lewis, 1997). The difficulty is that when senior officials show the sort of leadership suited to business organizations, political sensitivities arise. Strong leadership relevant in other contexts may not work easily in the public service because leaders in official positions can render ministers redundant. This is a difficulty that was observed on numerous earlier occasions, including attempts to implement the recommendations in the Fulton Report on the Civil Service and the Next Steps Report.

Questions need to be asked about the meaning of public sector accountability, including to whom and how, but the answers cannot be of the once and for all time variety. Sometimes accountability is simply within a hierarchy (especially at the lowest levels); at other times it is to superiors; ministers; the legislature and its committees; professional standards; rules of procedure; the electorate; even, ultimately, for some individuals, to their ideal of how a civil servant ought to behave. In the public sector, the questions have to be asked again and again as particular experiences and contexts change and as the political environment leads to different emphases and different requirements. As with other aspects of ethics in public service, increasingly sophisticated and comprehensive rules may appear to remove the unavoidable discretionary aspects of decision making. Discretionary decision making by responsible and accountable officials is a fact of life in a well developed liberal democracy. Nevertheless is should be recognized that accountability is a key element in the political sphere of government. Dangers arise when politicians, speaking in public and motivated by expediency, emphasize the need for accountability in others while disregarding its relevance for themselves. This can be especially important when ministers avoid their responsibility by deciding that matters of an operational nature are the responsibility of public servants, but they themselves decide where the line should be drawn between policy and operations.

Decisions about the distinction between policy and operational matters arose from time to time in the UK throughout the twentieth century, perhaps because the twentieth century saw the creation of nationalized industries and other forms of public ownership. Much publicity was given in the 1990s to the creation of executive agencies within government. In the final year of the century the European Commission became a similar focus of attention as a result of the Report of the Committee of Independent Experts.

Democratic standards

The Report of the Committee of Independent Experts is a powerful and remarkable document: its outspokenness was unexpected and its consequences unprecedented. It was not only critical of fraud, it was also critical of mismanagement, a concept which it said 'refers in general to serious or persistent infringements of the principles of sound administration' (Committee of Independent Experts, 1999, 1.4.3). The Report emphasizes the need for decisions to be taken 'solely in terms of the public interest' and in accordance with 'proper standards in public life' (1.5.4). It found numerous deviations from these criteria, some of which indicated disregard for the most elementary rules of administrative practice. The report also raises questions about other practices in the Commission – questions which seem relevant to the public service in many individual states at the beginning of the new millennium. For example, it refers to the practice of having public programmes implemented by private contractors and says the concept needs to be carefully considered and that private contractors must be subject to contractual provisions in the general interest (5.8.2; 5.8.3). It is the general interest that must be paramount in a democracy. It should be emphasised, however, that democratic standards in this context require much more than ensuring that there are democratic elections. This may sound a routine, even trite, observation, easily dismissed because it seems so obvious and not new; but it needs saying again and again. Responsible liberal democracies require good administration. Good administration involves known and conscientiously applied principles of accountability, control, and efficient administration. Liberal democracies also require relevant values to be upheld, and these values were well expressed in the principles of public life laid down in the First Nolan Report on Standards in Public Life, referred to on a number of occasions in the earlier chapters of this book.

The Nolan principles, which the Committee said applied to all aspects of public life were: selflessness, integrity, objectivity, accountability, openness, honesty and leadership. To each of these principles the Nolan Committee attached a sentence or two of explanation and these are given in a note at the end of this chapter. The principles, which were set out for the benefit of all who serve the public in any way, provide a valuable framework for evaluating recent experience and considering the future.

Numerous other suggestions emerge from the earlier chapters in this volume. They may not appear as startlingly new, but the evidence suggests they need reiterating. The promotion of ethics in public service *requires* repetition in this context. The topic cannot be looked at in a once-and-for-all way. It requires continuous attention if the principles of public life in liberal democracies are to be practised and maintained in a healthy condition. It is necessary to ensure, as has already been argued, that discretionary decision making (the key element in ethical behaviour) is *discretionary*. Such decisions cannot and should not in a democracy be replaced by systems of increasingly precise rules. The human element cannot be removed. This is because the political environment, which conditions the daily work of public administrators, is never static: adapting to change and reconsidering issues from first principles is a requirement of modern life. It is the nature of ethics in public service that discretionary decisions are made, requiring fresh consideration of each problem. The elements of decision making may vary from time to time and from place to place and there must be an appropriate balance between the needs of accountability (to government, to parliament and to the public), hierarchy and good administration, the principles of practice evolved from liberal democracies, and the values of politicians, officials and citizens. That many of the details are represented as specifically appropriate in liberal democracies does not seem to matter much. After all, many countries in the twenty-first century are liberal democracies. Those that are not, or are among the group of less developed democracies, like to be seen as aspiring to be democracies. Democratic government may be an unattainable ideal; the actualities of the practical world may continuously present new challenges; there may be increasing opportunities for refining principles and practice; but perhaps the key feature relevant to this discussion is continuous attention and effort to strive towards the ideal. The tasks of administrators in the new millennium are likely to be increasingly tasks of refinement: considering all the relevant factors, ignoring irrelevant factors and, in many cases, making decisions that set complexities of infinite shades of grey into frameworks that are increasingly expected to be black and white.

Notes

The Nolan Committee's Seven Principles of Public Life:
Selflessness: Holders of public office should take decisions solely in terms of the public interest. They should not do so in order to gain financial or other material benefits for themselves, their family, or their friends.
Integrity: Holders of public office should not place themselves under any financial or other obligation to outside individuals or organisations that might influence them in the performance of their official duties.
Objectivity: In carrying out public business, including making public appointments, awarding contracts, or recommending individuals for rewards and benefits, holders of public office should make their choices on merit.
Accountability: Holders of public office are accountable for their

	decisions and actions to the public and must submit themselves to whatever scrutiny is appropriate to their office.
Openness:	Holders of public office should be as open as possible about all the decisions and actions that they take. They should give reasons for their decisions and restrict information only when the wider public interest demands.
Honesty:	Holders of public office have a duty to declare any private interests relating to their public duties and to take steps to resolve any conflicts arising in a way that protects the public interest.
Leadership:	Holders of public office should promote and support these principles by leadership and example.

References

Barry, Norman (1991), *The Morality of Business Enterprise*, Aberdeen: Aberdeen University Press.
Bridges, Edward (1950), *Portrait of a Profession*, London: Cambridge University Press.
Chapman, Richard A. (1988), *Ethics in the British Civil Service*, London: Routledge.
Dale, H.E. (1943), *The Personnel and Problems of the Higher Civil Service*, London: Oxford University Press.
Lewis, Derek (1997), *Hidden Agendas*, London: Hamish Hamilton.
Nolan, Lord (1995), *First Report of the Committee on Standards in Public Life*, Cm. 2850-I, London: HMSO.
Robson, William A. (1960), *Nationalized Industry and Public Ownership*, London: Allen and Unwin.
Sampson, Anthony (1962), *Anatomy of Britain*, London: Hodder and Stoughton.
Snoeyenbos, M., Almeder, R., and Humber, J. (1983), 'Cost Benefit Analysis and the Ford Pinto', in Snoeyenbos, Almeder and Humber (eds), *Business Ethics*, New York: Prometheus Books.

Index

Aberbach, J.D. 185-6
access to information 191
accountability 5, 6, 8, 41, 47, 81-2, 114, 117, 127-38, 141-62, 166-7, 169, 176-81, 185-200, 218, 220, 224-30
accountable 24, 30, 113, 173, 197-8, 225-6, 228
accountants 122
accounting 121
Adjudication Panels 20
Administrative Review Council 178
advice 108
affirmative action 45
age 35
agencies 5, 76, 79, 111, 114-17, 131, 141-2, 154, 160, 165, 168-9, 174-5, 179-81, 189, 191, 224, 226, 228
 see also monitoring agency
agent 170, 177-8, 181
Albert, Prince 90
American 144
 see also United States
Amsterdam, Treaty of 46, 57, 59
anonymity 87-8, 205
Aquinas, Thomas 71, 73, 83
Aristotle 71-5, 78-9, 83, 89, 215, 217
Army 102
arrogance 208-10
asbestos 15

assurance 179
Aston 16
Attorney General's Department 174-5
audit 167, 180
Aukland 153
Australia 6, 47, 142, 151, 155, 170, 174, 176-7, 180
Australian Post 178
Australian Public Service 6, 175
authorities (of departments) 99
authority 71, 93-8, 100, 108, 148, 161, 167
autonomy 186-7
Aviemore Highland Centre 10

Ball, Ian 154
Bamforth, Nicholas 61
bankruptcy 10
Barker, Sir Ernest 72, 89
Barratt, John 15-16
Barrington, C.G. 99
Basic Law 194, 198-9
Bazoft, Fazad 80
behaviour 23
Beijing 195, 198-9
Belgium 209
beliefs 123
benchmarks 174
Bentley, Arthur F. 71-2, 75-7, 79, 83, 89
Berkeley, Arthur Mowbray 101-2
Berlin, Sir Isaiah 23, 33

bias 24, 159-60
bird flu 196
Birmingham 16
Blair, Tony 47-8, 51
Blake, John 121-2
Board of Trade 98, 107
Board of Works 98
Boston, Jonathan 153-5
Boucher, Dale 174-5
Bourbon Restoration 205
Bradford City Council 10
Bradley, A.W. 57
bribery 102-3, 170
Bridges, Edward 222
Brind case 51
Bristol 156
Britain 2
British government 80
Browne, John 24, 28
Bryce, James 73
'Building Stable Communities' 13, 15
bureaucratic 5
Burke, Edmund 156
business-like 219-20, 227

Cabinet Office 39-44, 48
Camden 13, 38, 42
Campbell, Colin 185
Campos, Ed 155
Canada (including Canadian experience) 56-7, 63, 132, 142, 144, 151, 160, 203
Canadian Charter of Rights and Freedoms 56-7, 62-3, 67
Canadian Constitution Act 62
Canadian Supreme Court 56
carelessness 106
Carter, Jimmy 144
case law 101
Castle, Barbara 37
Cave Creek 152
Cavendish ward 13

censorship 88
certification 95, 97, 106
Chadwick, Edwin 97
Champion, Mrs 103
Chan, Anson 191, 195, 199-200
change 123
Chapman, Richard A. 116, 181
character 106
Charity Commission 107
charter(s) 3, 136, 179-80
  see also Canadian Charter, citizens' charter
cheating 102
Chek Lap Kok 196
chickens 195
Chief Executive 198, 200
China/Chinese 6, 100-1, 188, 191, 194, 198
Chope, Christopher 12
citizen engagement 132
citizens' charter 131, 136
City District Office 189
Civil Service Act 94
Civil Service Code 51, 94
Civil Service Commission 4, 93-108
Civil Service Commissioners 44
Civil Service Reform Act, 1978 144
Civil Service Selection Board 105
Clay Cross 11
Clovis 209
code(s) 4-7, 11, 20, 23, 25, 30, 33, 41, 51, 87-8, 94-5, 112-13, 116, 120, 128, 174-6, 180-1, 222, 227
coherence 117
colonial traditions 7
colony 6
commercialization 174-6
Commissioner for Privacy 191
Commissioner for Standards 29-33
Commissioners *see* European

Commission of the European Union 82
Commission for Racial Equality 38
Committee of Independent Experts 82-3, 88-9, 228-9
common good 73-4
communities 167, 177
Community *see* European
competence 196
competition 174
competitiveness 40, 175
competitive tendering 165, 168, 170, 172-3, 220
Complaints Task Force 131
Comprehensive Social Security Assistance 196
conduct 16, 106, 173, 222
Conduct of a Member of the House, Select Committee 27
conflict 123, 168, 170, 224
Conservative government(s) 11, 17, 146
Conservative party 12-13, 16, 18, 151
consistency 117, 121
constitution(s) 7, 72, 117, 119, 161, 203-15, 220-4
constitutional care 175
constitutional role 85
constitutional supremacy 62
Constitution Unit 52
consultation 97, 223
consumerization 130, 132, 137
consumers' charter 131
contract(s) 132, 166-70, 172-3, 225
contracting (out) 5-6, 39, 47, 115, 165-81, 219-20
contractors 229
control 33, 128-37, 146, 165, 167, 169, 179, 187, 191-2, 224, 229
convenience 82
convention(s) 3, 18, 112, 120-1, 221

Convention *see* European Convention on Human Rights
Convention rights 60-2, 65-7
Cooper Terry L. 113, 118
Cordle, John 27, 31, 33
corruptible 79
corruption 9-16, 20, 23, 31-2, 87, 93, 101, 104, 107, 113, 189
cost-benefit 223-4
Council of Civil Service Unions 42
Council of Europe 66
Court of Appeal 15, 53
courts 53-66
Coussey, Mary 42
Covent Garden 12
Craig, Paul 54, 59, 61
Crane, Sir James 10
Crédit Foncier 211
Cubbon, Sir Brian 20
cultural diversity 179
cultural theory 128
culture(s) 5-6, 36, 43, 67, 93, 104-5, 108, 119, 141, 143, 160, 173
see also enterprise culture
custom(s) 119-23, 221
customers 165, 179-80, 192, 225

Dahl, Robert 150
Dale, H.E. 225
Dale, Tony 154
Dasent, Sir George 101
Day, Patricia 127
decency 181
decentralization 35, 41, 46
decentralized budgeting 20
deficit spending 211
delegation 35, 41-2, 46
democracy 71, 77, 82-4, 86, 89, 111, 113, 127-38, 141-62, 219-22, 225-6, 228
see also direct democracy, representative democracy
democratic accountability *see*

accountability
democratic standards 228-30
deontology 203-4
Department of Administrative Services 176
Department of Conservation 152-3
Department of Finance 177
Department of Health 40
Department of the Environment 13-14
Department of the Gironde *see* Gironde
Department of the Prime Minister 154
Department of Trade and Industry 40, 80, 145
deregulation 132
development 23
devolution 41, 108, 174
Dickens, Linda 39
Dilulio, John J. 159
direct democracy 133-5
Director of Audit 196-7
Director of Social Welfare 196
disability 35, 42
discretion 1, 4, 5, 7, 24, 51, 82, 105, 118, 127-8, 135-6, 141-2, 148, 161, 167, 179, 197, 227-30
see also managerial discretion
discretionary authority 148
district boards 190
discrimination 37-8, 43-4, 46
District Auditor 12, 14, 15, 19
doctrines 56
Doig, Alan 26, 28, 31
Doncaster 9
Downey, Sir Gordon 31-3
duc de Perigny 208, 213
duc d'Orléans 212
due process 120
du Gay, Paul 173
duties 7, 82, 84, 89, 95, 106, 120, 123, 165-7, 179, 209

Dutt, Michael 14
duty *see* duties
dysfunctions 128, 152

East India Company 95
Eaton, Dorman B. 93
education 4, 33, 52, 102, 107, 116, 131, 134, 158, 190, 222
effective 132, 134, 169, 174-5, 192-3, 205, 212, 215
efficiency/efficient 93, 96, 107, 113, 115, 119, 128-9, 132, 159-60, 165, 168-70, 174-5, 178, 180, 188, 191-2, 226-7, 229
elderly welfare 199
electoral 15
electoral corruption 12
elite(s) 186, 188-9, 191
empathy 179
Employment Development Group 40
Employment Relations Act 40
empowering 172-3
Endacott, G.B. 188
enforcement 175
enterprise culture 165-81
entrepreneurial 220
equality 135, 227
equal opportunities 3, 35-48
Equal Opportunities Commission 38, 42
Equal Pay Act 37, 40
Equal Treatment Directive 45
equity 113, 129
ethic 85, 87, 135
ethics in government: definitions 1, 36
ethnic origin 35
ethnicity 42
ethos 4, 31, 36, 93, 104, 114, 119
European Commission 80, 83, 228
European Commissioners 83
European Communities Act 59

European Community 40, 82
European Convention on Human Rights 3, 51-4, 56-9
European Court of Human Rights 52, 56, 58-9, 62, 65-6
European Court of Justice 45, 57-8
European Union 45, 59, 88-9
Eustace, Rev J.M. 101
evolving 21
examinations 93, 102-3
  see also open competition
excellence 175
executive agencies 41
Executive Council 195
expediency 104

Factortame case 59
Fair Employment Act 40, 45
fairness 4, 32, 43-5, 108, 129, 135, 176, 178-9, 181, 227
Fairness at Work 40
Farrant, Graham 16
Ferry, Jules 212
fidelity 105
Finance and Public Administration Committee 178
financial irregularities 210-12
Finer 128
fire service 219
First Division Association 84-6
First World War 102
Fitzrovia 13
Fok, Katherine 200
Ford 223
Foreign Office 80, 100-1
Forest Service 153
framework 41
France 102, 133, 203, 213
Francis I 209
fraud 103, 107, 228
freedom(s) 56, 58-9, 173-4, 177, 186

Freedom of Information Act 175
Friedrich 128
Fulton Report 189, 228
functions 221

Gambia 27
gender 35, 37, 39, 41-2, 135
General Belgrano 145
general interest 229
gentrification 14
German administration 193
Germany 215
gifts 21
Gironde 205, 213-14, 216
Gladstone 107
globalization 7, 218
Glover, Malcolm 9
Goldfinch, Shaun 152
governance 72, 114-16, 153, 157, 159, 161, 167, 171, 185, 189, 193-5, 198, 203-15, 226
Government Performance and Results act 204
Gowthorpe, Catherine 121-2
Greater London Council 12-13, 38
Green Papers 87
Gregory, Robert 152-3
Grey, Earl 96
group(s) 75-8, 89-90, 118, 134-5, 137, 147-8, 222
group theorists 71, 83, 88-9

Haddon-Cave, Philip 198
Haileybury 95, 97, 102
Hamilton, Neil 24, 28, 31-2
Harrison and Sons 103
Hartley, Peter 14
Haussmann, Baron 7, 203-15
Hayler, Paul 14
Head, Sir Edward 107
health care 131, 190
  see also public health
Heclo, Hugh 144

238 *Index*

Hencke, David 31
Hiebert, Janet L. 57
High Court 14, 19, 53
High Court of Judiciary 54
Hitler 215
HM Customs and Excise 40
Hodge, Margaret 11, 18
Holy Land 209
Home Office 54, 60, 66, 85, 98
honesty 117, 229-30
Hong Kong 6-7, 185-200
Hood, Christopher 128, 130, 172
horizontality 67
Hotel de Ville 206, 209
House of Commons 23, 97
House of Lords 51, 54, 59-60, 63
housing 11-12, 15-16
  see also public housing
Howell, R. 107
human rights 52,55, 59, 61-4, 67
  see also rights
Human Rights Act 51-67
human rights legislation 3, 21, 47
Hunt, Murray 67

ideal(s) 23, 25, 33, 36, 73, 78, 89, 111, 115, 129, 172, 186, 228, 230
idealist 79
ideal state 72
illegal/illegality 15, 47, 54, 145
impartiality 4, 108, 113
Imperial Edict 100
improper 14-15, 102, 145
impropriety 29, 47, 102
inaccuracy 106
incompatibility 62-4, 66
independence 88-100
India 37, 98
Indian Civil Service 95, 102, 105-6
India Office 102
indulgence 106
industry 107

Industry Commission 171-2
inefficiencies 101
influence 28, 94, 98, 106, 144, 221
informing process 97
Inland Revenue 40, 97
Inner London Education Authority 38
inputs 157-60
inspection 167
Institute of Personnel Management 38
institutions 3
integrity 82, 87, 93, 117, 174, 191, 195-6, 229-30
interest(s) 24-5, 27-32, 76-9, 82, 84, 86, 89-90, 104, 118, 123, 134, 137, 147-8, 186, 192, 194, 222
Iran 81
Iran Contra affair 144
Iran/Iraq War 47, 80
Iraq 80-1, 88, 145
iron-triangles 147
Irish Daily Independent 103
irritability 47
irregularities 170
Islington 11, 18, 38, 42
Israel 196
iterative process 123

Jenkin, Patrick 11, 16
Jenkins, Roy 37
Jewson, Nick 43
Jones, Douglas 101
Jordan, Davis 207, 210
Jowett, Benjamin 143
judgment(s) 5, 7, 14, 31, 33, 56, 58-60, 66, 75, 99-100, 105, 153, 156, 166, 179, 205, 215, 227
judicial act 97
judicial authority 107
judicial officers 106
judicial review(s) 11, 47, 55-7, 59-62, 66

July Monarchy 205
justice 72, 89, 206

Kant 203
Kemp-Jones, Mrs E.M. 37
Kensington Gardens 12
Kenyon, Sir Bernard 10
Klein, Rudolph 127
Knight, Ted 11

Labour government 11, 16, 37, 51, 57, 150-1, 172
Labour party 9, 12-13, 15, 46
Lambeth 11, 38
Lankester, Sir Tim 145
Laski, Harold J. 71, 74-5, 77-9, 83
Lau, S.K. 185
Lawton, Alan 112
leadership 106, 220, 227, 229-30
Leathes, Stanley 107
Lefevre, John George Shaw 95, 99, 106-7
legislation 161, 219
Legislative Council 190-1, 196-8, 200
Leigh, Ian 54
Lester, Anthony 37
Leung, Antony 199
Leung, Elsie 199
Lewis, Derek 227
Lewis, Robert 14
Lewis, Sir George Cornewall 96
lighting 205
Light, Paul 132
Liverpool 11
Livingstone, Ken 12, 38
Lloyd v. McMahon 12
local government 2, 9-21, 121, 168, 172
Local Government Act 1988 38
London County Council 12, 18
Long, Norton C. 157
Lords cricket ground 12
Loughlin, Martin 16, 18

Louis Napoleon *see* Napoleon III
Louis Philippe 205, 212-13
loyalty 19, 123, 146, 167, 206, 222
Lustgarten, Laurence 54
lying 203-4
Lynn, Laurence E. 161

Macaulay, Lord 95-8, 105-6
McConkie, Stanford S. 112
McKinsey and Company 187, 189, 193
MacLehose, Sir Murray 189
Magill 14
Maitland, J.G. 99
Major, John 29, 43, 47
maladministration 131
Malaysia 146
malfeasance 132
Malmesbury, Earl of 100
Malta 10
Management and Personnel Office 37
managerial discretion 175
managerial freedom 173
managerialism 132
Manchester City Council 42
Mandelson, Peter 40
Mann, Horace 103
Manusco, Maureen 25
March, J. 119-20
market 167-8
marketization 88
market-mimicking 166
market testing 169
Mason, David 43
Maudling, Reginald 10, 27, 31, 33
Meadows, Thomas T. 100
Melbourne 177
Members' Interests (Declaration), Select Committee 26-7
merit 35, 43-7, 88, 108, 132-3, 166, 176
meritocratic 97

240 Index

Mesopotamia 102
Method II 105
Militant 11
Mill, John Stuart 97
ministerial responsibility *see* responsibility
Minister of Conservation 152
Ministry of Defence 80, 145
Ministry of Works and Development 153
minorities 89
misconduct 14-15
mismanagement 82, 228
mission statement 174
misuse 21
modernize/modernization 55, 57, 193, 227
monitoring 175, 177-9
Montanheiro, Luiz 185
Moore, Mark 161
moral 7, 17, 44, 73-4, 79, 105, 111-15, 119, 121-2, 141-2, 153, 166, 174, 204, 215
morale 220
moral default 106
moral issues 23
moral obligations 38
moral standards 1, 23, 218, 220
see also standards
Morrell, David H. 85
Morrison, Herbert 12, 18
Morrison, Speaker 26
Mulgan, Richard 177, 179

Napoleon I 205-8, 214
Napoleon III 204-6, 208-9, 211, 213-14, 216
National Assembly for Wales 60
National Health Service 40-1
National Highway Traffic Safety Administration 223
national interest 147
nationalization 222

nationalized industries 224, 228
national law 212
National Party 153
natural justice 32
natural law 203
Nazi 215
Neave, Marcia 178
negligence 101
negotiation 98
Nelson 13
networks 167, 171, 177, 180-1
network theorists 72
neutrality 85-6, 113
Newby, Eddie 10
Newcastle 10
New Deal 147
new institutionalism 119, 121
new public management 5, 38, 132, 173-4, 186, 203, 220, 224
New Zealand 6, 142-4, 149-55, 160-1
Next Steps 228
Nicaragua 145
Niskanen, William 149
Nolan Committee/Report 11, 21, 25-6, 29-31, 33, 113, 115, 229
Nolan, Lord 11, 29, 83
nomination 95
nonfeasance 132
Norfolk County Council 16
norms 120-2, 124, 127, 137, 141, 174, 179
Northcote, Sir Stafford 95, 98, 143-4
Northcote/Trevelyan Report 94, 96-8, 104
Northern Ireland 40, 45, 53, 60
North Rhine-Westphalia 45

objectives 5, 170
objectivity 229-30
obligations 120, 123, 165, 167, 179-80

OECD 36, 43, 46-7, 113, 115
office-holding 165-8, 170, 173, 181
Office of Management and
  Budget 148
Office of Public Service 43
Official Secrets Act 1889 103
Olsen, J. 119-20
Ombudsman 19, 177-8, 187, 191,
  196-7
open 113, 135, 137, 151, 178, 218
open competition/open competitive examination 44, 96, 98-9,
  104, 106
open consultation 171
open government 130, 187, 191
openness 4, 20, 47, 82, 88, 108,
  135, 218, 229-30
operational/operations 228
Opportunity 2000 39-40
order 120
Order(s) in Council 94-9, 104
Orleanist regime 205, 212-13
O'Toole, Barry J. 166
outcome(s) 44-5, 47-8, 118-19,
  121, 123, 134, 142-3, 153-4, 158-61, 165, 176-7, 179, 197
outputs 142, 148, 150, 152-4, 157-61, 165
outsiders 31
outsourcing 20
Overseas Development
  Administration 146
ownership 6
owner/trustee 141-62
Oxford 143
Oxford Military College 101

Pakistan 37
Pallot, June 153-5
Palmerston, Lord 94, 99
Paris 205-7, 209-14
Paris Commune 206
parliament 2, 20, 23-33, 51-61, 82, 86, 94, 96-8, 104, 129, 135, 145-7, 150, 176, 212, 226, 230
parliamentary sovereignty 55, 57
Partington, Frederick William 102
partnering 172
patronage 93, 97, 132-3, 135, 186
Patten, Chris 191, 195, 198
Patten Report 45
Paynter, Reginald H. 103
Peking Gazette 100
performance indicators 170
performance measurement 88
performance related rewards 88
performance standards 178
personation 102
persuasion 94
Philippe-Auguste 209
Phillips, Bill 13-15
Pinto 223
planning 13
Plato 71, 78, 84, 217
pluralistic accountability 143
police force 219
policy 228
Policy Analysis and Review 149
policy communities 171
policy formulation 186
political appointments 131-3, 144
political environment 2, 5, 7-8,
  219-21, 225-6, 228, 330
political meddling 212-14
politicization 2, 16, 18
polyarchy 151
Pontefract 10
Ponting, Clive 145
Poplar 36
Porter, Dame Shirley/Lady 12, 14-15
positive action 44
Pottinger, George 10
Poulson, John 10, 12, 27
Powell, Enoch 27
practice(s) 23, 112, 119, 121-2

Pradhan, Sanjay 155
pragmatism 39
precedent 100, 121
Prefect of the Seine 205, 208-11, 213-14
preferences 121
press 100
presssure 107
principal-agent 171
principles 4, 36, 47, 56, 82, 89, 97, 110, 112-17, 121-2, 129, 156, 167, 174, 204-5, 214, 224, 226-7, 229-30
principles of public life 25, 229
prisons 177
Prison Service 227
Privacy Act 175
private finance initiative 20
privatization 220
privileges 25
probation 96, 105-6, 108
probity 33, 179
procedure(s) 3-5, 30, 32, 131-2, 222, 228
process(es) 3, 30, 33, 47-8, 85-6, 114, 118-20, 124, 218
   see also accounting
productive spending 211
professionalism 17
Professional Standards, FDA Sub-Committee 88
promotion 41-4, 47, 105, 108
proportionality 56
propriety 93
prosecution 103
provider 170, 177
public accountability see accountability
Public Accounts Committee 21
public authorities 60-6
public censure 32
public choice theory 6, 142, 146-9, 154, 156, 161, 169

public good 156, 162
public health 206
public housing 190, 199
public interest 4, 7, 47, 71-90, 93, 100, 102, 104, 135, 137, 145, 153, 175, 186, 206-7, 222, 225, 229
   see also general interest
public service 106, 143, 147
Public Service Act 175
Public Works Fund 211-12
purchases 168, 170-1, 177, 180
purchaser/provider 141-62
Putnam, R.D. 185

'quality of life' 15
quangos 132
Quebec 205
quotas 45, 47

race 38, 42
Race for Opportunity 40
Race Relations Acts(s) 37, 45
Race Relations Board 37
racial discrimination 37
rate-capping 18
Rates Act 11
rational choice theorists 156
Reagan, Ronald 144-5
reciprocity 117
recruitment 41, 43-4, 47, 116
Redcliffe-Maud, Lord 10
re-engineering 108
reform(s) 90, 104, 127-38, 150-1, 172, 180, 190-3, 196-8
Register of Interests 27, 29, 31, 33
regulation 165, 181
Reiter, Nick 16
religious affiliation 35, 45
reporting 177
representative democracy 175
reputation 100
respect 98

responsibility 5, 7, 18, 30, 41-2, 86-7, 117-19, 121-2, 124, 129, 142, 146-7, 152, 154-5, 165-7, 171, 175-7, 180, 196-7, 205, 225
responsible/responsibly 6, 82-3, 89, 119, 130, 157, 223, 228-9
responsiveness 129, 141, 174-5, 179
restructuring 35, 41, 46
review 56, 167
revision 3
rights 2, 23, 25, 54, 56, 58, 60, 79, 89, 134, 136, 179-80
  see also human rights
rituals 121
Roberts, Albert 27, 31, 33
Robson, William A. 224
Rockman, Bert 144, 186
Rohr, John A. 118
roles 25
Romilly, Edward 95
Rotherham 9
Rouban, L. 133
Rousseau, J.J. 84
royal commissions 85
Royal Irish Constabulary 103
Royal Military College 103
Royal Ulster Constabulary 45
rule of law 175
rules 4, 21, 23, 26-7, 30, 32, 56, 94, 98, 102, 107, 116, 119-20, 131, 134, 145, 180, 222, 228-9
Rushdie, Salman 80
Ryan, Sir Edward 95, 97, 106-7

safeguard(s) 3, 23, 166
Sandhurst 103
Sandinista 145
sanitation 205
Salmon, Lord 10-11
Sampson, Anthony 222
Saudi Arabia 81

scandal 114, 210
Scandinavia 133
Schattschneider 134
Schick, Allen 153-5
Scotland 63
Scott, Graham 154
Scott Inquiry see Scott Report
Scott Report 80-3, 88-9, 145
Scott, Sir Richard 83
Scottish Parliament 60
Scrutiny Committee(s) 20
secrecy 143, 152
Seibel, W. 193
Seine 212
selection 35, 43-4
selflessness 229-30
Senior Executive Service 144
Seven Principles of Public Life 83, 113
Sex Discrimination Act 37, 40, 45
Sex Discrimination (Removal) Act 36
sexual orientation 35
Shanghai 100
Sheldon, Robert 33
Shergold, Peter 176
Shetland islands 16
Short, Edward 27
simplification 120
sleaze 196
Smith, T. Dan 10
social engineering 13
social housing 131
socialization 25, 116
social justice 37-40, 46, 117
social policy 134, 136
Society of Civil Servants 4
Society of Local Authority Chief Executives (SOLACE) 9
Sorbonne 205
Southampton 103
South Yorkshire County Council 11

sovereignty *see* parliamentary sovereignty
Soviet Union 215
Special Administrative Region 6, 186, 192-4, 198
stability of purpose 105
Stalin 215
standards 2-4, 7-8, 11, 23, 27, 29-30, 33, 83, 85-6, 93-4, 100-8, 111, 113, 116, 121-2, 124, 135-6, 147, 173-6, 179-80, 206, 222, 224, 227-8
see also democratic standards
Standards and Privileges, Select Committee 25, 28, 31-3
Standards Committee 20
Standards in Public Life 83
Standards Officer(s) 20
Star Chamber 149
Stationery Office 102
Stepan, A. 188
Strafford, Earl of 101
Strasbourg (Court) 52-3, 58, 63-4, 67
strategic/strategies/strategy 13, 64, 77, 127, 132, 150, 153, 155, 157, 159-62, 187, 190, 192, 204
strategic alliances 172
strategic results areas 153
structural 24
Structures 5, 25, 122, 124, 218, 220-1
stubbornness 106
Superannuation Act (1859) 95
supervision 181
surcharge 12, 20-1
symbolism 120
symbols 120-1

team building 172, 181
teaming 172
tendering 174
tender process 177

testimonials 106
Thatcher, Mrs Margaret 11-13, 18, 121, 145, 149, 151
Tomlin Royal Commission 97
trading funds 191
tradition(s) 127, 133, 147
Trafalgar Square 13
training 5, 33, 42, 44-5, 52, 116, 127, 141, 167, 212, 222
transparency 168
transportation 205
treasury 36-7, 97-100, 107, 150-1, 219, 224
Treaty of Amsterdam *see* Amsterdam
Trevelyan, Sir Charles 95, 97, 143-4
Truman, David B. 71, 77, 83, 89
trust 168, 171, 195
trustee 143, 154-61
trusteeship 6, 157
Tung, Chee-hwa 195-6, 199-200
Twistleton, Edward Turner Boyne 107

Uhr, John 175
unfair 87
unified (civil service) 93-4, 96-8, 104, 108
uniform 108
United Kingdom 142, 149-50, 160, 203, 226-7
United States 81, 93, 113, 133, 142, 144, 147-51, 155, 203-4, 221
unity 97
unlawful(ness) 52, 61, 63
unpunctuality 106
unreliability 106
unsatisfactory 106

value-laden 226-7
values 4-6, 25, 47-8, 108, 111-23,

127-9, 132, 153, 166-7, 174, 176-81, 188, 194, 197-8, 204, 218-19, 221-6, 229-30
Van Wart, M. 116-18
vices(s) 207-10
vigilance 3
virtue 112-13, 206-7, 220

Wahlke, John C. 156
Wakefield 9
Walker, David 31
Walrond, Theodore 101, 103
Wandsworth 12-13
Wan, Ka-shuen 199
Warner, Judith 14
Weber, Max 143-4, 167
Weeks, David 14

welfare services 190
  see also elderly welfare
West Indies 37
Westminster, City of 12, 14-20
Westminster, Palace of 12
Westminster system 166
West Yorkshire County Council 10
West Yorkshire Police Authority 9
Weybridge 103
Widdicombe, David (Committee/Report) 11, 16, 18, 20
Wilkinson, Ellen 3
Willetts, David 28
Wilson, Sir Richard 227
Wood, John 97
Wright, N. Dale 112

Yeoh, E.K. 200